THE DODGE BROTHERS

Great Lakes Books

*A complete listing of the books in this series
can be found online at http://wsupress.wayne.edu*

Editors:

Philip P. Mason
Wayne State University

Dr. Charles K. Hyde
Wayne State University

Advisory Editors:

Jeffrey Abt
Wayne State University

Susan Higman
Detroit Institute of Arts

Sidney Bolkosky
University of Michigan–Dearborn

Norman McRae
Detroit, Michigan

Sandra Sageser Clark
Michigan Bureau of History

William H. Mulligan, Jr.
Murray State University

John C. Dann
University of Michigan

Erik C. Nordberg
Michigan Technological University

De Witt Dykes
Oakland University

Gordon L. Olson
Grand Rapids, Michigan

Joe Grimm
Detroit Free Press

Michael D. Stafford
Milwaukee Public Museum

David Halkola
Hancock, Michigan

John Van Hecke
Wayne State University

Richard H. Harms
Calvin College

Arthur M. Woodford
St. Clair Shores Public Library

Laurie Harris
Pleasant Ridge, Michigan

THE DODGE

BROTHERS

The Men,
the Motor Cars,
and the Legacy

CHARLES K. HYDE

 WAYNE STATE UNIVERSITY PRESS   DETROIT

© 2005 by Wayne State University Press,
Detroit, Michigan 48201.

ISBN-13: 978-0-8143-3246-7   ISBN-10: 0-8143-3246-3

Library of Congress Cataloging-in-Publication Data

Hyde, Charles K., 1945–
The Dodge brothers : the men, the motor cars, and the legacy / Charles K. Hyde
p. cm. — (Great Lakes books)
Includes bibliographical references and index.
ISBN 0-8143-3246-3 (cloth : alk. paper)
1. Automobile engineers—United States—Biography.   2. Dodge Brothers—
History.   3. Dodge, John F. (John Francis), 1864–1920.   4. Dodge, Horace E.
(Horace Elgin), 1868–1920.   I. Title.   II. Series.
TL140.D63H93 2005
629.222'092'2—dc22
2004023802

To the Memory of
John Francis Dodge (1864–1920)
and Horace Elgin Dodge (1868–1920)

CONTENTS

TABLES

PREFACE

The roots of this book extend back to late 1980, when I wrote a brief history of the sprawling Dodge Main plant in Hamtramck, Michigan, before its demolition. This was my first venture into Dodge history and I quickly learned of the absence of any comprehensive history of John and Horace Dodge and the automobile company that bore their names. I discovered that Chrysler's historical archives contained a great deal of material on Dodge Brothers before the Chrysler Corporation bought the firm in 1928. Once I finished a history of the Chrysler Corporation, I turned my attention back to Dodge Brothers. This has been a difficult research effort because many Dodge Brothers business records, especially the correspondence, have not survived. Some business and family records have found their way into more than a dozen archives, but other materials are in the hands of private collectors and are not easily accessible.

Any serious work of history depends in large part on the cooperation and assistance of archivists and librarians. I owe a great debt to Barbara M. Fronczak, now retired, whose responsibilities as manager of the DaimlerChrysler Information Resource Center included the DaimlerChrysler Historical Collection. Brandt Rosenbusch, the current manager, graciously allowed me to return to the collection to focus on the Dodge story.

The archives at Oakland University's Meadow Brook Hall in Rochester, Michigan, were another source of much valuable information about both brothers and the Dodge Brothers firm, but mostly related to John F. Dodge. Lisa Baylis Ashby, former executive director at Meadow Brook Hall, and Maura Overland, a former curator of collections, encouraged me to examine the materials held there. I am grateful for the enthusiastic cooperation and encouragement of Sally Victor, former acting executive director of Meadow Brook Hall, and Brandy Hirschlieb, curator of collections, when I spent several months in the archives in 2003.

I am also grateful for the help and guidance of many other archivists. Mark Patrick of the National Automotive History Collection of the Detroit Public Library deserves special thanks. Tom Featherstone, photo archivist at the Archives of Labor and Urban Affairs, Walter P. Reuther Library, Wayne State University, helped steer me through his institution's massive collection of photographs and scanned the images that appear in this book. The patient, professional staffs of the Burton

Historical Collection, Detroit Public Library, and the Benson Ford Research Center, the Henry Ford, offered invaluable assistance. Patricia Zacharias, manager of the Catlin Library of the *Detroit News*, guided me through that newspaper's indexing system.

My research took me to several cities where the Dodges worked and lived before settling permanently in Detroit. Several reference librarians and museum professionals were extremely helpful: Michelle Klose at the Niles (Michigan) Community Library; Carol Bainbridge at the Fort St. Joseph Museum in Niles; Barbara King at the St. Clair County Library, Port Huron, Michigan; and George Livingstone at the Willard Public Library, Battle Creek, Michigan. I would particularly like to thank my colleague and friend Alan Douglas for helping me navigate through the historical records of Windsor, Ontario.

Several members of the Dodge Brothers Club were also extremely generous in sharing photographs and other materials with me. I am especially grateful to John W. Parsons, Jr., who graciously allowed me to examine his large collection of Dodge Brothers materials, and to John Bittence, who helped me better understand the various Dodge Brothers offerings of the period 1925–29. Other Dodge Brothers Club members who shared materials with me include Mel Bookout, Thomas "Jack" Carpenter, and John Velliky. Several Dodge Brothers Club members read earlier versions of this book and offered countless suggestions and advice. I am particularly grateful to John C. Bittence, John W. Parsons, Jr., and Harry M. Trebing. Ron Fox, owner of a rich collection of Dodge family materials, generously allowed me to examine his collection. I am deeply indebted to all of the individuals I have named above, and I hope I have not forgotten anyone. Naturally, any errors or omissions that may be found in this book are my responsibility alone.

INTRODUCTION

Automotive historians are familiar with the lives and accomplishments of John and Horace Dodge, but most general readers are not. The Dodge brothers were relatively obscure figures to their contemporary public when they worked as manufacturers of parts for the Olds Motor Works and the Ford Motor Company from 1901 through 1914. They then manufactured their own automobiles for only six years, but by the time they both died in 1920, they had earned considerable recognition and respect for their work and their contributions to the Detroit community. Unlike Henry Ford, who developed an apparatus to promote and control his public image, the Dodge brothers preferred that people knew them through the Dodge Brothers automobile. They were an important force in Detroit society, mainly in the 1910s, when they both played an active role in politics, civic service, and philanthropy.

Two popular histories of the John and Horace Dodge families published in the 1980s were the first full-length books on the Dodge brothers, but neither focuses primarily on the automotive story. Only one-third of the first history, Jean Maddern Pitrone and Joan Potter Elwart, *The Dodges: The Auto Family Fortune and Misfortune* (South Bend, IN: Icarus Press, 1981), focuses on John and Horace Dodge. Roughly half the second volume, Caroline Latham and David Agresta's *Dodge Dynasty: The Car and the Family That Rocked Detroit* (New York: Harcourt Brace Jovanovich, 1989), examines their lives and accomplishments. Both chronicle the lives of four generations of the Dodge family.

Some historians continue to understate the importance of John and Horace Dodge to the automobile industry. A case in point is Douglas Brinkley's recent history of the Ford Motor Company, *Wheels for the World: Henry Ford, His Company, and a Century of Progress* (New York: Viking Penguin, 2003). Brinkley contends that in 1903, Dodge Brothers supplied the fledgling Ford Motor Company with barebones untested engines for Ford's Model A and nothing else. For the first three years of Ford Motor Company's operation, Dodge Brothers supplied Ford with the entire Ford automobile except the wheels, tires, and bodies. Brinkley views Dodge Brothers merely as an insignificant, marginal supplier to the Ford Motor Company.

This is the story of two small-town machinists who became enormously successful automobile manufacturers in the early years of the Michigan auto industry.

It began in Niles, Michigan, in the southwest corner of the state, where the brothers grew up in a family that included a father and two uncles who were machinists by trade. The family left Niles in mid-1882 and lived in Battle Creek, Michigan, for a little more than two years before moving to Port Huron, Michigan, at the southern end of Lake Huron. They remained in Port Huron for two years before moving to Detroit in late 1886. Their father, Daniel Rugg Dodge, was in effect an itinerant machinist after the family left Niles.

John and Horace Dodge worked in Detroit and in Windsor, Ontario, directly across the Detroit River, from late 1886 until they established their own machine shop, Dodge Brothers, in 1900 in Detroit. They honed their skills as machinists during this period and moved into the ranks of foremen and superintendents.

They began in Detroit at the Murphy Boiler Works, where they did rough machining from late 1886 until 1892. They then took jobs in Windsor at the Dominion Typograph Company, which manufactured and repaired typography equipment for newspapers and book publishers. The work at Dominion Typograph involved precision machining, which was new to them. After Horace Dodge invented and patented an improved bicycle bearing in 1896, John and Horace Dodge established a partnership with Fred Evans, who had worked for Dominion Typograph. They leased the Dominion Typograph building and manufactured the Evans & Dodge Bicycle there from 1896 until 1900. Sometime in 1900, the Dodges sold their interests in bicycle manufacturing and returned to Detroit to open a general machine shop under the name "Dodge Brothers."

By late 1900 or early 1901, the Dodges had their first automotive contract; they were to manufacture engines for the Olds Motor Works. After successfully completing additional contracts for Olds for transmissions, they agreed in February 1903 to become the principal supplier of parts and components for the Ford Motor Company. They worked exclusively for Ford from then until July 1914, when they ended what was a very lucrative business relationship to manufacture their own nameplate.

John and Horace Dodge made their own automobiles from November 1914 until their deaths in 1920. Dodge automobiles were mid-priced vehicles that incorporated sturdy design and construction along with some innovative features. Dodge Brothers, for example, was the first American automaker to use all-steel bodies exclusively. They also introduced a series of light-duty delivery trucks built on their automobile chassis. The Dodge brothers showed their manufacturing prowess by turning out unprecedented numbers of the recoil mechanisms for two 155-millimeter artillery pieces during the First World War.

Introduction

After John and Horace Dodge died in 1920, Dodge Brothers continued to operate successfully under the direction of Frederick J. Haynes and other managers
whom John and Horace Dodge had groomed to run the firm. The company
remained under Dodge family control until 1925, when John Dodge's widow,
Matilda Rausch Dodge, and Horace's widow, Anna Thomson Dodge, sold the business to the New York investment banking firm of Dillon, Read & Company. They
ran Dodge Brothers for three years without much success and then sold the business to the Chrysler Corporation in 1928. The Dodge brand has survived to this
day, and Dodge remains a flagship division of the DaimlerChrysler Corporation.

ABBREVIATIONS

BHC   Burton Historical Collection
             Detroit Public Library

BHL   Bentley Historical Library, University of Michigan
             Ann Arbor

DCHC   DaimlerChrysler Historical Collection
             Detroit, Michigan

HF   Collections of the Henry Ford
             (formerly the Benson Ford Research Center,
             Henry Ford Museum and Greenfield Village)
             Dearborn, Michigan

MBHA   Archives of Oakland University's Meadow Brook Hall
             Rochester, Michigan

NAHC   National Automotive History Collection
             Detroit Public Library

ONE

Growing Up in Niles, Michigan, and the Long Road to the Dodge Brothers' Machine Shop in Detroit

Together the two Dodge brothers spent their boyhood surrounded by the simplicity of Niles, Mich. They ran barefoot through the woods together and fished side by side with bamboo poles in the St. Joseph River.

Detroit News, 15 January 1920

Two fiercely independent but inseparable redheaded brothers—John Francis Dodge and Horace Elgin Dodge—grew up in the small town of Niles on the St. Joseph River in Berrien County, which is in the extreme southwest corner of Michigan. The Dodge brothers spent most of their adult lives working as skilled machinists and manufactured complete automobiles for only a brief six years before their deaths in 1920. They emulated their father, Daniel Rugg Dodge (1819–1897), and two uncles who had earned their living as machinists. John and Horace Dodge were the seventh generation of Dodges in America, pioneer Yankees who left New England in the middle of the nineteenth century for the economic opportunities afforded by the Midwest.

John and Horace Dodge spent their childhood and youth in Niles and attended public schools there until the family moved to Battle Creek in 1882. The brothers showed independence and initiative, a willingness to work hard, and mechanical abilities from an early age. More important, John and Horace Dodge became close friends and partners in most endeavors and continued this relationship until death separated them more than fifty years later.

Chapter One

The Dodge Family in Niles

The appendix to this book outlines the history of the Dodge family in America, which began in 1629. Constructing more than a bare-bones history of the Dodge family in Niles is problematic because of the paucity of detailed records. The published accounts of Dodge family life in Niles, particularly the childhoods of John and Horace Dodge, are anecdotal at best and quite unreliable. For example, Caroline Latham and David Agresta have Ezekiel Dodge (John and Horace Dodge's grandfather) spending much of his life working as a skilled machinist in Salem, Massachusetts, and then moving to Niles in the early 1830s. Ezekiel, however, first appears in Niles in the U.S. Census of 1860 and had probably just arrived there.[1]

The 1850 federal census shows Daniel Rugg Dodge (age thirty), future father of John and Horace Dodge, living in Newbury, New Hampshire, with his father, Ezekiel Dodge, and thirty-five-year-old Lorinda Dodge, presumably his wife. The census records no children of Daniel and Lorinda Dodge. When Daniel appears in the next census, he is living in Niles with his father and two children, Charles F. Dodge (age five) and Laura Belle Dodge (age three). Lorinda Dodge died sometime between 1857 and 1860. At the 1870 census, Daniel (age fifty-one), identified as a machinist, was married to Maria Dodge (age thirty-five), born in Indiana. She was the former Maria Duval (Duvall) Casto, shown in the 1860 census as the twenty-five-year-old daughter of William and Indie Duvall Casto, both born in Pennsylvania. The 1860 census identifies Maria Duval Casto, born in Indiana, as a "seamstress." Daniel Rugg Dodge's second marriage yielded three children—Della Ione (born in 1863), John Francis (25 October 1864), and Horace Elgin (28 May 1868). Daniel Rugg Dodge's family in 1870 included five children—Charles (sixteen), Laura (fourteen), Della (seven), John (five), and Horace (two). The 1880 census for Niles shows Daniel Rugg Dodge married to Maria Dodge, with only three children living with them—Della, John, and Horace.[2]

Daniel Dodge, along with his brothers Caleb and Edwin, earned their living in Niles as machinists. Although Niles was about twenty miles from Lake Michigan, its location on the navigable St. Joseph River enabled it to become a thriving commercial and industrial town by the 1850s. Berrien County's population, a mere 325 in 1830, leaped to 5,011 in 1840, with 1,420 in Niles alone. By 1860, county population reached 22,378 and Niles had 2,699 residents. During the 1860s, the population of Niles increased 55 percent to 4,197, but then growth slowed in the next decade, with population increasing only 10 percent to reach 4,630 in 1880.

According to the published Dodge family histories, Daniel and Caleb were business partners operating a machine shop on the St. Joseph River in Niles in the 1860s

Maria Casto Dodge (1823–1906). Courtesy of Oakland University's Meadow Brook Hall.

and 1870s, with Edwin working there periodically. The limited surviving business records from this era, the *Michigan State Gazetteer and Business Directory* for 1867–85, and surviving city directories suggest a different history. For instance, there is no evidence that the machine shop was on the waterfront. The earliest Dodge reference came in 1867, when the *Michigan State Gazetteer* listed a "Kimmel Dodge" operating a machine shop in Niles. This probably refers to Caleb Kimball Dodge.

A similar directory for 1870–71 includes "C. K. Dodge, Machinist, Niles." The Berrien County directory for 1871 includes listings for "Caleb K. Dodge, foundry and machine shop, nr. M. C. [Michigan Central] Depot" and "Edwin A. Dodge,

Dodge Railroad Standpipe Company, Fifth Street at the Michigan Central Railroad, factory buildings below the tracks. Detail from *Niles, Mich. 1889*, drawn and published by C. J. Pauli & Company, Milwaukee.

Machinist," but no reference to Daniel Dodge. The 1875 *Gazetteer* listings for Niles include "C. K. [Caleb Kimball] Dodge and L. F. [La Forrest] Dodge, Founders, Machinists and Manufacturers of Railroad Stand Pipe, near MCRR [Michigan Central Railroad] depot." La Forrest Dodge was probably Caleb's nephew or cousin. The 1874–75 Niles city directory shows essentially the same business listing for the Dodge shops, with both Caleb and La Forrest Dodge living south of the MCRR and east of Fifth Street. It also lists Daniel R. Dodge as a "mechanic" living on Fifth Street north of Barron Lake Road. Two years later, the 1877 *Michigan State Gazet-*

teer repeats the 1875 listing, but for 1879, the entry is simply, "Caleb K. Dodge, founder and machinist."[3]

The last specific reference to Caleb Dodge is in the 1881 *Gazetteer,* which identifies him as a "founder," but also lists him as "superintendent of founders and machinists" for the "Dodge Railroad Stand Pipe and Machine Company [capital $10,000]." The company officers were J. C. Larimore [president], F. M. Gray [treasurer], and R. W. Montross [secretary]. Caleb Dodge was not a top official in the firm but an employee. The company listing for 1883 was virtually identical to that for 1881, except that the "superintendent of founders and machinists" is "F. L. Dodge," probably Frank L. Dodge, Caleb's son.[4]

An 1884 Sanborn insurance map for Niles shows an extensive two-story manufacturing works including a foundry with a cupola furnace, a machine shop/pattern shop, and a warehouse, all located south of the railroad tracks and immediately east of Fifth Street. It identified the works as "M'f'rs of the Dodge R.R. Stand Pipe, Not Running," with the additional information, "Dodge Est. [estate] Owners." The 1885 *Gazetteer* shows the "Dodge Railroad Stand Pipe and Machine Company," but with no mention of any Dodge by name. They apparently had permanently closed the plant by then. The Sanborn insurance map for 1889 shows the same manufacturing buildings as in 1884, still vacant and still part of the Dodge estate. An 1889 "bird's-eye" view of Niles shows the same set of buildings as those on the insurance maps. The 1900 Sanborn insurance map does not show any of the buildings. There was no specific mention of either Daniel R. Dodge or Edwin Dodge throughout the period 1867–85 because they were mere employees of brother Caleb.[5]

Growing Up in Niles

According to Dodge family oral tradition, Daniel Dodge and his family left Niles in 1882, following the death of Daniel's brother Caleb. Since John Dodge was seventeen years old and Horace was fourteen at the time, they had spent their formative years in Niles. Several dozen stories about John and Horace's childhood and youth in Niles have survived, as part of Dodge family tradition and lore. It is difficult to determine which stories are authentic, exaggerated, apocryphal, or simply fabricated.

Most of the tales of John and Horace's childhood in Niles, repeated in the two published Dodge histories, seem to come from two sources. When the Dodge brothers arrived in Niles on 8 August 1913 to visit their mother's grave at Silverbrook

Cemetery, John Dodge gave an extensive interview to the *Niles Daily Star* in which he described at length their impoverished childhood. After John's death in January 1920, Niles mayor Fred N. Bonine, a boyhood friend of John's, called a special joint meeting of the town council and the Reliable-Home Building and Loan Association on 15 January 1920 to pay tribute to John Dodge. That meeting generated a rambling, thirteen-page collection of historical snippets of the Dodge success story and reminiscences from those who were there about John's years in Niles.[6]

The legend of John and Horace's poverty-stricken childhood comes directly from John Dodge's interview that appeared in the *Niles Daily Star*:

> We were born out on North Fifth Street in a little wooden cottage, close to where your standpipe is located. In those days we were the most destitute kids in the town. Poor mother, how she used to worry about her boys. I am three years older than my brother and naturally mother always confided her trouble in me. When cold weather came and H. E. and myself were obliged to go barefooted and wear ragged clothes, we didn't grumble, but tried to make mother think it was all right.

John Dodge's story has all the earmarks of a fable. Many of the successful automobile manufacturers, much like Josiah Bounderby in Charles Dickens's *Hard Times,* deliberately exaggerated their poor childhood circumstances to give credibility to the "rags to riches" stories they liked to tell about themselves. Henry Ford was perhaps the most notorious of the fabricators. As for the Dodge brothers, some tales ring hollow, but other sources confirm most of the stories.[7]

Dodge family biographies repeat John Dodge's 1913 description of the two brothers growing up in Niles in poverty. Daniel Rugg Dodge was allegedly a poor businessman who did not adequately provide for his family. These claims do not, however, fit very well with other established facts of their early lives. Older sister Della Dodge completed high school (with honors), John Dodge earned his high school diploma in 1882, and Horace was still in school when the family left Niles. Families living in poverty in the 1870s could not afford the luxury of allowing their children to remain in school into their late teens. Besides, Horace Dodge allegedly saved his money and at age nine bought himself a violin, an unlikely purchase for a child living in grinding poverty.[8]

Horace Dodge's interest in music was a result of his relationship with one of Niles's successful businessmen, Joseph S. Tuttle. The 1860 census identifies Tuttle (age thirty-two) as a tanner. A decade later, the 1870 U.S. Census shows a "Joseph S. Tuttle," age forty-three, identified as a "leather manufacturer" and a widower

Joseph S. Tuttle House, Main and Fifth, Niles, Michigan. Courtesy of the Fort St. Joseph Museum, Niles, Michigan.

with three children. Ten years later, Tuttle (fifty-three) had a new wife, Nancy (age forty-two), and an additional child, Ruth M. (age seven).

Tuttle owned a large Victorian house on Main Street and allowed Horace to play the piano in his parlor. Tuttle was also a member of the Niles school board and was the superintendent of Sunday school at the Methodist Episcopal church the Dodge family regularly attended. Because of Tuttle's influence, Horace gave John a Bible as his first significant present. Horace Dodge, the product of a perfectly respectable lower-middle-class family supported by a skilled machinist, probably would have nevertheless coveted the material goods of one of the richest citizens in town.[9]

Many of the stories about John Dodge's childhood concern his experiences in school. John had perfect attendance during his first three years of grammar school and his teacher, Mary Manson, presented him with a book recognizing that achievement. She was probably the Mrs. Mary E. Manson listed in the 1874–75 Niles city directory. In January 1920, Mayor Bonine, former seatmate of John Dodge in grammar school, recalled an early school incident in which John Dodge threw a wad of paper across the room and startled the school cat, which knocked over and broke a vase. The teacher punished John by making him sit with a girl. An examination of old Niles school records reveals that John Dodge struggled to pass an arithmetic examination in February 1876 at age eleven. He needed more than an hour to finish the exam, struggling with long division.[10]

There is some evidence to corroborate other Dodge family stories that have been passed down from one generation to the next. John and Horace worked hard as youngsters and showed a good deal of ambition and initiative. John claimed that as a young boy, he drove a cow three miles twice a day and earned fifty cents a week for his efforts. As a teenager, John carried heavy sacks of bran from railroad cars to riverboats for fifty cents a day. He worked with Tom Davis, the African American son of the town ashman, a low-status job even in Niles. William Davis (age fifty-two) appears in the 1880 census tract, listed as "drayman" and identified as a "Negro." He had a son Thomas (age thirteen), identified as "mulatto." Later versions had John Dodge working *for* Tom Davis, when in fact he worked for William Davis. A photograph of Tom Davis in 1920 shows him still working as an ashman. Following John Dodge's death, Davis recalled that John was a hard worker and added, "I always think of him bending over carefully to pick up a sack of grain so as not to rip the patches on the seat of his trousers." When Tom Davis died in January 1927, the mayor of Niles ordered all businesses closed during his funeral.[11]

Growing up in Niles, the Dodges also became friends with Cyrus Bowles, an African American who worked in the Dodge machine shop. The 1880 census lists Bowles as a thirty-six-year-old "teamster" born in Virginia and classed as a mulatto. According to local legend, Bowles taught the Dodge brothers how to fish, fashioned whistles for them from willow twigs, and relayed stories about growing up on a Southern plantation. The Dodges' experiences with Davis and Bowles probably explain in part their willingness to pioneer (along with Henry Ford) in hiring African Americans to work in their factories in the 1910s.[12]

The Dodge boys exhibited glimmerings of their mechanical genius even as youngsters. When John was in high school, schoolmate Fred Bonine was the first person in Niles to own a high-wheel bicycle. Bonine's family was wealthy and the bicycle supposedly cost two hundred dollars. Family legend holds that John and Horace, fiercely jealous of Bonine, fabricated their own high-wheel bicycle from scrap. They fashioned the high wheel by hand and used a wheel from a baby carriage for the small rear wheel. They proudly rode their homemade creation around town for two years, and it worked as well as any store-bought model. The story is plausible.[13]

Although John and Horace were close companions throughout their youth, they developed distinct personalities and interests. Horace was painfully shy compared with John and was overly sensitive about his name because of constant teasing from his peers. He used "Elgin," later "H. E.," and other variants for many years. Horace developed an early appreciation of music and taught himself to play the violin he had bought at age nine. He also became fascinated with boats, an important part of the landscape of Niles. Horace's love of boats, not entirely shared by brother John, remained strong for the rest of his life.[14]

John and Horace Dodge had a limited and sometimes ambiguous relationship with their hometown after achieving fame and fortune as automobile manufacturers. After Maria Casto Dodge died in 1906, the brothers visited their parents' graves in Niles each summer. In June 1912, they commissioned Lloyd Brothers Company of Toledo to build "a monument and nine grave markers" at the Silverbrook Cemetery to mark the graves of the Dodge and Casto families. John Dodge instructed the company to correct one inscription on the monument from "Castle" to "Casto." Lloyd Brothers charged the Dodge brothers $1,125 for the work, completed by October 1912. The monument and grave markers remain in place today.[15]

During their visit to Niles in August 1913, the brothers offered the city a gift of $100,000 to build a park honoring their parents. John Dodge told a reporter, "This amount sounds big but really is nothing to us now. H. E. and myself are worth $50 million and we have made the [sic] most of it in the last 10 years. We want to do something for Niles right away and I have suggested a donation of $100,000. We will double this amount if your citizens will advance a judicial manner in which it can be spent." The offer went before the city council, but after its members questioned the need for a park and determined that the city might have to spend money to maintain it, the council rejected the offer.[16]

The Dodge brothers later aided Niles in a substantial way less than a year before the death of John Dodge. Late in 1918, the Michigan Central Railroad decided to transfer its freight car classification yards from Michigan City, Indiana, to Niles. The move would bring an influx of upward of eight hundred families to Niles, resulting in a need for about four hundred new houses. Mayor Fred Bonine approached the Dodge brothers for assistance, and they agreed to help. John and Horace Dodge still wanted to do something to help Niles, even though the town's refusal to accept their earlier offer angered and embarrassed them. At Bonine's urging they lent $500,000 to the Reliable-Home Building and Loan Association of Niles (organized on 22 April 1919) to help finance the construction of housing for the railroad workers. By late July 1919, 151 homes were already under construction, easing the transfer of the freight yards, which took place in October.[17] Ironically, there was

Dodge Family Monument, Silverbrook Cemetery, Niles, Michigan. Author's photograph.

no public acknowledgment of the Dodge connection to Niles until the dedication of a State of Michigan historic marker on 16 November 1996 at the site of the Dodge boyhood home on North Fifth Street.[18]

The Dodge brothers did, however, have fond memories of their boyhood and the people of Niles who helped them grow up. In 1919, John Dodge learned that Joseph Tuttle had suffered financial reverses in his old age and was going to lose his home. Dodge bought the house and gave Tuttle a life lease on the property and an annuity so that he could live comfortably for the rest of his days. News that Cyrus Bowles was seriously ill reached John Dodge in late 1919. Dodge sent a letter in December 1919 to Fred Bonine offering to pay for a "proper Burial" for Bowles in case of his death. Ironically, Bowles, nearly eighty at the time, outlived John Dodge.[19]

The Battle Creek and Port Huron Years

Daniel Rugg Dodge left Niles sometime in 1882, taking with him his entire family—wife Maria, daughter Della, and sons John and Horace. There are contradictory accounts of their lives after they left Niles. Latham and Agresta argue that

Daniel Dodge moved his family to Battle Creek, intending to operate a machine shop there, but then moved to Port Huron sometime in 1886 and finally to Detroit later in the same year. Pitrone and Elwart argue that Daniel Dodge went directly to Port Huron in 1882 and remained there until moving to Detroit in late 1886. They also claim that Daniel Dodge tried unsuccessfully to operate a machine shop in Port Huron for four years before seeking a better life in Detroit. Both sources have John and Horace Dodge working in Port Huron for the Upton Manufacturing Company, which made agricultural machinery.[20]

The historical evidence of their whereabouts in 1882–86 is far from definitive. The scenario best supported by the available evidence suggests that the Dodge family lived in Battle Creek in 1882–84 and then moved to Port Huron in late 1884, after their employer, the Upton Manufacturing Company, transferred its operations there. Daniel Dodge almost certainly left Niles because he was unable to find work following the death of his brother in July 1882. Why Daniel Dodge moved to Battle Creek remains a mystery.

William Brown began manufacturing threshers in Battle Creek in 1851, but in 1858 the firm became Upton, Brown & Company, with James Stephen Upton as the controlling partner. The enterprise, renamed the Upton Manufacturing Company in 1874, left Battle Creek in October 1884 after a group of Port Huron investors bought $100,000 in stock in the company to lure it to their city. In 1890, the firm became the Port Huron Engine and Thresher Company, one of the largest American manufacturers of steam traction engines for farm use over the next quarter century.[21]

After leaving Niles, the Dodge family went first to Battle Creek, but the circumstances of their departure from what later became the "Cereal City" are not clear. The family does not appear in the 1882 city directory for Battle Creek, probably compiled well before their arrival that year. The directory issued two years later included "Daniel R. Dodge, machinist," living on the south side of Jackson Street, west of McCamly. The same volume included a listing for "Upton Mnfg. Co., threshing machines and engines," on East Canal Street at Jackson Street.[22]

By March 1884, civic boosters from Marshall, Michigan, and from Port Huron were vying to lure Upton Manufacturing to their cities, while a group of Battle Creek capitalists was attempting to keep the firm from moving. James Stephen Upton apparently needed an influx of new capital for expansion. The Marshall group initially offered twelve acres of land and an investment of $100,000 in stock. It is not clear why Port Huron got the nod, but in August 1884, Upton decided to close the factory in Battle Creek and move to Port Huron in October. Upton Manufacturing did not expect many of its 150 employees to make the transfer. By late October 1884, the firm had transferred its machinery to Port Huron, although the company planned to keep an office in Battle Creek "for the purpose of collections and attending to business here." Edward Frank Upton, one of James Upton's sons, left Battle Creek for Port Huron in late November to work in the office of Upton Manufacturing at its new home.[23]

If Daniel Rugg Dodge had worked for Upton Manufacturing Company in Battle Creek and then moved his family to Port Huron in October or November 1884, this would explain why there is almost no surviving evidence of the Dodges in Port Huron. The 1884 Michigan census of St. Clair County, completed in June of that year, does not list them, probably because they had not yet arrived there. Nor do the Port Huron and St. Clair County directories for 1885 or 1888 include them. If they arrived in Port Huron late in 1884 and then left for Detroit in late 1886 or early 1887, the directories would not have "captured" them in Port Huron. The directories for 1885 and 1888 included the Upton Manufacturing Company and identified the firm as a manufacturer of agricultural tools. No directories exist for 1886 or 1887 for Port Huron.[24]

One piece of evidence, other than Dodge family lore, that places the Dodges in Port Huron is Eugene H. Moak's informal history of Upton Manufacturing completed in December 1982. Moak cites the recollections of his father, also Eugene H. Moak (1866–1930), who worked as an apprentice at Upton Manufacturing with John and Horace Dodge. William Jenks's history of St. Clair County confirms that Moak worked as an apprentice for $4 a week, and Moak's 1930 obituary states that he began work at Upton Manufacturing in 1885 at age nineteen. Moak claims that John Dodge first became a skilled machinist while working for Upton Manufacturing. Although John Dodge was two years older than Moak, the two became good friends and John Dodge made Eugene Moak a machinist's hammer as a gift.[25]

We know very little about the period the Dodge family spent in Battle Creek and Port Huron, five years in total. Both John and Horace probably labored full-time and presumably began informal apprenticeships learning the trade of a machinist. Since the Upton Manufacturing Company made threshing machines and steam engines, the Dodge brothers must have gained valuable experience working iron and steel. The years in Battle Creek and Port Huron were much like the adolescent transition between childhood and adulthood. When the Dodge family left Niles in July 1882, John was seventeen and Horace a mere fourteen. When the family arrived in Detroit in spring 1887, John was twenty-two and Horace eighteen, both young adults.

In 1887 Detroit was a mid-sized city of about 200,000 with an industrial base that included scores of foundries and machine shops. Over the next fourteen years, the Dodge brothers became accomplished machinists, experienced managers, and successful businessmen. They came of age professionally. The brothers worked as machinists at the Murphy Iron Works in Detroit from 1887 until 1892, when they took new jobs in Windsor, Ontario, just across the Detroit River. They worked at Dominion (later, Canadian) Typograph Company, manufacturer of typography equipment, from 1892 to 1897. With Fred Evans, they manufactured the Evans & Dodge Bicycle in part of the Canadian Typograph factory from 1896 until 1899, when they took positions with the National Cycle and Automobile Company. During their Windsor days, they lived in Detroit and traveled to work by ferry. The pair then established their own enterprise, "Dodge Brothers," in 1900. They operated a machine shop in Detroit that initially made replacement parts for typography machines, special-purpose machinery, and steam engines for pleasure boats.

Early Days in Detroit

Daniel Rugg Dodge and his family, minus Della Dodge, likely arrived in Detroit in spring 1887. This would explain why they do not appear in Detroit's city directory for 1887, compiled at the end of 1886 or very early in 1887. The *Detroit City Directory for 1888* lists Daniel Dodge, age sixty-seven, as a "machinist" living at a house at 135 Porter Street, on the near west side of Detroit, a few blocks from the Detroit River. The same volume lists Daniel's wife, Maria Casto Dodge, along with "John F. Dodge, foreman," and "Dellie I. Dodge, machinist," as boarders. The following year, "Dellie I. Dodge" transformed himself into "Horace E. Dodge." Della Dodge had remained in Port Huron and in February 1892 married Uriah Eschbach, the former superintendent of the Upton Manufacturing Company.[26]

John Dodge went to Detroit in search of a job and found one at the Murphy Iron Works, which specialized in manufacturing steam boilers for stationary and marine engines. Thomas Murphy first appears in the 1880 city directory for Detroit, listed as "founder and machinist." An advertisement in that year's directory shows that he manufactured "Murphy's patented grate bars, smokeless furnaces, and feed water heaters." The 1882 directory identifies his company as "Murphy's Iron Works, General Machinists and Founders," but says that the firm made the "Murphy Smokeless Furnace," along with marine and stationary steam engines.

Thomas Murphy appears in later directories as the proprietor of the Murphy Iron Works but also as the secretary-treasurer of the Detroit Tug & Wrecking Company and the Windsor Tug & Wrecking Company. Murphy's manufacturing plant was at 190–200 West Congress Street from 1880 until 1892, when Thomas Murphy moved to larger quarters at the former Russel Wheel and Foundry Works at the foot of Walker Street at the Detroit River. The Congress Street plant was only a few blocks from where the Dodges lived on Porter Street.[27]

A *Detroit News* article published when John Dodge died in January 1920 recalls his first days in Detroit. He called on John Trix, president of the American Injector Company, looking for work. Trix had nothing to offer John Dodge, but found him so deserving of work that he spent the rest of the day going from factory to factory with him in search of a job. The quest ended at the (Thomas) Murphy Boiler Works. John Dodge later told a fellow workman at the Murphy shops, "I reached Detroit with 50 cents, but I spent 25 cents to have an aching tooth pulled out." According to the newspaper article, John Dodge worked alone at Murphy Iron Works through winter 1886–87 and then brought Horace to Detroit in spring 1887 to join him there. It is likely that John Dodge's parents moved to Detroit then.[28]

A 1890 survey of agricultural implement and iron works conducted by the Michigan Bureau of Labor and Industrial Statistics identifies all of the forty-six workers at Murphy Iron Works by trade and pay. The list includes a twenty-six-year-old single man, native-born with native-born parents, employed as a foreman at $16.50 a week, certainly John Dodge. The list also includes a twenty-one-year-old single man, native-born with native-born parents, who earned $13.50 a week as a machinist, mostly likely Horace Dodge. The age is wrong, possibly a typographical error, because Horace would have been twenty-two. The fact that both men were paying $5.00 a week for room and board suggests that these are John and Horace. The Dodge brothers left the Murphy Iron Works after about six years, seeking greater opportunities in nearby Windsor, Ontario.[29]

Sometime in the early 1890s, before John and Horace changed employers, John suffered from severe chronic coughing, which was soon diagnosed as tuberculosis. He was unable to work for several months, but according to family lore he recovered completely by consuming large quantities of medicine made by the Detroit pharmaceutical firm, Parke, Davis & Company. The firm produced Elixir 130, officially labeled "Terpin Hydrate and Codeine Elixir," which had an alcohol content of 42 percent. Dodge family tradition holds that John Dodge, previously a teetotaler, developed a dependence on alcohol as a result. This may well be the Dodge family's rationalization of John and Horace's periodic and well-documented alcohol abuse.[30]

During John's disability, Horace worked part-time at the machine shop of Leland, Faulconer & Norton in Detroit to help cover John's living expenses. Horace no doubt gained valuable experience working for Henry M. Leland, who had brought to Detroit the high standards for accuracy already attained in the machine shops of Leland's native New England. John's health problems would have made it difficult for him to continue to do the heavy work required in a smoke-filled shop like Murphy Iron Works, and his condition may have prompted the two brothers to look for new jobs.[31]

Working in Windsor

John and Horace took positions in 1892 in Windsor with the Dominion Typograph Company, first listed in the Windsor Business Directory section of the Detroit city directory in 1891 under "Typograph Manufacturers." Fred S. Evans was the secretary-treasurer of the firm. The listing remained the same through 1899, but the firm's name changed in 1894 to Canadian Typograph Company. The Dodge brothers first appear in the *Windsor Directory* as employees of Dominion Typograph in 1894, with the entries, "H. E. Dodge, machinist," and "J. F. Dodge, foreman." There and in subsequent directories, the plant is in the Medbury Block, on Sandwich Street just west of Ouellette. According to Pitrone and Elwart, the Dodge brothers first became familiar with micrometers and calipers, which permit greater precision in machining parts, while working at Dominion Typograph.[32]

Walter G. Griffith, who was an apprentice at the Typograph plant in 1890–95, recalled the arrival of John and Horace Dodge at the plant. The company had placed an advertisement in the *Detroit News* for "an assembly man, a floor man." The Dodge brothers came to the plant to see the superintendent, Mr. Piper, looking for work for both. Piper said that he wanted only one man, to which John Dodge replied, "We're brothers and we always work together; if you haven't got room for two of us, neither of us will start. That's that!" Piper agreed to hire the pair and told them to report the next Monday. Griffith recalled that John was the more aggressive and hardworking of the two brothers. Horace still went by the name of "Ed." Both drank heavily on weekends at various taverns in Detroit, but seldom got into fights because they usually drank with each other, apart from others.[33]

At some point while he was working as a machinist in Windsor, Horace Dodge devised an improved bicycle bearing, which incorporated an enclosed mechanism by which the bicycle axle rode on four sets of ball bearings. His innovative design

Evans & Dodge Bicycle advertisement, Windsor *Evening Record*, 16 April 1896.

had the advantages of being dirt-proof and offering a smoother ride with less effort. Horace and John jointly applied for a patent on the improved bicycle bearing on 20 July 1895 and the U.S. Patent Office granted a patent on 15 September 1896. An advertisement in the (Windsor) *Evening Record* in mid-April 1896 guaranteed the bicycle, described as a "roadster," to be "absolutely dust proof." By then, the Dodge brothers had already created a partnership with Fred S. Evans to manufacture a bicycle using the patented bearing, leasing part of the Canadian Typograph plant for that purpose.[34]

Fred Evans had already been manufacturing bicycles before he became business partners with the Dodges. The *Windsor Directory* for 1896 identifies the Canadian Typograph Company as "Manufacturers of Type Setting Machines & Bicycles," em-

Maple Leaf emblem on fork of Evans & Dodge Bicycle. Courtesy of DCHC.

ploying J. F. Dodge as "mechanical superintendent" and H. E. Dodge as "foreman." The listings for 1897–98 and 1899 remain essentially the same as those in 1896 and identify the Dodges as employees of Canadian Typograph Company, Ltd., which manufactured typesetting machines, bicycles, and other products. A second business directory for 1899 lists the firm in two places—under "Manufacturers and Dealers in Bicycles" and as "Typograph Manufacturers." Starting in 1896, Fred Evans and the Dodges manufactured the Evans & Dodge Bicycle, also commonly called the "E. & D. Bicycle" or the "Maple Leaf Bicycle." The metal emblem on the fork had the intertwined letters "E and D" on a maple leaf.[35]

The Evans & Dodge Bicycle had great success in the market, in part because Fred Evans was a good salesman. His company was the only Canadian bicycle manufacturer to exhibit its wares at the New York Cycle Show in February 1897. He spent ten days at the show and reportedly sold fifty "wheels" to dealers in Philadelphia and additional ones in New York City. By November 1897, the plant in Windsor already had one hundred employees and Evans planned to double production and employ additional workers. In January 1898, the Canadian Typograph Company announced plans to open branch offices and retail stores in London, Ontario, and in Montreal. To promote sales of the E. & D. Bicycle and the use of bicycles generally, the Canadian Typograph Company offered bicycle-riding instruction at the Windsor Curling Rink starting in March 1898. Instruction was free for E. & D. owners and cost all others $2.00 for five lessons. Their advertisement advised, "You can learn at the rink without publicity and under the instruction of capable instructors." They offered separate sessions restricted to "ladies" in the mornings and mixed sessions the rest of the day.[36]

Changes in the structure of the American and Canadian bicycle industries at the close of the nineteenth century seriously affected the Dodge brothers' careers. Forty-two American bicycle manufacturers merged in 1898 to form a cartel, the American Bicycle Company (ABC). Later that year, ABC decided to build a bicycle factory in Canada's industrial center in Hamilton, Ontario, to avoid paying Canadian duties, seriously threatening the Canadian bicycle manufacturers. In mid-December 1899, one Windsor newspaper reported that John Dodge was in Indianapolis supervising the removal of bicycle manufacturing machinery that he shipped to the new ABC factory in Hamilton, while Evans had moved his family to Toronto, the company headquarters. Under the leadership of Fred Evans, the Canadian manufacturers consolidated in 1899 into the National Cycle & Automobile Company, Ltd., and became the Canadian subsidiary of the American Bicycle Company.[37]

National Cycle took control of Evans's manufacturing facilities and discontinued the E. & D. Bicycle. National Cycle, however, continued to pay the Dodge brothers royalties to use their patented bicycle bearing and offered them good jobs as well. John became general manager of the National Cycle plant in Hamilton in December 1899, while Horace remained in Windsor at the former Canadian Typograph factory. National Cycle gained control of bicycle manufacturer E. C. Stearns Company of Toronto and planned to ship all of its machinery to the Hamilton factory. John Dodge met with the manager of Stearns, Frederick J. Haynes, ordered him to ship the machinery, and brusquely offered him a job, which Haynes accepted. The two became close friends and Haynes eventually managed Dodge Brothers.[38]

The five largest independent Canadian bicycle makers merged in September 1899 to establish a Canadian cartel, the Canada Cycle & Motor Company Limited (CCM). After CCM bought National Cycle in summer 1900, the Dodge brothers sold their interests to CCM for $7,500 and established their own machine shop in Detroit. Their nine-year stint in Canada gave them much-needed experience as machinists and as managers. Besides, they finally had some capital to go into business on their own.[39]

John and Horace Dodge also went through major changes in their personal lives in the 1890s. Both married and fathered several children apiece. John Dodge

John F. Dodge, ca. 1900. Courtesy of Oakland University's Meadow Brook Hall.

and Ivy Hawkins, a dressmaker, married in September 1892, when they were both twenty-eight. The newly married couple lived in the Dodge family home at 854 Trumbull in Detroit, while Daniel Dodge, Maria, and Horace moved to 534 West Warren Avenue in 1892 and lived at 524 Lincoln from 1894 on. John and Ivy Hawkins Dodge had three children—Winifred (b. March 1894), Isabel Cleves (b. February 1896), and John Duval (b. August 1898). John Dodge remained in the house on Trumbull until 1907, when he moved into a mansion on East Boston

Horace E. Dodge, ca. 1900. Courtesy of Oakland University's Meadow Brook Hall.

Boulevard, in a fashionable Detroit neighborhood where several automobile moguls lived, including Henry Ford.[40]

Horace married Christina Anna Thompson in July 1896, in Windsor, Ontario, during a lunch break from work. Horace was twenty-eight and she was twenty-five when they married. Christina Anna Thompson was from a working-class family and had worked at a bakery in Detroit. At the time of their marriage, she was giving private piano lessons to young students and was going by the name Anna. She quickly dropped the "p" from her last name to become Anna Thomson Dodge. The newlyweds lived in the house at 524 Lincoln in Detroit with Daniel and Maria Dodge. After Daniel Dodge died on 19 July 1897 at age seventy-nine, Maria Dodge continued to live with Horace and his wife until late 1901, when she moved into John Dodge's home following the death of Ivy Dodge. Horace and Anna had their first child, Delphine Ione, in February 1899 and their second, Horace Elgin Dodge, Jr., in August 1900. These were the only children born to Horace and Anna Dodge. They named Delphine after John and Horace's sister Della, who had changed her name to the more sophisticated Delphine about the time she married.[41]

Dodge Brothers Machine Shop

In October 1900, the Dodge brothers used the proceeds from the sale of their interest in CCM to open their own machine shop in Detroit. At that time, John Dodge was nearly thirty-six and Horace was thirty-two. There are contradictory accounts of this transaction. Latham and Agresta, probably following Glasscock, claim that the Dodges received $7,500 in cash and a promise for continued royalties for their patented ball bearing. According to Pitrone and Elwart, CCM went bankrupt and all the Dodge brothers received was their choice of machinery from the Windsor factory. The latter scenario cannot be correct because CCM remained solvent through the First World War. Besides, picking machinery that would be right for their new machine shop would be problematic, as well as shipping the machinery across the border. The Latham and Agresta scenario seems more consistent with the facts.[42]

The 1901 Detroit city directory includes a listing for "Dodge Brothers (John F. and Horace E.), Machinists & Engineers, Manufacturers of Special Machinery, and Machinery Repairs" at 133–137 Beaubien Street. They took out a quarter page of advertising in the same issue of the city directory and listed in more detail the kinds of work they were prepared to do. They described themselves as "Builders

DODGE BROS.,
Machinists and Engineers
133-135-137 Beaubien Street.
Builders of Simple, Compound, Triple and Quadruple
Expansion Marine and Stationary Engines,
We also build and repair any kind of machinery, do all kinds of difficult punch, die and tool work;
do internal, external and surface grinding, milling, gear cutting, and punch press work; in short,
we are prepared to do any class of work that can be done in a first-class modern shop.
Linotype Machines Repaired Skillfully and Promptly.   Telephone M. M. 519.

Advertisement for Dodge Brothers machine shop, from the *Detroit City Directory for 1901*.

of Simple, Compound, Triple and Quadruple Expansion Marine and Stationary Engines," but further explained, "We also build and repair any kind of machinery, do all kinds of difficult punch, die and tool work; do internal, external and surface grinding, milling, gear cutting, and punch press work; in short, we are prepared to do any class of work that can be done in a first-class modern shop. Linotype machines repaired skillfully and promptly."[43]

The *Detroit Free Press* ran a lengthy feature article on the Dodge machine shop on 1 September 1901 and praised the operation enthusiastically: "It may be truthfully stated that the plant of this firm on the ground floor of the large structure known as the Boydell Building, 133 to 137 Beaubien Street, is one of the most thoroughly equipped and up-to-date in the city. The newest ideas in everything that can in any way assist them in their work have been adopted." Virtually all the secondary sources have assumed that the Dodge brothers had just opened the shop in September 1901. The *Detroit City Directory for 1901* claimed to cover the city "for the year commencing Aug. 1, 1901," so the Dodge brothers must have operated their machine shop before September. By all reports, when they first began work in the Boydell Building, the Dodge brothers employed a total of twelve men and boys. The extensive operations described in the *Detroit Free Press* article suggest a workforce of about fifty.[44]

Ransom E. Olds (1864–1950) had already contracted with Dodge Brothers in early 1901 to build engines for his curved-dash Olds runabout. He followed with a contract in June 1901 for 2,000 transmissions. Olds was not likely to give substantial work to a firm that was not already an ongoing enterprise with a factory, machinery, and experienced employees. A lengthy newspaper article on the Dodge

Boydell Building, Beaubien Street, Detroit. Author's photograph.

Brothers Hamtramck factory gives September 1900 as the date John and Horace Dodge started in business as Dodge Brothers.[45]

Ransom E. Olds was in many respects the founder of the Michigan automobile industry and the most important early automotive pioneer in the United States. His father, Pliny F. Olds, established a machine shop in Lansing, Michigan, in 1880 under the name P. F. Olds & Son. Ransom Olds became a partner in the firm in 1885, and on his initiative, the Olds shop began making small steam engines equipped with a gasoline burner. He began experimenting with steam-powered carriages around 1887 and produced several prototypes, but decided to focus on gasoline engines after visiting the Chicago World's Fair in 1893. Ransom Olds introduced his first gasoline-powered carriage in June 1896 and began manufacturing them for sale in the Lansing factory in fall 1897. The Olds gasoline automobiles were a success in the market, but Ransom Olds lacked the capital needed for expansion. Samuel L. Smith, a Detroit capitalist who had made a fortune in Michigan copper mining, agreed in spring 1899 to invest $200,000 in the venture provided that Olds moved the operation to Detroit. The resulting enterprise, the Olds Motor Works, built the first automobile factory in Detroit shortly thereafter.[46]

The Olds Motor Works manufactured the lightweight "curved-dash" Olds run-about, the first American automobile to sell in significant numbers. More important, the Olds Motor Works attracted future automotive pioneers with substantial contracts for automobile components, and it was a training ground for other automotive leaders. The Olds Motor Works provided the first automotive contracts for the Wilson Body Company, Hyatt Roller Bearing Company, Dodge Brothers, and the Leland and Faulconer Manufacturing Company. Henry Leland, the manager of Leland and Faulconer, launched the Cadillac Motor Car Company in 1904 and the Lincoln Motor Company in 1917. During the brief time the Olds Motor Works was in Detroit, it employed future automobile entrepreneurs such as Jonathan Maxwell (Maxwell Motor Car Company) and Roy D. Chapin (Chalmers Motor Company and Hudson Motor Car Company).[47]

The lack of substantial business records limits our understanding of the Dodge Brothers enterprise in those early days. Fortunately, an invoice book covering the period from 15 October 1900 through 28 October 1901 has survived and offers some insights. Each page of the book was stamped "Dodge Bros., Successors to Canadian Typograph Co., Ltd." The vast majority of invoices during the first ten months of operation reflect a continuation of the work they had done in Windsor. They may have acquired Canadian Typograph's customers as part of the sale of their interest in bicycle manufacturing.

The volume includes more than one thousand invoices for repairs to typography machines, for replacement parts for typesetting machines or presses, and for "matrices," the molds in which letters are cast. Dodge Brothers supplied these services and products to roughly two hundred newspapers in the United States and Canada. Most of the invoices were for amounts less than $30. Despite offering a 25 percent discount on bills paid within 30 days, they faced the curse of small, struggling firms—past-due bills. On 1 December 1900, they notified the *Sarnia Post* that their bill was two months old. Nearly a year later, they reminded the American Car & Foundry Company of St. Louis of an unpaid bill for $193.60. John Dodge was apologetic when he asked this large company for payment: "We are very sorry to have to make this request of you, but as we are just getting our plant established, you can readily understand that we are not overburdened with ready cash."[48]

A close reading of the invoices reveals the efforts to diversify away from the work for the printing industry. Starting in early 1901, Dodge Brothers completed dozens of small jobs for companies as diverse as railroads, breweries, and telephone companies. The Dodges actively solicited work by letter as well as by word of mouth. On 26 March 1901, John Dodge sent a letter to F. F. Whitney, the general foreman of the Wabash Railway, in St. Thomas, Ontario: "As we understand that you have no repair facilities in Windsor, we would respectfully call your attention to the superior facilities that we possess for doing all kinds of machine repair work." The Dodges received a letter from L. D. Cord inquiring about their willingness to work on naphtha or gasoline-powered launches. They told Cord that they had no experience with this type of engine, but forwarded his letter to the Michigan Yacht & Power Company (formerly owned by Ransom Olds) on 7 October 1901. The Dodge Brothers cover letter added, "Trusting that when you receive inquiries for steam launches you will give us a chance to bid on the machinery."

In July 1901, Dodge Brothers sent out dozens of notices to various newspapers with unpaid balances—"Gentlemen: As we have disposed of our interests in the Typograph (Company), we would be obliged for a prompt settlement of the above." They had severed whatever financial relationship they had retained with Canadian Typograph Company after they had sold their interest in CCM. From July 1901 on, the Dodge Brothers machine shop did no additional work on typography machinery or typeface.

John and Horace Dodge had perhaps already decided that their future was in the manufacture of automobile components. Besides, they probably had to concentrate all their efforts on fulfilling the Olds transmission contract. They sent a letter on 30 July 1901 to the Browne & Sharp Manufacturing Company of Providence, Rhode Island, the premier American manufacturer of precision machine tools, indicating that, with one exception, they were pleased with a large order of machine tools that had just arrived. They had some questions about how a surface grinder was set up to handle work pieces. On 14 October 1901, Dodge Brothers sent an inquiry to the Fellows Gear Shaping Company of Springfield, Vermont: "We have been asked to figure on a quantity of Automobile Transmission Gears." They asked Fellows to quote them a price for cutting (specified) gears in lots of 2,000, 4,000 and 6,000, with Dodge Brothers providing Fellows with the machined metal blanks. The Dodges may have been anticipating a new Olds transmission contract.

The *Detroit Free Press* article of 1 September 1901 offers the only detailed view of the Dodge Brothers operations until the Dodges opened their large factory complex in Hamtramck in 1910. The author of the article was particularly impressed with the orderly, efficient way in which the shop was laid out and managed: "The machine room is a revelation to those who have been accustomed to dimly-lighted, litter-obstructed so-called machine shops. Perfect order prevails, no unpleasant odors of burnt oil are perceptible, no pounding of loose-jointed machinery jars upon the nerves, and the numerous employees have an orderly and neat appearance that is decidedly refreshing." The result was high-quality, precision work that came as a result of using machine tools with skill and care. The reporter observed, "Exactness (of measurement) is an absolute certainty, mistakes of calculation are rare." The article, however, says little about the products they were fabricating, with no mention of the work for Ransom Olds.[49]

An article that appeared in *Automobile Topics* in 1914 claims that the Dodge brothers "were the first to establish in Detroit a machine shop of the type where really close and accurate work could be done. They installed machine tools of a size and character that nobody else in Detroit had the courage to consider." Recalling Henry Leland's earlier highly successful Detroit machine shop featuring precision work, where Horace Dodge worked briefly in the early 1890s, the assertion that the Dodge machine shop was the first to do precision work is at best exaggerated.[50]

The *Detroit Free Press* article of 1 September 1901 describes Dodge Brothers as a general-purpose machine shop equipped to perform a variety of metalworking operations. The newspaper article details the types of work they were doing at the time:

> While the variety of work for which this plant is specially equipped covers almost everything imaginable in mechanical construction and repairs, there are some lines in which they are conceded as to be almost unequaled, as for instance in the construction of special machinery of any device no matter how intricate it may be, the making of special tools, all kinds of repair work, difficult punch and die work, milling of every kind, external, internal, and surface grinding, planer and drill work, lathe work, high speed marine engines, either compound, triple, or quadruple expansion, and steam yacht building.

The Dodge brothers not only designed and built steam engines for power yachts, but they may have designed the boats as well. The September 1901 article includes a discussion and photograph of their own steam launch, the *Lotus*. At the turn of the new century, the Dodge brothers entered this vessel in a race covering a twenty-mile course. The *Lotus* won the race by a wide margin, averaging nearly twenty-eight miles an hour, and broke all previous speed records on the Great Lakes in the process. The *Detroit Free Press* claimed that the Dodge launch was the fastest steam-powered pleasure boat in the world.[51]

At the time of John Dodge's death in January 1920, Adolph Vocelle, the superintendent of the forge at the Dodge Brothers factory, recalled the details of the race

Steam launch *Lotus* (1900). Courtesy of Oakland University's Meadow Brook Hall.

that the *Lotus* won in 1900. Vocelle claimed to have known John Dodge since Dodge first came to Detroit in 1886 and had worked for Dodge Brothers since 1900, when they opened their first machine shop in the Boydell Building. After the Dodges had boasted that their launch was the fastest on the Detroit River, a boating enthusiast set up a race with a cup as the prize. Six or seven boats entered. While the other boat operators were getting up steam in their boilers and running their steam engines without engaging the screws, John Dodge built up steam pressure in the boiler, but did not release steam into the engine proper. The competition thought that the Dodges did not have enough steam to race. When the starter's gun went off, John Dodge allowed steam into the engine and the *Lotus* "jumped almost out of the water and shot forward, really starting the race about 200 yards ahead of her competitors." As a result of this stratagem, the *Lotus* won the race by a wide margin.[52]

The Dodge brothers, especially Horace, maintained a keen interest in racing, in speedboats, and in building engines to power these fast boats. Manufacturing marine engines remained one of their long-term interests. Their first steam launch, *Lotus,* was not their last. In mid-June 1904, an explosion and fire at the Detroit shipyard of Peter H. Studer destroyed a nearly completed steam launch belonging to Dodge Brothers and valued at $1,800, but still lacking the engine. Studer rebuilt this forty-foot launch, the *Hornet,* completing the work either later that year or in early 1905. This would be the start of a series of larger and more elaborate boats built for Horace and John Dodge, which will be discussed in chapter 5.[53]

Once the Dodge brothers began making automobile components for Ransom Olds and Henry Ford, they specialized almost exclusively in automotive work, but until that happened, they took on almost any work offered to them. A *Detroit News* feature article on John Dodge, published in October 1915, is one of the few sources of detailed information on the brothers' hard work and their style of "hands-on" management in those days. There were only two keys to their Boydell Building machine shop—each brother had one, so one or both were always present at the start and end of the workday. When John Dodge was not working as a machinist along with Horace, he was scouring the city for more orders. The two brothers routinely locked up at the end of the day, went out for a sandwich, and then returned to work until midnight before finally going home. They would spend time planning the next day's work, preparing blueprints, making estimates, preparing the accounts, and sending out letters to customers or suppliers. John Dodge estimated that during the two years they occupied the Boydell Building, he spent a total of only six weekday evenings at home.[54]

During the eighteen-year period between their departure from Niles and the start-up of the Dodge Brothers machine shop, John and Horace Dodge gained valuable shop floor experience in the machinist's and related trades. At the Murphy Iron Works, they did rough machining on large pieces for large products, particularly steam boilers. Their time in Windsor not only allowed them to learn the subtleties of precision machining but also gave them experience in manufacturing a precision product, the bicycle. John Dodge, more than brother Horace, took on broader managerial responsibilities at Canadian Typograph and later at National Cycle. When they returned permanently to Detroit sometime in fall 1900, they had not only the capital to launch their own business but also the broad experience and "seasoning" that made success more likely.

TWO

Automotive Suppliers
to Ransom Olds
and Henry Ford, 1901–1914

I went all over the Dodge Brothers plant and assembling room today,
and even into the room where the half-dozen draughtsmen are kept
under lock and key (all the plans, drawings and specifications are
secret, you know), making drawings and blueprints of every part,
even to the individual screws, and was amazed at what had been
accomplished since last October.

John Wendell Anderson to Wendell Abram Anderson
4 June 1903

John and Horace Dodge established a machine shop in Detroit in late 1900, operating under the name "Dodge Brothers." They started as a general-purpose
machine shop, but soon made the first of several crucial decisions that enabled
them to become successful manufacturers and wealthy men. By late 1900, they
supplied engines to the Olds Motor Works, the first substantial automobile manufacturer of any note in Michigan. Six months later, they were manufacturing transmissions for Olds. Their first plant, in the Boydell Building in Detroit, proved
inadequate for their needs and they built a larger factory on nearby Monroe Avenue,
occupying the new factory in late 1902. The Dodge brothers made a second major
decision, more risky than the first, but ultimately a brilliant one. They agreed in
February 1903 to become the major supplier of components for Henry Ford, before
the current Ford Motor Company even existed. As a supplier to and a major stockholder in Ford, the Dodge brothers quickly earned profits and dividends much
greater than expected.

Chapter Two

Automotive Suppliers

The Dodges became suppliers for the Detroit automobile industry when they began building engines for Ransom Olds in late 1900. Olds had established a factory in Detroit in September 1899, and from the outset he relied on outside suppliers for components. After Henry Leland from the Leland and Faulconer Manufacturing Company helped Olds correct a noisy transmission, Olds awarded him a contract to build transmissions sometime in late 1900. At this time, Olds gave the Dodge brothers a contract for engines. No historical record explains the initial Olds-Dodge connection. Dodge Brothers had operated a machine shop in Detroit for about a year and Olds must have known their reputation for quality work. The Olds Motor Works displayed a Dodge-built engine at the Detroit Auto Show held in February 1901 at the Detroit Light Guard Armory.[1]

In the early months of 1901, Olds concentrated on the production of his popular lightweight runabout, the curved-dash Olds, also known as the "Merry Oldsmobile." Following a disastrous fire on 9 March 1901 that destroyed most of the Detroit factory, including the engine department, Ransom Olds relied even more on outside sources. He signed a contract with the Leland and Faulconer Manufacturing Company on 27 June 1901 to manufacture 2,000 engines. The Dodge brothers continued to make engines for Olds, but Leland's engines were better because he had more exacting manufacturing standards. Henry Leland's son Wilfred, hardly an unbiased observer, claimed that the Dodge-built Olds engine developed three horsepower, while the Leland-build engine of the same specifications developed 3.7 horsepower.[2]

According to Frederick L. Smith, who was an officer of the Olds Motor Works at the time, one result of the fire of 9 March 1901 was more work for the Dodges. Ransom Olds likely contracted with Dodge Brothers to build 2,000 transmissions, making the agreement at roughly the same time (June 1901) as his contract with Leland to build engines. The secondary sources, however, offer conflicting accounts of the size and timing of the transmission contracts. Pitrone and Elwart state that the first contract was for 3,000 transmissions, but they do not specify a date. Latham and Agresta also refer to a contract for 3,000 transmissions, but place it in early 1902. The figure of 2,000 in June 1901, paired with Leland's contract for 2,000 engines, makes more sense. Olds most likely signed a second transmission contract with Dodge Brothers in early 1902 for 3,000 more units. This would be consistent with the curved-dash Oldsmobile production of 2,500 cars in 1902 and 3,924 the following year.[3]

The Dodge brothers' operations quickly outgrew the Boydell Building, and in late 1902 or early 1903 they moved into a new machine shop they had built at 232–240 Monroe Avenue in Detroit, only two blocks away. The City of Detroit issued a building permit on 8 September 1902 for a two-story brick building, 50 feet wide and 138 feet long, at 238–240 Monroe Avenue. Detroit issued the permit to H. W. Chamberlain, probably the architect who designed it. This building, described as a "Manufactory," had a value of $18,000. Dodge Brothers is first listed at the Monroe Avenue address in the 1903 city directory for Detroit. The June 1903 issue of *Cycle and Automobile Trade Journal* includes two photographs of the Monroe Avenue machine shop, one exterior view and one interior shot.[4]

John and Horace's fortunes changed permanently and positively in late 1902. Henry Ford, who was on the verge of launching his third company and a new car, asked the Dodges to become his major parts supplier. According to Pitrone and Elwart, Horace Dodge examined the plans for Ford's new automobile, did not like what he saw, and insisted that Ford modify the designs of the engine and rear axle. No historical evidence exists to support this claim. John Wendell Anderson, who was the Ford Motor Company's attorney and therefore was privy to its early dealings with the Dodges, makes no mention of any design changes. In explaining the Dodges' decision to not renew existing contracts with the Olds Motor Works and with the Northern Manufacturing Company, he simply stated, "After going over Mr. Ford's machine very carefully, they threw over both offers and tied up with Mr. Ford and Mr. Malcomson." John Wandersee, who had worked for Henry Ford since 1902, believed that changes in the Model A design came from Henry Ford and C. Harold Wills, Ford's chief designer, not from Dodge Brothers. Similarly, a lengthy obituary for Horace Dodge that appeared in *Automobile Topics* in December 1920 does not mention Horace's changing the design of the Ford car.[5]

Alexander T. Malcomson, a successful wholesale coal merchant who was the first investor in Henry Ford's newest venture, led the negotiations with the Dodge brothers. At a meeting in Malcomson's office in February 1903, John Dodge proposed a payments schedule. When James Couzens, Malcomson's chief clerk, strongly objected, saying, "I won't stand for that," John Dodge roared at him, "Who the hell are you?" Malcomson calmed the waters, explaining, "Couzens is my advisor in this," and they struck a deal.[6]

On 28 February 1903, the Dodges agreed to supply Ford with 650 sets of "running gear" (engine, transmission, and axles, mounted on a frame) at $250 each, for a total of $162,500. The running gear, also called a "machine," included the entire working automobile except wheels, tires, and bodies. If the Dodges could document

Dodge Brothers Monroe Avenue factory, ca. 1908. Courtesy of Oakland University's Meadow Brook Hall.

Interior of Monroe Avenue factory, *Cycle and Automobile Trade Journal*, June 1903.

their investment in this work, Ford Motor Company would make payments of $5,000 to them on March 15, on April 15, and with the delivery of the first sixty "machines" on May 15. If Ford failed to make the required payments, the Dodge brothers could sell all unsold machines and keep the proceeds; this provision would have at least left Dodge Brothers with some assets to sell. The Ford Motor Company struggled to make all of its early payments to the Dodges. In early July 1903, Dodge Brothers delivered the first machines to Ford's rented assembly building on Mack Avenue in Detroit, conveying them on horse-drawn hay racks.[7]

To begin production for Ford, the Dodge brothers spent more than $60,000 for retooling and raw materials before receiving any revenues. They had trouble getting paid by Ford right from the beginning. The Dodge brothers met with Alexander Malcomson in mid-March 1903 and demanded immediate payment of the first $5,000 due them. They also made it clear to Malcomson that they expected to receive the next payment of $5,000, due on 15 April 1903. Malcomson admitted that he did not have the money to pay the Dodges, and they threatened to take ownership of the machines and sell them, as their contract permitted. Malcomson returned that afternoon to the Dodge plant with Henry Ford, James Couzens, and banker John S. Gray, a potential investor they were trying to woo. On the heels of the visit to the Dodge Brothers machine shop, Gray invested $10,500 in return for 105 shares in the company. This last-minute infusion of capital kept the Ford Motor Company afloat and kept the Dodges in the fold.[8]

John and Horace Dodge had other problems with Malcomson in the early months of their relationship. Theodore F. MacManus and Norman Beasley claim that Malcomson announced in a two-page advertisement in a trade magazine in May 1903 the formation of a "Fordmobile Company," which would produce a car selling for $850. The advertisement also states that the Fordmobile Company had leased the Dodge machine shop and that Dodge Brothers had already finished 80 percent of the 650 chassis they had agreed to build. None of these claims was even remotely true, and John Dodge was so furious that he forced the publisher to print a correction and demanded an apology from Malcomson.[9]

Henry Ford and his fellow investors started their enterprise with very little cash. The newly incorporated Ford Motor Company of 16 June 1903 issued stock with a nominal value of $100,000, but had only $19,500 in cash paid in. A *Detroit Evening News* article of June 1903 announcing the launch of this new car company notes that "Dodge Bros.' factory at 240 Monroe Avenue has been practically turned over to the new company and 130 men are employed in the manufacture of everything except the tires, wheels and bodies." The June 1903 issue of *Cycle*

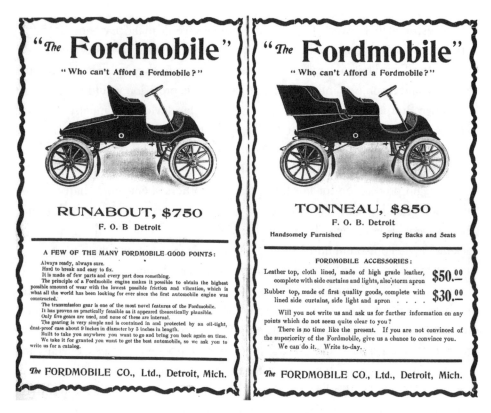

"Fordmobile" advertisement, *Cycle and Automobile Trade Journal*, June 1903.

and Automobile Trade Journal shows an interior view of the Monroe Avenue plant and claimed that Dodge Brothers employed 136 men there. In contrast, Ford had only forty men at his assembly plant on Mack Avenue in Detroit. The caption for the exterior of the Monroe Avenue plant erroneously states that the Ford Motor Company leased the building, and the article wrongly labels an accompanying photo "Interior Ford Motor Co.'s Machine Shop."[10]

With the Ford Motor Company habitually behind in its payments, the Dodges agreed in June 1903 to write off overdue payments of $7,000, extend Ford an additional $3,000 in credit (a note due in six months), and in return receive 10 percent of the Ford Motor Company's stock. From that point until they introduced their own automobile in 1914, the Dodges worked exclusively for Ford, and they held stock in Ford Motor Company until 1919. The fortunes of the Dodges and Henry Ford remained intertwined for more than fifteen years.[11]

The Dodge brothers' decision to become Henry Ford's chief supplier of components involved risks, but it was not an uninformed rolling of dice. Donald Finlay

Davis argues that the Dodge brothers took a huge gamble because they withdrew from lucrative contracts from Ransom Olds and from the Northern Manufacturing Company to work for Ford. He argues that the Dodges risked "their hard-earned independence on Henry Ford, a two-time loser who had offended most of Detroit's financial elite." In fact, they simply swapped masters (Ford for Olds) and gambled that Ford would succeed. Davis relies on a single letter from John Wendell Anderson to his father, discussed below, for the information on the Dodge brothers' decision to give up other contracts to work exclusively for Ford. Anderson had little firsthand knowledge of the Dodge business and erroneously calls the Northern Manufacturing Company the "Great Northern Automobile Company."[12]

Ransom Olds and the Northern Manufacturing Company may have proposed new contracts to the Dodge brothers, but all automotive work was risky. When John Dodge testified at great length in 1916 about the Dodges' original contract with Ford, he did not mention his company turning down "safe" contracts to work for Ford, although such a contention would have strengthened his case against Ford. Besides, by early 1903, Ransom Olds had left the Olds Motor Works after a serious policy rift with the majority stockholders, and the firm was already shifting its production from Detroit to Lansing. John Dodge was an astute businessman who was quite familiar with the major Detroit automakers and probably saw no future with Olds. In trying to find a supplier to manufacture the entire chassis, Ford Motor Company did not have any viable alternative to working with Dodge Brothers. Olds was an independent firm producing its own nameplate, and the Leland and Faulconer Manufacturing Company was already committed to providing the major components for the Cadillac automobile. Dodge Brothers was the only experienced and willing manufacturer.[13]

John Dodge later recounted the details of the 1903 contract in testimony given in his 1916 lawsuit to force Henry Ford to distribute the Ford Motor Company profits to the stockholders. He estimated that the Dodge brothers invested between $60,000 and $75,000 in machinery and materials to start production for Ford. John Dodge admitted, "We had a rather foolish contract or we would have compelled them (the Ford Motor Company) to pay over much more. We were not as wise then as we, perhaps, should have been." They should have demanded a larger advance payment on the contract.[14]

In the same lawsuit, the Dodges' attorney, Elliott G. Stevenson, aggressively questioned Henry Ford about his own contributions as well as those of the Dodge brothers to the newly formed Ford Motor Company. Ford admitted that the Dodges made the entire Ford car except the body, wheels, and tires. He also conceded that while the Dodge brothers risked everything they owned to make the Ford car, he risked very little to start the Ford Motor Company. He invested no money or property in the venture in 1903 and contributed only his experience and the design of the first Model A Ford. A contemporary observer of the early automobile industry, C. B. Glasscock, emphasizes a critical characteristic of the original Ford Motor Company—none of its investors or officials other than Henry Ford and the Dodges had any mechanical abilities or manufacturing experience.[15]

Shortly before the incorporation of the Ford Motor Company in June 1903, John Wendell Anderson (1867–1945), an attorney working for Henry Ford's chief financial backer, Alexander Malcomson, wanted to invest in Ford's venture. John W. Anderson wrote to his father, Wendell Abram Anderson, a La Crosse, Wisconsin, physician, asking for a loan so he could invest in this fledgling automobile company. Dr. Anderson borrowed the $5,000 that enabled his son to buy fifty shares of Ford Motor Company stock and become a director to boot. Anderson's letter to his father confirms the pivotal position of the Dodge brothers in the Ford venture. He claimed that the Dodges had borrowed $40,000 since signing their agreement to make the Ford "machine" and that all of the drawings and blueprints for the new model were kept under lock and key at their plant. This made perfect sense, because the Dodges were manufacturing virtually the entire Ford automobile. Potential buyers of the Ford car placed orders based on a single visit to the Dodge plant.

John Wendell Anderson also revealed to his father much of the cost structure of bringing the new Ford car to market. Henry Ford purchased all of the components and did nothing more than assemble the pieces at his Mack Avenue plant. The basic components included the machine ($250) supplied by Dodge; the body ($52) and seat cushions ($16) from the C. R. Wilson Carriage Company; a set of four wheels ($26); and a set of four tires ($40), for a total of $384. Anderson assumed that most customers would order the optional "tonneau" (a detachable rear seat), which would cost an additional $50, for a total of $434. Assembly of the components, which was the only work Ford completed, was a mere $20 per car. Ford's workforce consisted of ten or twelve "boys" paid $1.50 a day and a single foreman. Adding $150 per vehicle to cover all salaries, commissions, advertising, and other expenses brought the total cost per car to $604. Ford would sell his automobile, equipped with a tonneau, for $850, yielding a healthy profit margin.[16]

The relationship between the Ford management and the Dodges was not without friction. Design and manufacturing problems were expected with an "all-new" car like the Model A, designed and put into production with little time to test components. The Dodges initially attached Kingston carburetors to the engine, but these were not satisfactory. The Schebler carburetor that came next was not much better, but Ford then settled on an improved model built by the Holley Carburetor Company.[17]

The Dodges were responsible for some of the initial quality problems. They did not always assemble the Model A brakes with enough care, requiring repairs by the Ford dealers. August Degener, a machinist who first worked for Ford in October 1902 and was involved in the assembly of the first Ford cars at the Mack Avenue plant, reported an early defect in the Dodge-built engines: "First 2 cylinder motors came from Dodge in July. Did not get any power out of the first motors. It took a week before we found out we had no hole in the muffler." In another incident, Ford's tester, Fred Rockelman, went to the Dodge plant to complain about their shipping engines with loose flywheels. When he threatened to stop accepting the machines they were shipping, the Dodge brothers nearly started a fistfight with Rockelman. According to Rockelman, once he proved that the hole drilled in the flywheel was too big for the crankshaft it was supposed to accept, "they were gentlemen enough to apologize and said they would correct that."[18]

Whatever friction there was between the two firms, the contracts continued. In early December 1903, John Dodge proposed that Dodge Brothers would deliver seven sets of "engines and running gear" a day in February 1904, eight a day in March, and then fifteen per day in April through July, for a total of 1,891. The price would be $275, up from $250 in their earlier contracts. He also proposed that Ford Motor Company loan Dodge Brothers a sum of $25,000 by 1 March 1904, "for the purpose of putting up an additional shop and installing additional machinery to enable them to give us the increased number of machines." Dodge Brothers would repay the loan, without interest, in equal installments of $8,333.34 on 20 June, 20 July, and 20 August 1904. The Ford directors unanimously approved this arrangement.

In late August 1904, Ford Motor Company and Dodge Brothers signed an agreement under which Dodge would supply 2,000 "rigs" during the first six months of 1905 for the same price as in 1904. Malcomson wanted to reduce the contract price, claiming that Dodge Brothers was no longer facing much risk, but James Couzens resisted this effort and defended the Dodges.[19]

The Dodge Brothers *Time and Pay Record* covering a period of thirty-three months between September 1903 and May 1906 shows their near total dependence on the Ford Motor Company. These detailed accounts break down labor costs according to the job or type of work completed. Surviving time records begin with the two weeks ending 10 September 1903, but the summaries of work cover the entire year. Dodge Brothers paid out $35,296.02 in wages and salaries for the calendar year 1903.

JOHN F. DODGE
DETROIT
DODGE BROS., MFRS. OF SPECIAL MACHINERY

Cartoon, John F. Dodge, from *"Our Michigan Friends As We See 'Em"* (1905).

HORACE E. DODGE

DETROIT

DODGE BROS., MFRS. OF SPECIAL MACHINERY

Cartoon, Horace E. Dodge, from *"Our Michigan Friends As We See 'Em"* (1905).

General accounts labeled "shop tools, shop work, fixtures, engineering time, and pipe fitting in new shop" accounted for only $3,035.61 of the total, while they charged most of the remainder ($31,441.41) against a half-dozen Ford Motor Company accounts, with "machine work" ($11,260.75) and "painting and assembling" ($10,669.94) making up more than two-thirds of the total. For the year ending 31 December 1903, the Dodges charged $819 in labor costs to "transmissions for Northern Manufacturing Company."

The Dodge Brothers pay records reveal much about the Ford-Dodge business relationship. The labor value of all work at Dodge more than doubled from 1903 to 1904 (to $77,289.47), increased another 17 percent to $91,054.75 in 1905, and stood at $44,820.80 for only the first four months of 1906, suggesting a substantial growth in 1906 versus 1905. These figures reflect only part of the value of the Ford contracts, probably less than half, because much of the cost of the Ford machines that the Dodges produced was for raw materials, mainly iron and steel.

Labor costs at Dodge Brothers charged against the various Ford Motor Company accounts were usually about 95 percent of the total labor charges at Dodge. The exception was in 1905, when work on several boat engines and a boathouse amounted to $6,733.82. This probably included work done on engines for the *Hornet,* one of a half-dozen boats for which the Dodges provided engines. By 1905, the accounts distinguish among the various Ford models in production or under development. In 1905, the Dodge brothers completed drawings, built patterns, and did a variety of machine work for the Model H and the Model K Fords. The Model H was apparently a prototype that never went into production. Over the first third of 1906, the Dodges also provided components for Models F and K.[20]

The detailed pay records reveal a good deal more about the Dodge operations. Despite claims by Nevins and Hill that the Dodge shop relied heavily on piece rates, they paid nearly all workers by the hour. For the two weeks ending 10 September 1903, hourly wages ranged from five cents for apprentices and boys to 32.5 cents for the most highly skilled machinists. A typical workweek consisted of ten-hour days Monday through Friday and a five-hour day Saturday.[21]

Dodge employment levels grew considerably between September 1903 and May 1906 but with wide swings, depending on the size of the Ford contracts. After remaining at a steady level of 120–135 in the last four months of 1903, Dodge employment climbed quickly to 250 in early April 1904 and peaked at 276 in late June, probably reflecting the Ford contract for delivery of 150 machines per month. For the last five months of 1904, employment varied from 146 to 192. A new Ford contract for the delivery of 2,000 machines in the first six months of 1905 accounts for another upward swing in employment to a new peak of more than 250 workers in March and early April. However, employment at the Dodge machine shop then slumped to 110–120 workers in July–October 1905 before rebounding to 210 in late January 1906 and rising gradually to 270 in late May 1906. Some of these seasonal fluctuations in employment reflected the changing of models at Ford.[22]

Although Ford sometimes complained about the poor quality of some components coming from the Dodge factory, these problems were never serious enough to threaten their business relationship. Dodge Brothers sometimes could not keep up with Ford's requirements for parts. In a detailed letter to the Dodge brothers in April 1906, James Couzens listed the most serious parts shortages Ford faced and asked for quick deliveries so that assembly could continue without further disruption. He listed eighteen different components needed for the Models B, C, and F, including radiators, cylinders, connecting rods, crank cases, front springs, and gasoline tanks.[23]

From the early days of the Ford-Dodge business relationship, Henry Ford gave the Dodges broad responsibility for his cars while also trying to become more independent from them. John Wandersee, Ford's chief metallurgist for several decades, gave Dodge Brothers credit for revamping the Model A into the Model C (runabout) and the Model F (touring car) by designing larger engines. According to Wandersee, "The (design) work was all done at Dodge Brothers. Whether Mr. Ford revised it there or not, I couldn't tell. I would say the Dodge Brothers started putting out the Model C and F late in 1904." He also claimed that Ford assembled the Model B, introduced in fall 1904, with parts built by suppliers other than Dodge Brothers. The American Ball Bearing Company made the rear axle and drive train, and various job shops in Toledo and Cleveland made other components for it. Henry Ford was keeping his options open and applying leverage to Dodge Brothers at the same time.[24]

In 1906, the Ford Motor Company for the first time manufactured a substantial part of its component requirements. Ford and Couzens established a new corporation, the Ford Manufacturing Company, in November 1905, with the announced intention of producing a large share of the needed engines and transmissions in-house. Henry Ford may have wanted to establish a degree of independence from Dodge Brothers, but he launched this new enterprise mainly to force Alexander Malcomson to sell his shares in the Ford Motor Company. Malcomson, who wanted the company to concentrate on expensive models, frequently clashed with Ford. All of the Ford stockholders except Malcomson, John Gray, Vernon Fry, and Charles Woodall received shares in the new firm (John Dodge was named vice president) so they would enjoy profits from manufacturing the Ford car while reducing Ford Motor Company's (and Malcomson's) profits.

The Ford Manufacturing Company made components for the new, inexpensive ($600) Model N, including its engines and transmissions. The A. O. Smith Company of Milwaukee made the frames and the C. R. Wilson Company supplied the bodies. Dodge Brothers was left producing parts for the more expensive ($2,800) Model K. In January 1906, the directors of the Ford Motor Company approved contracts with Ford Manufacturing and with Dodge Brothers for the delivery of chassis by 1 March 1907. Ford Manufacturing was to provide 10,000 Model N chassis at $206 each, while Dodge Brothers would supply only 1,000 Model K chassis at $437.50 each. This stratagem worked. Malcomson sold his quarter interest in Ford Motor Company to Henry Ford on 12 July 1906 for $175,000. In early 1907, Henry Ford merged the Ford Manufacturing Company back into Ford Motor Company.[25]

Fortunately for the Dodge brothers, most of the Ford models were successful in the marketplace. They received a contract from Ford to deliver 2,000 machines during the first six months of 1905 alone. Ford moved into a large new factory at Piquette and Beaubien in Detroit in late 1904. There, Ford assembled his Models B, C, F, K, N, S, and R, and, starting in 1908, the Model T. With the exception of the Model N, Dodge Brothers supplied substantial components for all of the Ford automobiles. Ford's production, only 1,745 vehicles in the year ending 30 September 1905, jumped sharply to 8,423 units the following fiscal year. With the Model T and perhaps earlier, the Dodge Brothers supplied Ford with particular components, rather than the entire chassis. In January 1907, for example, Ford ordered 6,600 transmissions and 6,600 differentials for delivery in the first six months of the year. Once the Model T was in production, Ford turned out 10,607 cars in the year ending 30 September 1909 and 18,664 the following year. The Dodge Brothers Monroe Avenue plant quickly became woefully inadequate, although it was the largest and best-equipped machine shop in Detroit.[26]

Keeping pace with Henry Ford's demand for components was a constant challenge for the Dodge brothers. The City of Detroit issued a second building permit (2 February 1904) to the prominent Detroit architectural firm of Malcomson & Higgenbotham for a one-story brick manufacturing building at 226–234 Monroe Avenue. The building would be 90 feet wide and 138 feet long and would have a value of $8,000. The job records of another Detroit architect, Field, Hinchman & Smith, document further expansion of the Monroe Avenue plant. They built an enameling oven in November 1904, constructed a powerhouse and an additional

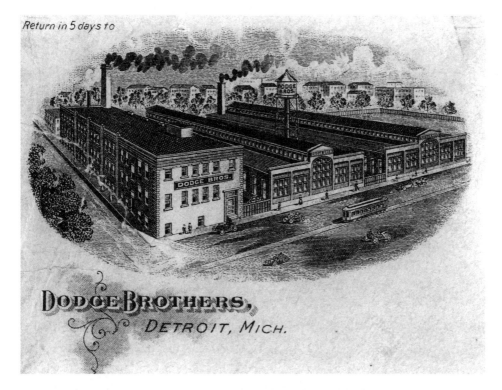

Return in 5 days to

DODGE BROTHERS,
DETROIT, MICH.

Dodge Brothers Monroe Avenue factory, from company letterhead, ca. 1908. Courtesy of Oakland University's Meadow Brook Hall.

manufacturing building in April 1907, and added a brass foundry in October 1907. The illustrations on Dodge Brothers company letterhead over time show the physical expansion of the plant.

Even with these additional buildings, the Dodge brothers were so cramped at the Monroe Avenue site that they leased additional space in 1909 at 284–290 Rivard in Detroit, some five blocks northeast of their Monroe Avenue plant. They used the building on Rivard until February 1911. By 1910, Dodge Brothers employed 1,000 men and planned to triple that number once they had sufficient space. The long-term solution was a new manufacturing facility built in 1910, the same year Henry Ford opened his Highland Park factory, which soon produced Model T Fords in unprecedented quantities.[27]

Although the Dodges' business relationship with Ford had a rocky start, they earned substantial profits from the Ford contracts and, more important, received substantial dividends from their Ford stock. Combined dividends from Ford amounted to $98,000 for the year ending 30 September 1904 and $200,000 for the following fiscal year. Ford Motor Company paid no dividends for the year ending in September 1906 and only $10,000 the next year, but then the dividends soared to $500,000, $3.6 million, and $2.3 million for the fiscal years ending on 30 September 1908, 1909, and 1910, respectively. John and Horace together collected one-tenth of the total and were no longer the struggling businessmen they had been in the first few years of running their machine shop.[28]

Personal Lives

John Dodge's private life during the first few years of the new century included considerable trauma and turmoil, particularly compared with Horace's more staid and stable existence. John's wife, Ivy Hawkins Dodge, died in October 1901 from tuberculosis, leaving him a widower with three children—Winifred (age seven), Isabel (age five), and John Duval (age three). Anticipating Ivy's death, John had to borrow money from relatives to buy a cemetery plot. John and Horace jointly purchased a plot on 28 August 1901 from the Woodward Lawn Cemetery Association (later shortened to Woodlawn Cemetery). The plot cost $210, with the Dodge brothers making a deposit of $84 and three payments of $42 each, all due within twelve months.[29]

In the wake of his wife's death, John moved his seventy-six-year-old mother, who was confined to a wheelchair, from Horace's house into his own. He hired Isabelle Smith, a close friend of Horace's wife, Anna, as his housekeeper, to help care for his motherless children. John Dodge quietly married Isabelle Smith on 8 December 1903 in Walkerville, Ontario, a small town opposite Detroit. Horace and Anna Dodge were the only witnesses and John Dodge consciously kept the marriage secret. He called his second wife "my housekeeper" throughout their marriage of nearly four years.[30]

When Dodge Brothers moved into their new plant on Monroe Avenue, they hired additional employees, including a stenographer, Matilda Rausch. The daughter of the owner of the Dry Dock Saloon near the Detroit River, she had completed courses in typing and shorthand at Gorseline Business College. She was working at the E. J. Kruse Cracker Company in Detroit when she applied for the position with Dodge Brothers. John Dodge soon asked Matilda to accompany him to the Detroit Opera House and to other social activities and was her sole escort at the time he married Isabelle Smith. About two years after his marriage to Isabelle Smith, he sought a divorce, which she refused to grant. She did, however, leave

The John Dodge family at the Redwoods in California, 1908. Left to right: John F. Dodge, Matilda Rausch Dodge, John Duval Dodge, Winifred Dodge, and Isabel Dodge. Courtesy of Oakland University's Meadow Brook Hall.

the family house on Trumbull Avenue. The two finally agreed to a divorce, which was completed on 29 October 1907 just as secretly as their marriage ceremony had been conducted. The "official" settlement of the divorce suit, filed in a small town in northern Michigan, was for $2,000, but the divorce likely involved a larger private settlement from John Dodge.[31]

John's path was now clear to marry Matilda Rausch, which he did on 10 December 1907, with only Horace and Anna Dodge present as witnesses. The Reverend C. S. Allen married John (age forty-two) and Matilda (age twenty-four) at the minister's house. Matilda then accompanied John to their large new home on East Boston Boulevard in Detroit and met his three children for the first time. A wedding dinner followed, but with none of the Rausch family present. John Dodge's third marriage produced three children—Frances Matilda (b. 1914), Daniel George (b. 1917), and Anna Margaret (b. 1919).[32]

Both brothers enjoyed substantial changes in their lifestyles as a result of their sudden prosperity. After living for many years in a modest home on Trumbull

John F. Dodge residence, 33 East Boston Boulevard, Detroit. Courtesy of Oakland University's Meadow Brook Hall.

Horace E. Dodge residence (Rose Terrace), Grosse Pointe, Michigan. Courtesy of Albert Kahn Associates, Inc.

Avenue, perhaps worth $5,000, John Dodge built a sprawling mansion costing $250,000 on fashionable East Boston Boulevard in Detroit. One of the premier Detroit architectural firms, Field, Hinchman & Smith, designed the house, which was completed in 1906. Two years later, John Dodge bought a 320-acre farm near Rochester, Michigan, about twenty-five miles north of downtown Detroit. He paid $50,000 for this rural estate that would become a country retreat for him and his brother. Horace, who had lived in a modest house on West Forest in Detroit since 1904, built an enormous red sandstone Jacobean style house on the Detroit River in upscale Grosse Pointe, which was completed in late 1911. Aptly named Rose Terrace, Horace Dodge's estate included extensive rose gardens extending to the Detroit River. Albert Kahn, who also designed several Dodge factory buildings, was the architect of this mansion.[33]

By 1910, John and Horace Dodge were wealthy men, thanks to their work for Ford Motor Company and their ownership of Ford stock. They had accumulated the trappings of wealth, especially the large homes both enjoyed. In many respects, they had merely reached a plateau in their climb to much greater success and fortune. An enormous new manufacturing plant was to serve as the jumping-off point for the next stage of their illustrious careers.

The Hamtramck Factory, 1910–1914

In mid-September 1909, the *Detroit News* announced the Dodge brothers' purchase of a twenty-four-acre parcel in Hamtramck Township, just outside the Detroit city limits. They paid Walter S. Harsha, a U.S. court clerk, $100,000 for what the paper described as "one of the choicest factory sites in the northeast section [of Detroit]." Ten months later, the same newspaper featured an architectural rendering of the plant and gave a brief description of the major buildings, although construction was just under way. They labeled the rendering, "Dodge Bros. Plant No. 3, Albert Kahn, Architect, Ernest Wilby, Associate." The newspaper estimated the total cost of the new facility, including equipment, at $750,000. By mid-January 1911, with construction completed, the Dodge plant warranted an eight-column, full-page feature article, dripping with praise of the plant's numerous innovative and "modern" features.[34]

Albert Kahn designed the first segments of the Hamtramck factory complex, including a machine shop, forge shop, powerhouse, and office building, all completed in 1910–11. Kahn was the premier Detroit industrial architect by this time,

Dodge Brothers Hamtramck factory, 1911. Courtesy of Albert Kahn Associates, Inc.

having designed factories for Packard, Ford, Chalmers, and others. The Dodges broke ground for the new complex on 1 June 1910 and began moving into the new buildings in late November. Kahn designed a steel-framed forge shop (75 feet wide and 400 feet long); a steel-framed brick powerhouse; and a modest brick office building. Kahn's most important work was the machine shop, a four-story reinforced concrete structure with flat-slab floors and ten-sided reinforced concrete columns. This was a U-shaped building, with two wings, each measuring 65 feet by 405 feet, joined at the northern end by a segment measuring 65 feet by 225 feet.[35]

John Dodge's 1910 diary affords a rare look at the working relationship that developed between an industrialist and his architect while planning a factory complex. Dodge noted on 26 April, "Gave Albert Kahn the first sketches for [the] new factory in Hamtramick [sic]." They had ten meetings in May and early June to complete the plans for the machine shop, forge shop, and powerhouse. Dodge approved the final plans for the machine shop on 3 June, Kahn put the project out for bids, and he awarded the construction contract to the firm of Bryant & Detwiler of Detroit on 21 June. Work continued on all three buildings, and John Dodge reported on 28 November that the powerhouse was operating and they were finishing the floors in the machine shop. By 7 December, the forge shop had a dozen steam hammers operating and was producing forgings. In little more than seven months, Kahn and Dodge had turned preliminary plans into completed

Dodge Brothers Hamtramck factory, 1913 letterhead. Courtesy of Oakland University's Meadow Brook Hall.

buildings. Everything did not go smoothly during those hectic months. In mid-May, John Dodge discussed a proposed brass foundry with Messrs. Boyd and Hunt from Kahn's office, but did not like their preliminary drawings. Kahn did not complete the brass foundry, which John Dodge awarded to the firm of Smith, Hinchman & Grylls. The design of the office building also involved long delays. Dodge reported on 3 June, "[I] went with Mr. Kahn to visit Burrows [sic] Adding Mach. Co.'s and [Hiram] Walker & Sons Offices. [I am] about to decided [sic] on plans for the office." Three months later, he was still examining plans for the office building.[36] Construction probably was under way in the fourth quarter of the year because a newspaper description of the plant in mid-January 1911 described the office building as finished.[37]

Because the Dodges were introducing new (for them) processes and machinery, including steam hammers and upsetting machines, both used in forging, they spent time visiting plants where these machines were already in use. John and Horace went by boat to Cleveland on the evening of 27 April 1910 and spent the following day in Erie, Pennsylvania, observing a 5,000-pound steam hammer in service at the Erie Forge Company. They spent 29 April 1910 in Cleveland discussing upsetting machines with two manufacturers, the Cleveland Hardware Company and the Acme Manufacturing Company. On 17 and 18 May 1910, John visited the factories of the Detroit Stoker Company and the Murphy Iron Works, both in Detroit, to examine boilers for the new plant. Their meticulous preparation was not limited to machinery. On 3 June, John Dodge and Albert Kahn examined office buildings Kahn had designed for the Burroughs Adding Machine Company in Detroit and for Walker & Sons in Windsor, Ontario.

When finished in early 1911, the Hamtramck plant was a vast improvement over the Monroe Avenue factory in every respect. The new plant provided 300,000 square feet of floor space, mainly in Albert Kahn–designed reinforced concrete buildings with enormous glass windows, which provided excellent lighting and ventilation. The Dodge Brothers Hamtramck plant looked much like Ford's nearby Highland Park plant, also designed by Albert Kahn and first opened in 1910. The Dodge plant, however, had no space devoted to automobile assembly. The power-house (100 feet wide and 110 feet long) was equipped with a pair of cross-compound Allis-Chalmers Corliss engines, each of 1,000 horsepower, driving 500-kilowatt generators. Instead of using a central compressor to provide air for tools, the plant used small electrically powered compressors. To keep floor space at a maximum, the plant used a forced-air heating system instead of steam or hot water. The brick and concrete office building, 55 feet wide and 150 feet long, provided two stories of offices and included a smaller third floor with a kitchen and dining room for office employees. Dodge Brothers also gave the factory workers a dining room that seated 1,500 and provided meals at cost.[38]

Dodge Brothers continued to use part of the Monroe Avenue plant, the brass foundry, for several years after opening the new plant in Hamtramck. In early March 1911, they asked the Detroit Illuminating Company for new (electric) meter readings at the Monroe Avenue plant, arguing that "All machinery has been removed from building No. 3 and considerable (machinery) from building No. 2, thereby reducing the load." Dodge Brothers sold the Monroe and Hastings plant in July 1911 to the Richmond and Backus Company for $60,000 on a ten-year land contract. However, as a condition of the sale, they retained the right to use the westernmost building (a brass foundry) for an additional two years. The automaker would pay one-quarter of all taxes on the property, would pay for heat for the building they used, and would credit the buyer with $900 in interest per year. The Detroit city directories for 1911, 1912, and 1913 list the "Dodge Bros. Brass Foundry" as the occupant of 224–226 Monroe Avenue. In 1914, the Richmond and Backus Company occupied the entire property at 224–240 Monroe.[39]

The Hamtramck plant remained largely unchanged from 1911 until 1914, when a wave of new construction brought on by the introduction of the Dodge automobile tripled the floor space. Two major exceptions, however, are worth noting. John Dodge had discussed plans for a brass foundry with Albert Kahn's office beginning in May 1910, but the two never agreed to proceed. Instead, the Detroit

Employee dining room, Dodge Hamtramck factory, ca. 1912. Courtesy of DCHC.

architectural firm of Smith, Hinchman & Grylls completed a steel-framed foundry 140 feet wide and 400 feet long for Dodge Brothers in 1912. The same firm designed the steel-framed heat treat building (1913), which was 70 feet wide and 400 feet long. This specialized plant received extensive coverage in the September 1914 issue of *Machinery* because of the innovative machinery used to harden steel. Smith, Hinchman & Grylls then served as the primary architect for Dodge Brothers for more than a decade.[40]

The Dodges switched architects because they were dissatisfied with Kahn's work in designing and supervising the construction of the first set of buildings at their new Hamtramck plant. Between 11 February 1911 and 18 March 1912, some thirteen months, they sent Kahn a total of 242 letters, nearly all of which complained about unfinished or shoddy work. A letter of 7 March 1911 cited the poor quality of work done by the contractor, Bryant & Detwiler, on the floors in the main building and their unwillingness to make the needed repairs. A letter in mid-September 1911 contained a list of eighteen defects in the main building that still needed attention. They reported serious problems with leaking roofs just two weeks later. In mid-December, John Dodge complained about Kahn's failure to get the blacksmith shop roof completed when the weather was good. He added, "We are certainly not well pleased with the way you have handled this job and we must insist that our work be given more attention."[41]

In addition, Horace Dodge was displeased with the work Kahn did in designing and managing the construction of Rose Terrace. Horace complained about the lack of progress in completing his home, blaming Kahn for not supervising Malow Brothers, the contractor: "I must say that I am thoroughly disgusted with them. They seem to think that it makes no difference with them whether they finish the work this year or next so long as they get it done." In early February 1912, Horace Dodge forwarded to Kahn an evaluation of the home's electrical circuits completed by A. E. Roach. While the original specifications provided that no more than ten outlets would be on any one circuit, more than ten circuits exceeded that limit and one had twenty outlets. Shortly after that, he made several serious complaints about the house. The most important was the inability of the furnace to produce enough steam to heat the radiators properly. The refrigeration plant made excessive noise, many drain pipes had become plugged, and several interior doors had shrunk from their original dimensions and needed replacement.[42] Given their dissatisfaction with Kahn's work, John and Horace Dodge's decision to use Smith, Hinchman & Grylls exclusively after 1912 is not surprising. Perhaps Albert Kahn was so busy and preoccupied with his contracts with Ford that he ignored "minor" clients like Dodge Brothers. Once the Dodge brothers broke with Ford, they perhaps did not want to share the same architect.

While Dodge Brothers was still manufacturing parts exclusively for Ford, the Hamtramck plant became a very large operation by any definition. In mid-1914, one visitor reported that the plant cut 34,000 gears a day. The foundry cast 25 tons of brass and 75 tons of gray iron daily, while the forge shops shaped 150 tons of steel per day. The annual parts production was impressive—240,000 transmissions; 225,000 rear axles; 190,000 front axles; 205,000 crank shafts; 855,000 connecting rods; 412,000 universal joint knuckles; and another two dozen major parts or assemblies, including steering gear, in numbers exceeding 200,000. According to the *Michigan Manufacturer and Financial Record* issue of 8 August 1914, Dodge Brothers manufactured 60 percent of the total value of the Ford cars produced between 1903 and 1914, including the legendary Model T. They made every major component except bodies, wheels, and tires.[43]

The machinery and equipment used at the Dodge Brothers plant during its operation as a parts supplier was elaborate, modern, and, in a few instances, innovative. The heat treatment department included a total of 43 recuperative, carbonizing, and annealing furnaces. Twenty cyanide furnaces that consumed 10,000 pounds of potassium cyanide per week to surface-harden steel used to make nearly seven million clutch discs per year. Dodge Brothers designed an elaborate system to keep the tempering oil used in the heat treat shop at a constant temperature. The forge shop had a total of 45 towering and Bradley hammers ranging from 400 to 5,000 pounds. The foundry was equipped with core ovens, a separate cleaning system of rattler and shot-blasting machines, and eleven rapid-fire furnaces.[44]

Typical of Dodge Brothers efficiency was the firm's use of low-pressure steam exhausted from its steam hammers to operate a turbine driving a 750-kilowatt electrical generator. This arrangement made a pair of Corliss steam engines in the powerhouse obsolete, so Dodge Brothers refitted them to produce compressed air or electricity as needed. Finally, the Dodge Brothers plant featured several advanced material handling systems. The foundry had an elaborate internal system for material handling, including battery-powered electric locomotives, a monorail system, and double traveling cranes. Two large traveling magnetic cranes located in the aisles between the forge, blacksmith, and heat treatment shops handled the enormous tonnage of scrap generated in these areas, while a heavy-duty overhead monorail crane extended throughout the rest of the complex. Dodge Brothers also used eight five-ton trucks, four half-ton motor wagons, and approximately 3,000 push platform trucks for material handling operations.[45]

Dodge Brothers apparently installed much of the material handling equipment described above in the course of converting the plant in 1914 to produce automobiles. The overhead cranes were perhaps part of the original installation. Dodge Brothers developed advanced material handling systems at the same time as Henry Ford or perhaps slightly earlier. As originally built, the Highland Park plant's material handling system was quite simple—overhead traveling cranes in the machine shop, an overhead monorail running throughout the first floor, freight elevators, and thousands of hand trucks. In describing the Highland Park plant on the verge of the opening of the New Shop in 1915, Arnold and Faurote reveal that Ford employed between 800 and 1,000 "truck-men, pullers, and shovers," who would mostly be eliminated when the new buildings opened. They argued that "handling of materials and work in progress of finishing is now the principal problem of motor-car cost-reduction."[46]

Despite the large size of their operations and their tremendous success, the Dodge brothers were also known for being fair and reasonable in their relationships with their employees and others. In November 1913, James Couzens, a fellow director from the Ford Motor Company and powerful political figure in Michigan, passed on to John Dodge a letter from a Frank Dodge (no relation), who was looking for a job. John Dodge replied,

> I should very much like to do something for this young man, but we have found it necessary to establish a rule that no one by the name of DODGE be given employment in our factory. We have had two or three cases and have always has [sic] a bad experience in each case.
>
> While you will not think it is much of a reason, it really has caused us considerable annoyance and we have decided that two members of the Dodge family are all that the firm should be burdened with.[47]

The Dodge brothers treated the competitors fairly as well. When Henry Joy was the president of Packard Motor Car Company, he was annoyed to learn that labor recruiters from Dodge Brothers waited outside the Packard factory gates and recruited Packard's toolmakers to take jobs at Dodge. Both companies were extremely busy with orders and Joy had trained the toolmakers at his own expense. Joy visited John Dodge, informed him about this practice, and asked Dodge to stop stealing his skilled tradesmen. John Dodge agreed that it was an unfair business practice and ordered his personnel manager to stop this type of recruiting.[48]

The Dodge brothers may have been "friends of labor" on one level, but they certainly did not want labor unions in their factory. In June 1911, Couzens wrote a letter to John Dodge urging Dodge Brothers to become members of the Employers' Association of Detroit (EAD). Referring to Ford's decision to join the EAD, Couzens explained that "after looking into it, [we] decided we could not afford to 'ride a free horse' and that they really were doing a good thing for the City of Detroit and employers of labor." In a follow-up letter, Couzens informed Dodge that he asked John J. Whirl, the director of the EAD, to make an appointment to visit him. The EAD kept labor unions out of the factories by controlling hiring and by identifying and then blackballing union activists. This alliance of factory owners helped to keep Detroit a bastion of the "open shop" from its formation in December 1902 until the mid-1930s. The Dodge brothers were members of the EAD by mid-February 1914, when their company was on the verge of automobile production and a much-enlarged labor force. The fact that organizers from the radical Industrial Workers of the World (IWW) were active in Detroit auto plants in 1912 and 1913 may have encouraged them to join the EAD. The IWW organized a strike at two Studebaker plants in Detroit in June 1913, and the union's campaigns among Ford workers late in 1913 was one reason that Henry Ford introduced the $5-a-day wage early the next year.[49]

Dodge Brothers was willing to reply to inquiries from the EAD about former Dodge workers who applied for jobs elsewhere, as it did regarding Joseph Hoppes, a machinist, in May 1911. Some scattered evidence suggests that they employed labor spies in their plant in May 1913. Three reports from three different spies, dated 13 and 14 May 1913, came to the Dodge management. Frederick Haynes wrote comments on all three reports. All the spies discussed the men's attitude toward the IWW and two of three men attended IWW meetings and reported on the speakers and the topics. The three reports that randomly survived were part of an original collection that could have included thirty reports or three thousand. The extent of the practice cannot be determined.[50]

The Dodge brothers demanded that their employees be hardworking and conscientious. John Dodge paid a surprise visit to the Hamtramck plant on Sunday, 5 November 1911, and did not like what he saw—the front gate to the plant was wide open, as were the doors to the office building and many offices. The watchman did not have keys to lock these doors or the front gate. John Dodge's letter to plant superintendent Adolph Vocelle the following day demanded immediate improvements: "Anyone could have come in the place and ramsacked [sic] it from top to bottom."[51]

Dodge Brothers attempted to provide a more humane work environment than would be found at other similar large factories. To make the work of their 200 forge workers a bit more bearable, Dodge Brothers made the following request of a local restaurant operator in July 1912: "We wish you would submit [to] us a price on 200 sandwiches and 200 bottles of beer to be delivered every working day, ice cold, to our Forge Plant about 9:30 a.m. during the months of July & August."[52] Clarence Krieg, a longtime Dodge Brothers employee (1911–51), offered a different perspective on this "humane" policy. He recalled sitting in a saloon across from the factory with seventeen other Dodge workers when John Dodge walked in and asked, "How many of you men belong at work?" No one replied. Dodge then said, "I'll buy a round [of drinks] for the house and when it's gone, you men who ought to be working better get back." They all scampered back to work. Krieg believed that Dodge Brothers supplied its men with beer to keep them from leaving the plant for the saloons. They stopped the practice after some men broke empty beer bottles on their machines.[53]

Contemporary observers of the Dodge business reported a rapid rise in the number of Dodge employees once the firm began to convert to automobile production.

When the Michigan Department of Labor conducted factory inspections in 1913, Dodge Brothers reported 130 employees at a Detroit foundry visited on 21 July and 2,574 at its Hamtramck plant, visited on 2 October. An article that appeared in the *Michigan Manufacturer and Financial Record* on 27 January 1913 claims that Dodge employed more than 2,000 men. The same publication gives Dodge Brothers 3,000 workers in April 1914. An article in *Automobile Topics* on 13 June 1914 cites employment of 5,000 men, which would be consistent with the ongoing plant expansion under way as Dodge Brothers prepared to manufacture its own car. H. Cole Estep wrote a lengthy article on the Dodge plant in *Iron Trade Review* on 6 May 1915 and claimed that the Dodges employed 5,000 while they were still engaged in making components for Ford.[54]

Even after Dodge Brothers moved into their large new plant in Hamtramck, their relationship with the Ford Motor Company was not without conflict. In late February 1911, the firm reported severe problems machining axle shafts for Ford at a sufficient rate to satisfy their contract. One problem was "the extreme hardness of the metal," but the main source of trouble was that Ford had changed the machining tolerances in the middle of the contract. The original drawings allowed tolerances of ±0.001 inch on the round part of the drive shaft and ±0.002 inch on the square part, levels of precision only recently obtained by Henry Leland and a few Detroit automobile manufacturers. When the Ford inspectors decided to lower the tolerances to ±0.0005 inch on both parts of the axle shaft, Dodge Brothers argued, "It is practically impossible to produce these pieces commercially within these limits." Their production of axle shafts was only 25 percent of the level a year earlier, and they were asking the Ford Motor Company for relief.[55]

Supply problems were not always Ford Motor Company's fault. In late April 1911, Dodge Brothers apologized for failing to supply Ford with prices for repair parts for earlier Ford models such as Models K and N. They blamed the move of their offices from Monroe Avenue to Hamtramck for disrupting their normal office functions. They explained to Ford in late July 1911 that they were unable to fulfill orders for rear axle assemblies, transmissions, and drive shafts on time because of shortages of materials.[56] The communications between the two companies were not always serious or critical. After John Dodge noticed that a recent issue of *Ford Times* had a poorly drawn illustration of the Ford Motor Company's inspection department, he gently kidded Henry Ford: "This illustration certainly must make some of our competitors smile, when judging by this illustration, our facilities for inspection consist largely of a six-foot rule and a pair of ice tongs."[57] The issue of *Ford Times* had a drawing with the caption, "Each Ford part is carefully inspected

Ford Motor Company branch managers meeting, 1907. James Couzens (top left), John F. Dodge (top right), and Horace E. Dodge (left of John Dodge). Courtesy of NAHC.

before being placed in stock to be sent out to Ford dealers." The only two "precision" measuring devices shown in the drawing were a six-foot folded ruler sitting on the inspection table and an enormous set of calipers that looked like ice tongs.[58]

Although Henry Ford never acknowledged their contribution, the Dodge brothers played a pivotal role in the success of his cars and his company. After some early hiccups, they gave Ford a steady supply of high-quality, reasonably priced parts and components. They worried about their near-total dependence on Ford, recognizing that he would eventually manufacture all of his own components. In the last contract drafted between the partners, the Ford Motor Company agreed to buy from Dodge Brothers at least 80 percent of its requirements of transmissions, rear axles and drive shaft assemblies, steering gear assemblies, bronze and brass castings, and drop forgings over the next nine years starting in July 1913. The contract required that Ford provide estimates of its minimum needs for the year in July, at the start of each year's contract renewal.[59]

Ford stockholders, *Ford Times,* June 1911. From the Collections of the Henry Ford, Negative No. 0–1707.

For John and Horace Dodge, the decision to break with Ford and manufacture their own car was not simple. They found the yearly haggling with Ford and Couzens over component prices a constant source of aggravation. In 1912, they agreed in principle to lease their factory to the Ford Motor Company starting in 1914. The lease agreement has not survived, so we do not know the precise provisions. A letter from Dodge Brothers to Couzens in July 1913 canceled the lease arrangement the two parties had signed on 13 August 1912, explaining, "One of the principal reasons for the making of this lease was to do away with the trouble arising annually when prices were agreed upon. Inasmuch as this lease has failed to overcome this trouble, we wish to exercise our right as given under clause ten of this lease to cancel the same upon twelve month's notice, to be given during the month of June of any year." John Dodge also resigned as director and vice president of Ford Motor Company in a letter to Couzens dated 18 August 1913. Ford Motor Company accepted John Dodge's resignation three days later.[60]

The Dodge brothers' decision to build their own car seemed like a logical step for them to take after making parts for Ford for eleven years. Richard Crabb argues that they were motivated mainly by a desire to produce a better car than the Model T. They believed that they could greatly improve Ford's car without driving up its price. Henry Ford's rigid refusal to consider improvements to the Model T further encouraged the Dodge brothers to strike out on their own.[61]

Theodore MacManus, whose advertising firm had Dodge Brothers as a client starting in 1914, provides a more personal version of their decision to break with Ford. MacManus recalled a meeting between the Dodge brothers and their legal counsel, Howard B. Bloomer, in downtown Detroit in 1913. Bloomer asked them point-blank, "Why don't you brothers build your own car?" John Dodge explained that they enjoyed lucrative contracts with Ford and hefty stock dividends and besides, they did not want the aggravation of having to sell cars. Bloomer reminded the Dodges that their total dependence on Ford could prove costly for their business. The following day, they resumed the discussion and both John and Horace Dodge conceded that Bloomer was right.[62]

John Dodge discussed their plans with *The Horseless Age* in late August 1913, and *Motor Field* printed essentially the same story in its September 1913 issue. He admitted, "We have been fussing with these plans [to make their own car] for a long time," and revealed that two years earlier, Dodge Brothers began buying property on Bismark Street south of the existing parts factory to permit plant expansion. They would destroy forty homes to make way for the new plant. He further explained, "Our business has grown too big to be dependent upon anyone else and we have decided to go into the manufacture of automobiles for ourselves."[63]

John and Horace Dodge rightfully wanted to end their dependence on Ford and the risks that their relationship with Ford entailed. Since the launching of the Ford Manufacturing Company in November 1905, Henry Ford had moved toward manufacturing a larger share of his components. Although the Highland Park plant included substantial assembly capacity, much of the new plant built in 1909–14 consisted of machine shops, foundries, and heat-treating facilities. Ford was greatly increasing his manufacturing capacity and experience with the move to Highland Park, and the Dodge brothers must have recognized their uncertain future as Ford's supplier.

After the Dodges notified Henry Ford in July 1913 that they would stop producing for him in a year's time, they turned their attention to their new challenges. Over the next eighteen months, John and Horace Dodge remade their manufacturing operations and redefined the thrust of their business. They stopped being the largest supplier of parts and components in the automobile industry, entirely dependent on the Ford Motor Company, and became an independent manufacturer of their own nameplate. They were remarkably successful at their new endeavor, and their company, along with their fortunes, grew even larger.

THREE

The First Dodge Brothers
Automobile

The Dodge brothers are the two best mechanics in Michigan. There
is no operation in their own shop from drop forging to machining,
from tool-making to micrometric measurement, that they can't do
with their own hands. . . . As a matter of fact, when the Dodge Bros.
new car comes out, there is no question that it will be the best thing
on the market for the money.

Michigan Manufacturer and Financial Record, 8 August 1914

Over a remarkable eighteen-month span, John and Horace Dodge designed and produced an entirely new automobile, introducing a proud new nameplate that has survived to this day. They designed and tested a new mid-priced car that offered many advanced technical features. They decided which components to manufacture in-house, which to buy from outside suppliers, and which suppliers to use. Surviving records allow us a unique view of this development process, which occupied most of their working lives in 1914.

While continuing to fulfill their contract to supply parts and components to Ford until June 1914, the Dodges simultaneously reworked and greatly enlarged their existing manufacturing facilities to produce their new car. They also created a national sales organization and a network of franchise dealers to sell the automobile, all from scratch. The two brothers launched an effective advertising campaign that generated enormous public interest in their new offering long before any Dodge Brothers cars were available for purchase.

Designing the Dodge Brothers Automobile

Before they broke with Ford, the Dodges hired Frederick J. Haynes in June 1912 to manage their growing manufacturing facilities and to oversee production of the automobile they intended to build. Haynes, who managed the H. H. Franklin Company automobile factory in Syracuse, New York, before coming to Detroit, had considerable experience running manufacturing plants, and was well-known to John Dodge. Born in Cooperstown, New York in 1871, his attorney father moved the family to Syracuse in 1881. After he finished high school, Haynes worked for a company that made carriage bodies, earning $4.50 a week, and then worked at a grocery store, making change, for $6.00 a week. He entered Cornell University in 1891 and studied mechanical engineering for three years, but had to leave for financial reasons and never finished his degree.[1]

Haynes gained practical work experience in the 1890s, initially in the machine shop of the Syracuse Bicycle Company, earning $4.50 a week. There, he showed evidence of his mechanical skills and willingness to take risks. After breaking many drills while working on a poorly designed jig, he went to the factory manager to complain about the tool design and to demand a transfer to the department that designed the tools. The manager agreed to do so and raised his pay to $7.50 a week. After a year, Haynes took a job with the Hunter Arms Company of Fulton, New York, after boldly offering to design the machinery and tools the firm would need for the new L. C. Smith bicycle it was preparing to build.[2]

After three years with Hunter Arms, Haynes became the superintendent of the E. C. Stearns Company bicycle factory in Toronto in 1899, a position he held for exactly one year. Late in that year, the National Cycle and Automobile Company absorbed the Evans & Dodge Bicycle Company in Windsor and the E. C. Stearns Company. Haynes met John Dodge, the new superintendent of National Cycle, on 15 December 1899. Dodge asked Haynes to prepare the machinery at the Toronto factory for shipment to the National Cycle plant in Hamilton, Ontario. When Haynes finished the task in two weeks, Dodge asked Haynes to join him in Hamilton. Largely as a test of his abilities, John Dodge ordered Haynes to clean out the Hamilton plant, including a battery of filthy paint ovens. After Haynes finished this unpleasant work, John Dodge made him the superintendent of the machine shop in Hamilton, and when Dodge left National Cycle later in 1900, Haynes became plant manager.[3]

Haynes later served as general manager of the Lake Shore Engine Works in Marquette, Michigan, in 1902–04. Lake Shore manufactured machinery and equipment used in the Lake Superior copper- and iron-mining industries. In 1903 John Dodge tried to get Haynes to supervise the Ford Motor Company assembly operations. He gave Haynes a tour of the Ford factory and offered him a three-year contract, with an annual salary of $2,500, but Haynes declined the offer, deciding to stay with Lake Shore. He did not think that the Ford Motor Company had very good prospects for success. Although Haynes might have been willing to work for John Dodge, he did not trust Ford or his lieutenants. His loyalty to Lake Shore meant nothing when a change in ownership later in 1903 resulted in his firing. Out of work, he returned to Syracuse and took a job with the H. H. Franklin Company in 1904 as the assistant engineer and later served as the plant manager.[4]

John Dodge had remained in contact with Haynes through occasional letters, and when the Dodge brothers decided to make their own car, he invited Haynes to Detroit in mid-April 1912 to hire him. When John Dodge wrote to Haynes asking him what salary he would need, he replied, "I don't care about the salary. I want the position." John Dodge sent Haynes a laconic response to this letter, simply stating, "I have your letter of the 12th. Things as you have outlined them will be perfectly satisfactory to me." Before Haynes departed Syracuse for Detroit, John Dodge suggested that Haynes bring his personal car, a Franklin Six, with him. Dodge wanted to examine the air-cooled Franklin carefully. Haynes became works manager for Dodge Brothers on 15 June 1912 without any agreement about his pay. Finally, John Dodge ordered his paymaster to give Haynes the same salary he had received at Franklin.[5]

Automotive trade publications began to speculate in 1912 about John and Horace Dodge's manufacturing future. In late May 1912, *Motor World* reported that Dodge Brothers planned to build their own automobile in the future but had made no firm decisions about the timing or the design of the car. Their motivation was simple—they no longer wanted to be totally dependent on Ford for their work. The article also claims that the Dodges were already testing several prototypes. The same trade magazine ran a story in late August 1912 predicting that the new Dodge Brothers car would appear soon and would definitely be a six-cylinder model. They had interviewed John Dodge and this was the story he gave them. The new Dodge Brothers car, which did not appear until November 1914, was in fact a four-cylinder model.[6]

John Dodge deliberately encouraged speculation about the new car. In an interview with *The Horseless Age* in August 1913, repeated in *Motor Field* the next month, John Dodge suggested that the Dodge Brothers car would be very similar to the Model T in terms of style and price. A lengthy article published in the *Detroit News* in mid-August 1913 claims that the Dodges had already designed the new car, which would be in production by June 1914, assembled in a new 2,100-foot-long factory at the Hamtramck site. Of course, none of this was true. In February 1914, *Automobile Topics* claimed that the new Dodge Brothers car would have "a Renault type of hood" and would sell for about $800. They further speculated that Dodge Brothers would produce 40,000 cars in their first year. Renault automobiles at this time were all air-cooled, so Renault hoods sloped downward in the front, extending beyond where the radiator would normally be. The Franklin Automobile Company used air-cooled engines in its cars in the 1910s, allowing for the elimination of the radiator and water pump.[7]

An article in *Chrysler Motors Magazine* in January 1936 shows a photograph of a clay model of an experimental air-cooled car with the Renault-style sloping hood. In the same article, George Kiernan, a longtime master mechanic with Dodge, also recalls an experimental six-cylinder engine with two radiators. When the Dodge brothers rejected this design and that of the air-cooled engine, they opted for a more traditional design. Kiernan claimed that he designed the water-cooled four-cylinder engine that went into the first Dodge Brothers cars. It is more likely that Kiernan worked under Horace Dodge's direction and that the new engine was the collective effort of Horace Dodge, George Kiernan, and dozens of engineers, draftsmen, and mechanics.[8]

The decision to produce a Dodge Brothers car required a reorganization of the Dodge Brothers enterprise. Dodge Brothers, legally established on 1 July 1914, was a corporation with $5,000,000 in capital stock, 50,000 shares valued at $100 each. John and Horace Dodge each held 24,995 shares, while Alfred L. McMeans owned the remaining ten shares. At the corporation's first board meeting, John Dodge was elected president and treasurer of the firm, Horace Dodge vice president and general manager, and McMeans as secretary. The new legal entity immediately bought all of the real estate, machinery, and inventories from the old partnership for $3,047,715.80. Three years later, the value of the capital stock doubled to $10,000,000 in July 1917 with the issuance of 50,000 additional shares. The only real change in the Dodge corporate structure before the death of John Dodge in January 1920 was the resignation of McMeans from the board of directors in December 1919. Howard B. Bloomer joined the board as McMeans's replacement.[9]

The Dodge brothers began production of their own nameplate in November 1914. They needed more than a year of preparation before the first car rolled off the line. Horace Dodge designed most of the new automobile and some of the machinery needed to produce it, doing the design work in a cottage on John Dodge's Meadow Brook estate. Tradition has it that John Dodge tested several brands of automobile tires by dropping them off a four-story building and studied the crashworthiness of one prototype car by driving it into a wall at twenty miles per hour.[10]

These stories aside, the work of selecting materials for the new car, designing the parts and components, and then purchasing or making all the needed parts was monumental. We can see the size and complexity of the work from a surviving three-volume set of notebooks, without title or author, containing materials relating to the purchase of raw materials and components for the Dodge Brothers car, along with information on the design of components and the purchase of machinery to manufacture the parts. The three volumes cover the period 13 March 1914–21 June 1916. Internal evidence strongly suggests that Frederick J. Haynes collected the materials.

The first volume, covering March 1913–July 1914, contains detailed cost and quality estimates for components ranging from frames, wheels, and tires to bearings, piston rings, and ignition systems from more than one hundred potential suppliers. The compiler typically collected information on three or four possible suppliers for each component. An entry of 8 July 1914, for example, examines the specifications and costs of batteries from six potential suppliers.

The first notebook also included proposals from important machinery suppliers, such as the Foote-Burt Company and the Ingersoll Milling Machine Company, and the Dodge evaluation of the machines and the proposals. A four-page section, "Rear Axle Housing Press Comparisons," examines presses manufactured by the Toledo Machine Tool Company, the E. W. Bliss Company, and the Ferracute Company. John Dodge made detailed suggestions for improving the operation of the Foote-Burt presses used to drill holes in engine blocks and then considered proposals from the manufacturers. By May 1914, Dodge Brothers had ordered nine different types of machines from the Foote-Burt Company. The compiler also listed several hundred component blueprints that he had checked and approved.

The second volume, covering July 1914–July 1915, has additional information relating to the purchase of components and machinery. Haynes also kept detailed notes regarding skilled mechanics, engineers, and managers seeking employment at Dodge Brothers, including their employment history and references. There is no evidence that Dodge Brothers hired any of these men, but the skills and experiences of many job-seekers were evidence of the Dodge Brothers' reputation within the auto industry. Several were skilled machinists or electricians seeking shop work. Two, R. A. Fisher and Charles D. Brown, sought such positions as machine shop foreman or superintendent, asking salaries of $2,000 and $3,300, respectively. Engineer A. J. Paige wanted a position in engine or chassis design at a salary of $2,500, while Harry Graves, chief engineer at the defunct Cartercar Company, was willing to take a job at $2,500 a year. Nelson Knox, who had held management jobs in the pressed steel business for eleven years, proposed to manage the Dodge Brothers stamping plant at an annual salary of $4,000. Finally, Alfred Thomson, who was the factory manager for Maxwell in Detroit, showed a willingness to work for Dodge Brothers at his current (January 1915) salary of $10,000 a year.

When the Dodges began to plan for their own press shop (stamping plant) to produce some of their own body panels, Haynes compiled four pages of notes (11 February 1915) on the layout of the plant, including the arrangement of machinery, the materials handling systems, and management of the dies. He later produced an elaborate chart (19 March 1915) comparing the capacity, features, and costs of two dozen different types of presses manufactured by the Toledo Machine Tool Company and the E. W. Bliss Company. Between 31 March and 23 April, Dodge Brothers placed orders for thirty-seven presses of twenty-three distinct types, splitting the orders roughly evenly between the Toledo and Bliss companies.

The new automakers had to consider more than just the physical production of their cars. Haynes created a list, "Our Office—Things to Do," which included a dozen administrative tasks identified by John and Horace Dodge as requiring attention, including cost accounting, purchasing, and handling of customer complaints. He labeled the page "How to Do Them," and included a list of men whom they could assign to handle these areas. Having the entire office force together in a single building would allow more cooperation among the staff and would make the administrative operations of Dodge Brothers more flexible and more efficient.

The third notebook, covering April 1915–June 1916, shows the continuous improvements that Dodge Brothers was making to components supplied by outside vendors or produced internally. The choice of which battery brand to install in the Dodge Brothers car came up again. The Willard battery was the original choice, based on cost savings over the Exide. In mid-October 1915, Dodge Brothers did another detailed comparison of the Exide and Willard batteries. The ten-page analysis, which provided fourteen points of comparison, gave Exide a slight advantage because the company was the largest and best-funded battery manufacturer in the United States, the firm sold its batteries worldwide, and its battery carried greater prestige than those of its competitors. The Exide was also nearly nineteen pounds lighter than the Willard (49.75 pounds versus 68.50 pounds). The only downside to the Exide was a higher cost (30 cents per car) than the Willard.

This volume also chronicles the visits made in May 1915 by the compiler to seven rolling mills that produced automobile sheet steel to help determine which would supply their sheet steel. The seven-page analysis included a comparison of the plants, equipment, and processes used at these rolling mills, along with the quality and cost of the sheet steel produced. We can also view the less-than-ideal relationship that Dodge Brothers had with the Edward G. Budd Manufacturing Company, their principal supplier of bodies. In short, these notebooks are a primer on launching a new automobile.[11]

Preparing the Dodge Brothers Factory

Preparing the Hamtramck plant to manufacture and assemble the Dodge Brothers automobile was a monumental, expensive undertaking. In June 1914, as the conversion was getting under way, *Automobile Topics,* with a bit of hyperbole, described the forthcoming transformation:

> Once the plant is released from contract work, the pulsations of engines, the hum of machine tools, the whir of belts, the shock of heavy steam hammers, the roar of heat-treating furnaces, the staccato of pneumatic devices, the rumble of overhead cranes, the hiss of molten metal, and noise and bustle incident to manufacturing in the Dodge way, all will blend in a sound that tells of Dodge car production on a scale commensurate with the mammoth capacity of the organization.[12]

Dodge Brothers enlarged the factory complex and restructured the existing plant and equipment to carry out the new work. The major additions included a four-story reinforced concrete assembly building (70 feet wide and 875 feet long), a body press shop (70 feet by 600 feet), carpenter shop, die shop, compressor building, and test building. They enlarged the original two-story office building (51 feet by 116 feet) to four stories and more than doubled its "footprint" to 72 feet by 220 feet. Dining rooms and rest rooms occupied the top floor.

The Dodges also built a quarter-mile test track of creosoted planks, including a hill climb, at the northern edge of the plant. While other automakers still "road-tested" their cars on city streets, Dodge Brothers built the first dedicated test track in the industry. Total spending on buildings was more than $1,000,000 in 1914–15, with the assembly building alone costing $500,000 and the body shop about $250,000. The expansion efforts increased factory workspace from about 500,000 square feet to nearly 1.4 million square feet. After designing the first cluster of buildings for the Dodge Brothers Hamtramck plant, Albert Kahn fell out of favor, and starting in 1912 the Detroit firm of Smith, Hinchman & Grylls designed virtually of the buildings for this sprawling complex.[13]

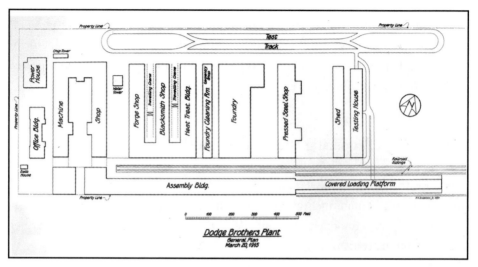

General plan, Dodge Brothers Hamtramck factory, March 1915. Courtesy of Richard K. Anderson, Jr.

During six hectic months in 1914, Dodge Brothers rearranged and retooled the Hamtramck plant at great expense. The transformation was so fundamental that the *Iron Trade Review* published an article describing the changes.[14] The new function of the plant required many new operations: a design ("experimental") department to engineer the new car; a testing department; an aluminum foundry; carpenter, tin, and pattern shops; a press shop for stamping frames; a body assembly department; a trim and upholstery department; a radiator shop; a motor assembly and testing department; a wheel shop; and a final assembly department. Dodge Brothers built a shipping platform, 900 feet long with a traveling crane, on the north side of the assembly building. Anticipating future expansion, Dodge Brothers required that the architects design all building foundations to support six stories, even if they built only two or four stories initially.[15]

The entirely new car design required replacing or rebuilding virtually every piece of equipment previously used for Model T parts production. This massive retooling included the patterns used in the foundry, dies for the forge shop, and tools, fixtures, and jigs used in the machine shop. The Dodge brothers had gained experience in quick retooling for new parts production after working for Ford since 1903. Horace Dodge designed much of the new machinery installed in the enlarged factory. After studying the enameling ovens used to dry painted car bodies, for example, he designed an improved oven that reduced heat loss from nearly 40 percent to about 4 percent. The scale of the conversion swamped Dodge Brothers' tool-

Test track and incline, Dodge Brothers Hamtramck factory, 1915. Courtesy of DCHC.

making force of 180 men, forcing the firm to hire four other Detroit companies to produce the required fixtures and jigs. Much of the new machinery was complex and expensive. Machining cylinder blocks for the engine required a dozen machine tools, costing a total of $59,000. A press used to stamp rear axle housings weighed twenty tons and cost $6,000. The forge shops alone had more than a dozen machines of that type. Dodge Brothers spent about $500,000 in retooling the plant for the new car. The force of men and women employed by Dodge Brothers also grew substantially during the transition from parts to automobile manufacturing. The firm had a workforce of about 5,000 during the first half of 1914, but by mid-April 1915 more than 7,000 were on the payroll, excluding the office staff.[16]

Niran Bates Pope, technical editor for *Automobile Topics,* wrote a nineteen-page booklet, *Dodge Brothers Works,* published in late 1919 by Dodge Brothers. Pope mainly describes the enormous plant as it appeared in 1919, but he also recalls visiting the plant in 1914 when automobile production was about to begin. He had asked the works manager, presumably Frederick Haynes, how Dodge Brothers was able to get such an enormous plant built and into operation so quickly. The works manager explained: "Chiefly because the Dodge Brothers themselves own the plant. If we had been obliged to get permission from a board of directors, from banking interests, or from outside stockholders, for the expenditures of millions that we have put into new buildings, new machinery, and new processes, it couldn't have been done. Things go smoothly when the actual owners are right in the factory and are the most enthusiastic of all in having the best."[17]

Launching a Sales Organization

Automobile manufacturers, parts suppliers, and car dealers all recognized the Dodge brothers as producers of top-quality, economical parts and components. By June 1914, nearly six months before anyone could buy a Dodge Brothers automobile, it was the dominant subject in automotive circles. *Automobile Topics* noted,

> So extraordinary a situation as has been created by Dodge Brothers, of Detroit, would not have seemed possible a few months ago. Practically all that the trade knows as yet is that Dodge Brothers are going to make automobiles and that a sales department has been created preparatory to marketing them; yet thousands of motor car dealers already have made application for the agency, and still other thousands are turning their eyes toward Detroit, to learn what might be expected. Without giving any details of their forthcoming offering, Dodge Brothers have become one of the big factors in the 1915 popular price car market.

The excellent reputation of Dodge Brothers, largely spread by word of mouth, was so great that by early November 1914, some 21,181 individuals, including many Ford dealers, asked to become Dodge Brothers agents without even seeing the new model.[18]

Dodge Brothers needed to have a sales organization in place well before the first cars came off the assembly line. In April 1914, Dodge Brothers named Arthur Irving Philp to the post of general sales manager. Philp had been the sales manager for the tire manufacturer Morgan & Wright and had served as general sales manager for the Studebaker Corporation. Philp divided the United States into sixteen sales districts and between late May and early July named experienced automobile salespeople to head each district. The district managers then selected the dealers. Philp also appointed Theodore MacManus as the firm's advertising consultant and Harry M. Robins as the foreign sales manager.[19]

MacManus recalled the beginnings of the Dodge sales operations. Philp interviewed dozens of advertising agencies to represent Dodge Brothers and finally settled on MacManus. Philp arranged a lunch meeting between MacManus and the Dodge brothers. When MacManus arrived, John Dodge immediately revealed his attitude toward advertising: "Horace and I go into the factory and sweat blood to save a tenth of a cent and you fellows turn right around and throw away ten percent." MacManus, impressed with John Dodge's honesty, began thinking about promoting the new cars as honest and practical, much like the brothers Dodge.[20]

Foreign automobile dealers and salespeople also expressed a strong interest in selling Dodge cars in their respective parts of the world. Sydney A. Cheney, a successful sales agent for Duncan & Fraser, Ltd., a Ford sales agency serving South Australia and Broken Hill, first wrote to Dodge Brothers in June 1913 asking about getting a dealership in South Australia. Cheney continued his efforts, after receiving letters from John Dodge saying that the car would not be in production for some time. Cheney quit his sales position, traveled to the United States, and arrived in Hamtramck in early October 1914 to visit Harry Robins in person and to ask for a Dodge Brothers dealership.

Robins explained that getting the Dodge Brothers car into production and launching an American sales organization preoccupied the firm so much that it would take no action on foreign sales any time soon. Cheney persisted in visiting Robins's office and finally had an interview with Philp. The stubborn Australian remained at the Dodge Brothers offices for three weeks, while hundreds of other visitors in search of a Dodge Brothers franchise paraded through the offices in Hamtramck. On 26 October 1914, Philp finally appointed Cheney as the district sales representative for Australia, but with the option of granting him a dealership for South Australia and for the Western Darling District of New South Wales. Cheney's persistence finally brought results.[21]

The Dodge brothers used advertising effectively to promote their new automobile among the general buying public. A series of billboard advertisements had only the words *Dodge Brothers* for several weeks, then included *Motor Car* for several more weeks, and, finally, *Reliable, Dependable, Sound.* They announced their new car in the *Saturday Evening Post* on 29 August 1914—"Dodge Brothers, Detroit, who have manufactured the vital parts for more than 500,000 motor cars, will this fall market a car bearing their own name." None of these advertisements included illustrations or specifications for the new automobile. The Dodges deliberately and effectively created enormous public anticipation by revealing nothing about the new car.[22]

The publicity buildup continued right through the public introduction of the Dodge Brothers automobile in early December 1914. The *Saturday Evening Post* became the firm's primary advertising venue, appealing to the general car buyer. In mid-October one ad proclaimed, "6,647 Solid, Substantial Business Men had, up to August 28, applied for the privilege of acting as Dodge Brothers' dealers." The reason was simple—"Dodge Brothers are sure to produce a car that will play a very large part in determining automobile values for the future." At the end of October, another ad reminded readers that the Dodge Brothers would bring to the manufacture of their car all of their experience, their insistence on accuracy, and their complete financial independence. Their plant was already accustomed to heating and forging more than 300,000 pounds of steel per day.[23]

Dodge Brothers also placed weekly advertisements in *Automobile Topics* from 11 July 1914 through December 1914, clearly intended to attract potential dealers. Full-page ads initially included only the Dodge Brothers logo, but in August they included a bird's-eye view of the factory in Hamtramck. On 15 August 1914 they added the note: "Copies of an illustrated sixteen-page pamphlet, 'Information for the Trade Concerning Dodge Brothers Detroit,' was recently mailed to motor car dealers. We will gladly supply any interested dealer who may not have received a copy." By late August, the advertisements also included an announcement about the number of dealers who had expressed a desire to sell Dodge Brothers cars. As of 21 August, inquiries had reached 6,126 and by 26 October reached 12,511 dealers. On 14 November, Dodge Brothers announced that it would show its cars in major U.S. cities. By late December, Dodge Brothers advertisements included images of the touring car and specific information about features and price.[24]

The widely accepted history of the initial production of early Dodge Brothers automobiles in November 1914 is at odds with much of the evidence about the earliest Dodge Brothers cars. Automotive historians have thought that the first production car, later named "Old Betsy," came off the assembly line at the Hamtramck factory on 14 November 1914. Guy Ameel, superintendent of final assembly for Dodge Brothers since the start of automobile production, served as John and Horace's chauffeur that day. With the brothers Dodge in the back seat, Ameel stopped the first Dodge Brothers car in front of John Dodge's mansion on Boston Boulevard in Detroit and a photographer recorded this important moment. At the introduction of the first Dodge Brothers car, John Dodge was fifty years old and Horace was forty-six. In contrast, Henry Ford, only a year older than John Dodge, was forty in 1903, the year he introduced his first commercially successful automobile, the Model A Ford.[25]

"Old Betsy" was more likely an experimental prototype car assembled several months before 14 November 1914 and not a production car at all. An article in

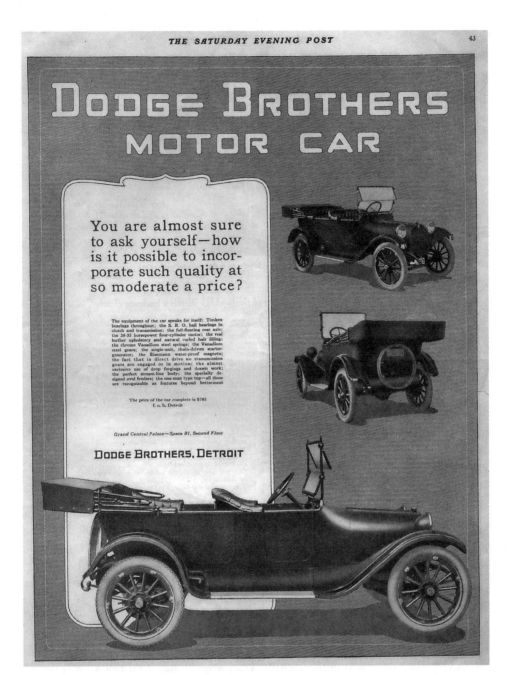

Saturday Evening Post advertisement, January 1915.

Horace Dodge (left rear) and John Dodge (right rear) in "Old Betsy" in front of John
Dodge's Boston Boulevard home, 14 November 1914. Guy Ameel is behind the wheel.
Courtesy of NAHC.

Automobile Topics from early October 1914 reports that Dodge Brothers had several "test cars" on the road, showing "decidedly gratifying" performance. The 7
November 1914 issue of *Automobile Topics* features an exclusive sneak preview of
the Dodge Brothers automobile that included three photographs of the complete
car, probably taken in early November. The Dodge brothers held a luncheon for
local newspaper reporters on 10 November at the Hamtramck plant and gave their
guests test rides in the new car. The *Detroit News* reciprocated by running a long,
gushing article in its afternoon edition, complete with a photograph of the new
model and the caption, "Dodge Bros. New Car Is a Model of Smartness, Grace
and Power." All these early cars had three ventilating louvers on each side of the
hood. These disappeared on Dodge Brothers cars sold to the public.[26]

An April 1917 article in the *Detroit News* reveals that "Old Betsy" was still in
use in the Dodge Brothers experimental department, having accumulated more
than 150,000 miles in test runs. The fact that the Dodge brothers did not retire
"Old Betsy" and keep the car for its historical value speaks volumes to their unsen-
timental, no-nonsense approach to their car business. According to Thomas J.
Doyle, the first Dodge Brothers dealer in Detroit, "Old Betsy" was not like other

experimental cars, which manufacturers often built with parts that were cast rather than forged, as an economy move. The Dodge brothers had so much confidence in their prototype that they went to the expense of producing the dies needed for forgings.[27] No one knows the fate of "Old Betsy," but it is likely that Dodge Brothers scrapped it when it was no longer serviceable.

The new Dodge Brothers automobile was vastly superior to the Model T Ford, already technically obsolete by 1914. The two cars were not direct competitors in any sense. The Dodge Brothers touring car carried a price of $785 versus the Model T Ford touring car's retail price of $490. The first Dodge Brothers model had a 35-horsepower four-cylinder engine (212.3 cubic inch displacement), with a three-bearing crankshaft, rated at 35 Brake Horse Power (BHP) versus the Model T's 20 BHP rating. It featured an all-steel body, lateral leaf springs at each wheel, and electric starting, making the new car technically up-to-date. The Dodge Brothers car also came equipped with a speedometer, a feature not found on the Model T Ford.[28]

According to Sydney Cheney, by early November 1914 Dodge Brothers had received 72,000 orders (and deposits) for their new automobile. The Dodge Brothers car continued to receive good press after it arrived at the dealerships. The first lengthy story about the new model that included detailed specifications and the price appeared in early December 1914 in the Atlanta *Hearst's Sunday American*. This paper ran two articles on the car on the same page, along with a three-column advertisement of the new Dodge Brothers car by the Atlanta dealership, the Pegram Motor Car Company. The article describing the vehicle in some detail noted, "If anyone expected some freakish model, he was disappointed, as the Dodge Bros. product is a perfectly normal motor car of standard lines and construction." The new model had a wheelbase of 110 inches and came equipped with a 35-horsepower four-cylinder engine, cone clutch, and pressurized fuel system. The article noted that the Dodge Brothers car was a larger, longer model than the competition was selling in the same price range. A companion article noted that more than 4,000 people had visited the dealership to examine the car over a four-day period.

The new car enjoyed the same kind of enthusiasm all over the country. Detroit Dodge Brothers dealer Thomas J. Doyle took delivery of the first Dodge Brothers car to leave the factory. Doyle reported a crowd of 6,000 on the first day he displayed the car. The fact that *Automobile Topics* reported the Dodge Brothers Detroit debut in its 14 November 1914 issue suggests that Doyle received the car a few days earlier. The first showing of the Dodge Brothers car in New York City drew 5,000 people on a cold and rainy day, and a similar exhibition in Chicago drew another 7,000. *Automobile Topics* reported in early December on first-day crowds

Caravan of Dodge cars arriving in Boston, 1915. Courtesy of DCHC.

of 5,000 in Boston, 4,000 in Cleveland, and dealerships in Omaha, Kansas City, and Minneapolis each drew more than 3,000 visitors. When the Murphy-O'Brien Company opened a new salesroom for the Dodge Brothers dealership in Omaha in late December, more than 8,500 attended the opening-day ceremonies. It is likely that the first batch of cars all went to dealers for display purposes. According to one source, it was not until 4 December 1914 that a customer took delivery of a Dodge Brothers car.[29]

The automotive press generally gave the new Dodge Brothers car enthusiastic reviews, praising its solid design and attractive looks. *Motor Magazine* of January 1915 gave it a good report card. Six months later, the British publication *Autocar* gave the new Dodge Brothers automobile very high ratings, unusual for the British auto press. The review noted that the new model had "many ingenious features, well-finished bodywork, and low selling price." The evaluation included an extensive road test and a thorough examination of all the mechanical features.[30]

The enthusiastic reception of the Dodge Brothers car extended well beyond the United States. Nearly a year after his visit to Hamtramck, Sydney Cheney established the Cheney Motor Company Limited in Adelaide, South Australia, in October 1915. Cheney received his first shipment of Dodge Brothers cars shortly after that. When he displayed the car for the first time in early November, a huge

1914 Dodge Brothers touring car. Courtesy of DCHC.

crowd waited outside his showroom for the doors to open. He sold his initial allot-
ment of seven cars by noon and the crowds continued for three weeks. One car in
that first shipment survives to this day. During the first year that Cheney operated
his dealership, he sold several hundred Dodge Brothers cars and by the third year
outsold all the dealers in South Australia, including the Ford franchise.[31]

John and Horace Dodge introduced their new nameplate in November 1914
with fanfare and great hope for its success. Dodge Brothers, however, was only
one of many companies making a mid-priced automobile. The touring car, the
most popular model, sold for $785 through 1917. In contrast, the Model T tour-
ing car sold for $490 starting in August 1914, but the price fell to only $360 two
years later. Maxwell Motor Company's touring car, which sold for $750 in 1914
and $670 the following year, was more directly competitive with the Dodge Broth-
ers touring car. General Motors' mid-priced cars, however, were markedly more
expensive than comparable Dodge Brothers models. For the 1915 model year
Oldsmobile offered a "Light 4" five-passenger touring car that retailed for $1,285,
while Buick offered two five-passenger touring cars, the Model C-25 ($950) and
the C-37 ($1,235). For the American market as a whole, cars selling for $676–$875
accounted for only 15.5 percent of the market in 1915 and 19.8 percent in 1916,

when fifteen substantial manufacturers competed in that narrow price range. The next highest price range ($876–$1,375) accounted for 15.3 percent and 20.1 percent of the market in 1915 and 1916, respectively.[32]

The combined effects of John and Horace Dodge's skills as mechanics, designers, and manufacturers allowed them at least a good chance to succeed in this highly competitive mid-priced automobile market. Their honest, no-nonsense approach to selling their cars and serving the needs of their customers also helped. Once committed to making their own nameplate, the brothers were remarkably skilled at promoting and selling the Dodge Brothers car. Their company enjoyed great success and quickly became a major player in the American automobile industry between 1915 and their untimely deaths in 1920.

FOUR

A Successful Car and a Successful Company, 1915–1920

Human haste, sweat and anxiety have been reduced to a minimum by a combination of ripe experience, far-sighted planning, and bold expenditure of money, and whatever strain is involved in enormous production falls on the machinery, not on the men. Nobody in the whole Dodge plant seems under tension.

"Dodge Brothers as Quality Producers of Cars"
Automobile Topics, 13 June 1914

Over the final seven years of their lives, John and Horace Dodge transformed their company from the largest supplier of automotive parts in the United States to a large-scale producer of a popular mid-priced car of their own design. The Dodge Brothers automobile was not merely another mid-range offering on the market but an innovative product because it incorporated all-steel bodies supplied by the Edward G. Budd Manufacturing Company of Philadelphia. Dodge Brothers developed an innovative, cooperative relationship with Budd in the process.

The Dodge brothers developed a strategy for selling their cars that was distinct from that of most other automakers. Much like Henry Ford, they froze the exterior appearance of their models, while making countless mechanical improvements. They also increased sales by introducing new models, including commercial vehicles. The Dodge Brothers automobile quickly became known as a durable, reliable car that delivered "dependability" to the customer. Their use by the U.S. Army in the Mexican campaign of 1916 and in the First World War only added to their reputation.

One of John and Horace Dodge's greatest accomplishments during their heyday did not involve automobiles. In October 1917, Dodge Brothers agreed to manufacture thousands of delicate recoil mechanisms for two types of 155-millimeter artillery pieces used on the Western Front. Relying on their skills and experience in the production of automobile components, they built a new factory and converted what had been a craft-based system of manufacturing into one based on mechanization using hundreds of machine tools. They achieved (limited) quantity production by summer 1918 and contributed substantially to the Allied war effort.

John and Horace Dodge achieved remarkable success as manufacturers of automobile components and complete cars. Their formula for success was quite simple—they had complementary skills, interests, and personalities, while they genuinely understood and liked each other. They remained honest and fair to their customers and employees alike. Their company survived and prospered after they died, and it later became a core component of the Chrysler Corporation. With their passing, the automobile industry and the greater Detroit community acknowledged their automotive significance and their important civic and charitable contributions as well.

"Bodies by Budd" and the Final Break with Henry Ford

One important feature of the new Dodge Brothers car seldom mentioned, much less emphasized in early accounts, was its all-steel body. In 1914, most automakers used either wood or metal/wood composite bodies, reflecting the manufacturing heritage of the body suppliers. Automobile body manufacturers such as Fisher and Wilson were originally makers of horse-drawn carriage bodies. The Dodges allied themselves with a Philadelphia manufacturer, Edward G. Budd (1870–1945), to outfit their entire production with all-steel bodies and enjoyed a long, if sometimes rocky relationship with this supplier.

Edward Budd had gained experience producing lightweight sheet steel stampings at the Philadelphia firm of Hale & Kilburn in 1902–12. Historically furniture makers, Hale & Kilburn had become the dominant producer of railroad car seats. They hired Budd to develop new methods to produce pressed parts for railroad seats and, in time, pressed steel panels for Pullman railroad cars. He was the general manager at Hale & Kilburn when the firm fabricated steel bodies for the 1912 Hupmobile, the first all-steel body production car in America. Budd and engineer Joseph Ledwinka invented acetylene and electric welding techniques for connecting the steel body panels and the necessary fixtures and jigs to hold the pieces together for welding. They also developed new techniques for making dies and invented new presses to produce the stamped sheet steel parts.[1]

Budd brought Ledwinka and twelve others with him when he established the Edward G. Budd Manufacturing Company in Philadelphia in June 1912. The company started with two substantial orders from the auto industry in 1912, one for 2,000 bodies for the Oakland and a $300,000 order from Willys-Overland for bodies for the Garford automobile. The payroll grew to 400 in 1913, but the bankruptcy of Garford Motors nearly drove Budd's company into receivership. John N. Willys, Garford's major stockholder, rescued Budd with a last-minute check for $100,000. Budd Manufacturing stumbled into 1914, surviving with orders from automakers Packard, Peerless, and Willys. On 17 June 1914, Joseph Ledwinka received a U.S. patent for the all-steel, all-welded automobile body, the foundation for Budd's early dominance in all-steel body production. Dodge Brothers gave Budd the large order for steel bodies that he needed to put his system into full production. The first Dodge Brothers body designs were the collective work of Ledwinka, Budd, and the Dodge brothers.[2]

John and Horace Dodge adopted the all-steel body in part because it was stronger and cheaper than the alternatives. The all-steel body had steel panels welded to a steel frame. The main cost advantage came from the painting process. On wooden or composite bodies, painting typically took ten or twelve days, with as many as twenty slow-drying coats applied by brush, each hand-rubbed before the next coat was added. Steel bodies permitted the use of baked enamel, which could be rapidly dried in ovens, where temperatures might reach 400 degrees. Finishing times typically dropped to five days.[3]

Dodge Brothers ordered 5,000 steel bodies in 1914 and followed with an order for 50,000 more for delivery in 1915. Dodge Brothers paid $42 per body and another $2 for each set of fenders. The Detroit automaker also agreed to pay up to $25,000 of Budd's tooling costs. The order was for open car bodies for touring cars and roadsters, making the Dodge Brothers car the first mass-produced car using an all-steel body. Because Budd was not able to estimate his costs accurately, the Dodges agreed to a contract with "flexible" prices to ensure that Budd would make a modest profit, but not an excessive one. According to Ledwinka, when the Dodge brothers signed the first contract with Budd, they told him, "At the end of the year, show us your books. If you have made too much out of us, we'll yell; if you've lost your shirt, we'll lend you something on your cuff buttons."[4]

A detailed list of the bodies and other stampings required for the first 40,000 cars, dated 2 June 1915, has survived. The list shows Dodge Brothers' heavy reliance on the Philadelphia firm. Budd delivered 33,500 touring car bodies, and the Wilson Carriage Company produced the remaining 1,500. (The Wilson bodies were of traditional wood-framed design, not the all-steel design used by Budd.) Budd was also responsible for all but fifty of the required 5,000 roadster bodies, and Dodge

Brothers would produce the remaining ones in-house. Similarly, Budd would fabricate 34,950 sets of fenders, the Hayes Manufacturing Company of Detroit 5,000 sets, and Dodge Brothers the remaining fifty sets. They divided the production of "splashers" (front fender inboard splash aprons) more evenly, with Budd making 22,000, Dodge Brothers producing 10,000, and Hayes the remaining 8,000. Budd and Dodge Brothers also split the production of running board brackets.[5]

Haynes visited the Budd plant in Philadelphia on 21 June 1915 in an effort to improve Budd's unsatisfactory record in keeping to its delivery schedule. He created a detailed record of Dodge Brothers' scheduled daily production for April through December 1915 and contrasted this with Budd's delivery of bodies and fenders. For the five weeks ending 19 June 1915, Budd fell behind in deliveries to the tune of 1,956 touring car bodies and 154 roaster bodies. Shortages of individual components caused enormous problems for assembly as well. Haynes reported that the factory had run out of left-side roadster doors. Budd had not started producing more until the supply was gone and the first new batch was defective.

Budd struggled to get all the necessary tools and machinery in place to satisfy Dodge Brothers' needs. On 21 June 1915, Haynes noted that the installation of body welding jigs for the touring car was a month behind schedule. Edward Budd promised to install additional presses in his fender department to speed production there, but he also threatened to increase his prices. The Philadelphia firm was still operating in the lower part of the "learning curve" and desperately trying to increase production, maintain quality, and satisfy Dodge Brothers. Stamping all-steel bodies in large quantities involved expensive dies and fixtures. Budd's factory location, far from Hamtramck, also made a smooth relationship with the Dodge brothers more difficult. Haynes remarked that the dies for the roadster, the low-volume Dodge Brothers model, cost Budd $32,184. Edward Budd was clearly betting his firm's future with the Dodge Brothers contract. The Philadelphia firm manufactured its 100,000th Dodge Brothers touring car body on 17 November 1916, number 200,000 on 18 February 1918, and number 301,987 on 21 June 1919. The two companies had joined at the hip. By 1916, Budd had a payroll exceeding 2,000 and was trying to hire another 1,500 to satisfy the ever-growing demand by Dodge Brothers for all-steel bodies.[6]

Despite this rocky beginning, production climbed steadily through 1920 (as shown in table 4.1). While Dodge Brothers enjoyed enormous growth and success during this time, John and Horace Dodge went through a bitter legal confrontation with Henry Ford over the payment of dividends to the Ford Motor Company

Table 4.1.
Dodge Brothers Factory Production, 1914–20 (Calendar Year)

Year	Units
1914	370
1915	44,630
1916	71,338
1917	101,587
1918	85,181
1919	121,039
1920	145,403

Source: Dodge Brothers *Master Parts Book, February 15,1927,* which lists the number of the first car produced on January 1 of each year. A different set of figures are found in a Memorandum, R. J. Kelley, Chrysler Public Relations Department to Frank Wylie, Dodge Division Public Relations Department, 31 May 1968, DCHC. Kelly derived the figures from statistics gathered by the Automobile Manufacturers Association. These totals include light commercial vehicles manufactured by Dodge Brothers.

stockholders. Henry Ford's only child, Edsel B. Ford, married Eleanor Lowthian Clay on 1 November 1916. The following day, John and Horace Dodge sued in the State Circuit Court, naming the Ford Motor Company, Henry Ford, and others as defendants. The suit sought to force the defendants to distribute 75 percent of the Ford Motor Company's surplus of $39 million as dividends to the stockholders.

The Dodge brothers planned to use future dividends from their Ford stock to help finance the expansion of their own business. Ford's statements and actions in 1916 forced them to seek legal recourse. Early in the year, Ford stated his intent to pay only nominal dividends (5 percent per month) on Ford Motor Company's book capitalization of only $2 million, or a total of only $1.2 million a year. By August 1916, the company's cash surplus was $52 million and ordinarily, the stockholders could have expected dividends of at least $25 million. Henry Ford announced that he would pay no special dividends and that he intended to spend the entire surplus on plant expansion at Highland Park and at the new River Rouge plant. By late October 1916, the Ford directors committed much of the surplus for plant expansion, prompting the Dodge brothers to file their lawsuit. Harold Wills testified that in January 1917, the Dodges offered to sell their stock to Henry Ford for a total of $35 million, but Ford simply said that he had no desire for any more stock. When asked by H. O. Richardson, a Minneapolis investor, in July 1917 if they would be willing to sell Ford Motor Company shares, they replied that they would sell their entire holdings of 2,000 shares for $36 million, or $18,000 a share.[7]

The Michigan Circuit Court issued its decision on 31 October 1917 and ordered Ford Motor Company to pay a special dividend of $19,275,000 within ninety days, less than 50 percent of the existing surplus. Ford appealed the decision to the Michigan Supreme Court and the case dragged on for more than a year. The Michigan Supreme Court filed its decision on 7 February 1919 and concurred with the order of the lower court for Ford to pay the special dividend, with interest. The court-ordered dividend amounted to $20,812,136, with the Dodge brothers getting 10 percent of the total.[8]

More important, in July 1919 Henry Ford purchased all the remaining Ford Motor Company stock, including the Dodge shares. Ford resigned as president of the Ford Motor Company in December 1918 and threatened to start a new company producing a car to compete with the Model T. This threat was nothing but a thinly disguised effort to intimidate the remaining stockholders to sell their stock at a low price. His tactics did not work with John and Horace Dodge. Ford paid them $12,500 a share for their 2,000 shares, a total of $25 million. Their business relationship with Henry Ford, begun in 1903, had finally ended. The Dodges had earned $5.4 million in dividends from their Ford stock since 1903 and additional profits of nearly $2 million from their contracts with Ford. Their original investment of $10,000 in the Ford Motor Company in 1903 yielded a total return of more than $32 million. After the legal battles ended, Henry Ford and the Dodge brothers had a remarkably cordial relationship, an appropriate finish for a business partnership unlike any other in the American automobile industry. According to John Wandersee, the news of John Dodge's death in January 1920 left Ford visibly shaken: "It was announced while we were on the train (to Pittsburgh) that John Dodge had just died and Mr. Ford's face dropped just like that. He just completely changed. He didn't look like the same man after, so he must have taken it pretty hard; he must have thought a lot of John Dodge." Perhaps Ford understood fully the contributions John Dodge had made to the Ford Motor Company.[9]

Sales Strategies

The Dodge brothers increased sales of their vehicles without engaging in annual styling changes by introducing additional models over time. Dodge Brothers offered only the touring car body during the first several months of production and then began offering a roadster body as an alternative. The roadster body, with seating for only two, used the same chassis and engine as the touring car and

1915 Dodge Brothers roadster. Courtesy of DCHC.

sold for $785. Dodge Brothers built a single roadster, in essence an experimental model, in late December 1914 to display at the New York auto show in January 1915. Although Dodge Brothers produced about 5,000 roadsters during calendar year 1915, the firm did not receive its first substantial delivery of fenders (450 sets) for this sporty model until March 1915. Dodge Brothers shipped the first production roadster (car number 14,356) to a dealer (Thomas J. Doyle of Detroit) on 5 June 1915.

The company produced only a touring car and roadster during the 1915 model year, but introduced the winter car versions of both in September 1915. These were simply a standard touring car or roadster with a detachable solid "winter top" with removable glass windows. This option cost $165, increasing the price of both models to $950, but enabled owners to use the car year-round. The Dodges had decided, much like Henry Ford, to "freeze" the appearance of their cars and thus avoid the costs of annual model changes.[10]

The "lineup" of cars did not change much until the 1917 model year, when Dodge Brothers increased the wheelbase on all its models from 110 inches to 114 inches and added a coupe and a two-door (center-door) sedan, both priced at $1,265. Their center-door sedan seated five passengers, but was not popular. The

1915 Dodge Brothers winter car. Courtesy of NAHC.

two-passenger coupe looked much like the roadster, but like the sedan, had wire wheels instead of the standard artillery-type wheels found on the other models.[11]

In mid-October 1917, Dodge Brothers introduced a screenside delivery vehicle, the commercial car, as a 1918 model. A closed-panel commercial vehicle, the business car, followed in late March 1918. Starting in May 1919, Dodge Brothers officially called these models the "screenside business car" and "panel business car." The new vehicles used a standard Dodge Brothers chassis equipped with heavier-duty springs than the standard car chassis. Both the screenside and panel versions had a carrying capacity of 1,000 pounds. Dodge Brothers promoted the use of special custom bodies with their business car chassis to produce ambulances, hearses, police cars, fire trucks, stake trucks, buses, and other specialized vehicles. Dodge Brothers did not supply special bodies for use on their chassis, but would "gladly assist dealers to obtain such equipments from reliable body builders." For model year 1919, Dodge Brothers sold 8,055 screensides, 4,073 chassis, 2,715 panel business cars, and 769 taxis, for a total of 15,612 commercial vehicles. Well before the Dodge Brothers associated with truck maker Graham Brothers in the early 1920s, the company had achieved much success with light-duty delivery vehicles. In 1920, business car and chassis production accounted for 10.8 percent of Dodge Brothers output.[12]

1916 Dodge Brothers center-door sedan. Courtesy of NAHC.

The last two significant additions to the model lineup before the deaths of the two Dodge brothers came in 1919. The first was a four-door sedan introduced in February 1919. It came with wire wheels and sold for $1,900. Dodge Brothers continued to offer the center-door sedan ($1,425) for the rest of 1919. In April 1919, the company introduced a five-window, three-passenger coupe ($1,750) to replace the Rex "convertible" roadster. Over the entire period of 1914–20, Dodge Brothers made remarkably few styling changes to its models. Unlike Henry Ford's practice of almost continuously lowering prices of the Model T Ford, Dodge Brothers prices rose over time, reflecting the various improvements incorporated into the new models. For the 1920 model year, Dodge Brothers offered five distinct car models—the touring car ($1,085), roadster ($1,085), sedan ($1,750), coupe ($1,750), and taxi ($1,850). In addition, the company sold chassis and two different business cars.[13]

Ford Motor Company followed a similar practice during the Model T era. It offered a single chassis, including the engine and drive train, but with a choice of body styles. For example, for the year beginning 1 August 1916, Ford customers could buy a runabout ($345), touring car ($360), couplet ($505), town car ($595), sedan ($645), and chassis ($325). Other car manufacturers were changing the

1918 Dodge Brothers screenside business car. Courtesy of DCHC.

1918 Dodge Brothers panel business car. Courtesy of DCHC.

1919 Dodge Brothers four-door sedan. Author's collection.

wheelbase, engine, and styling of their models frequently, if not annually. Both Oldsmobile and Buick frequently changed their wheelbase, engine, and model designations starting in 1908. Alfred P. Sloan, Jr., the president of General Motors in 1923–41, was the architect of a selling strategy known as "Sloanism," which included frequent changes in the appearance of car models. At a meeting with the top General Motors sales officers on 29 July 1925, Sloan claimed that only Ford and Dodge consistently avoided frequent model changes, but that Dodge had just changed its policy and Ford Motor Company was on the verge of doing so.[14]

Dodge Brothers, however, introduced mechanical improvements when necessary and convenient, with no connection to the model year. During the first thirty-two months of Dodge Brothers production, the firm made a total of 270 design changes requiring new parts, but most of these were very minor changes. A list of design changes through 1917 (compiled in 1926) identified fourteen significant improvements, all mechanical in nature. These included a vacuum tank, part of the fuel feed system used to deliver gasoline to the cylinders; "worm and wheel"–type steering; fourteen-inch brakes; a disc clutch; spiral bevel gears; improved radiators; and many improvements in the type or size of materials incorporated into housings, bushings, and the like. Dodge Brothers made another thirteen substantial improvements in design or equipment in 1918–20, including nine in 1919 alone. Only two of these, velvet upholstery and six half-inch pockets and flaps, both introduced in May 1919, could be considered "appearance and comfort" improvements. The rest were unvarnished mechanical upgrades.[15]

Continuous improvements to Dodge Brothers cars required quality engineering, and the Dodge brothers built an outstanding engineering department. In November 1915, they hired Russell Huff, the chief engineer at Packard Motor Company, to direct their engineering operations. Russell Huff (1877–1930), born in Leesburg, Ohio, earned a degree in mechanical engineering at Case School of Applied Science in Cleveland before joining Packard in 1900 at its plant in Warren, Ohio. When Packard moved to Detroit in 1903, Huff became assistant to Chief Engineer Charles Schmidt, whom Huff succeeded in 1905 at age twenty-eight. Huff remained at Dodge Brothers from 1916 until 1926, when he was vice president in charge of engineering.[16]

John and Horace Dodge only grudgingly accepted the need to advertise their cars and created an effective advertising operation within the firm. The man responsible for much of the early Dodge Brothers advertising was George Harrison Phelps, who began work at Dodge Brothers as an assistant to the general sales manager in October 1914 and became director of advertising in October 1915. Phelps was born in Millers Falls, Massachusetts, in 1883, graduated from Cornell University, and worked in a garage in Worcester, Massachusetts, before becoming the assistant manager of Buick's Boston branch in 1907. Two years later, he became the manager of Studebaker's New York City branch sales office. Phelps served as director of Dodge Brothers advertising until April 1922, when he established his own agency, which continued to produce the Dodge Brothers ads.[17]

Among other things, George Harrison Phelps wrote "The Creed of A Dodge Brothers Salesman," which embodied the Dodge Brothers philosophy in manufacturing and selling cars:

> I believe in Dodge Brothers Motor Car because into its making have gone the finest thoughts of those two Master Men whose name it bears. I believe in this car because I know that beneath the luster of a matchless exterior is the expression of honesty and integrity in material form. . . .

A Successful Car and a Successful Company

On offering Dodge Brothers Motor Car I know that I am selling a machine that is made of iron and steel and character—a vehicle that must and does symbolize and maintain a priceless reputation based on honor.

Phelps produced a four-page monthly newsletter for his sales force, including the dealers, from October 1914 through April 1922. The first page was usually a statement by Phelps relating to selling, either a philosophical statement or a pep talk. The rest of the newsletter typically included articles on new or updated models, new optional equipment, promotions and advertising campaigns, and personnel changes at Dodge Brothers.[18]

Phelps published a series of advertisements in 1916 emphasizing the growing acceptance of Dodge Brothers cars by the public. The campaign began with "A Year's Growth of Good Will," published on 1 January 1916. Later ads pushing the same theme appeared on 22 January, 24 June, 29 July, and 4 November 1916. The last advertisement noted that while Dodge Brothers had delivered more than 100,000 cars to customers, the lasting good will it enjoyed with the buying public was its most important asset. The company enjoyed success because its customers had faith in the integrity of Dodge Brothers manufacturing techniques.[19]

Dodge Brothers advertising was renowned for its simplicity. Sales brochures in 1914–15 and 1916 used the slogan, "It Speaks for Itself," without additional comment. A 1918 sales brochure had five blank pages except for the words, "UTILITY — ECONOMY — CONVERTIBILITY — ATTRACTIVENESS — VENTILATION," one to a page.[20]

Dodge Brothers customers were often the best promoters of the company's cars. Right before Christmas 1915, the Binghamton Motor Car Company of Binghamton, New York, asked its customers to write about their experiences with their Dodge Brothers automobiles. The dealership published twenty-eight letters in a booklet and listed a total of ninety-four Dodge owners at the end of the publication. All of the owners seemed genuinely pleased with the car's performance, reliability, and economy. Thirteen Dodge owners specifically mentioned the miles they had put on their car with no mechanical problems, ranging from 500 miles to 13,490 miles in just nine months.

A few of the letters bear repeating. E. Jeanette Roe wrote: "I am the proud owner of a Dodge and while I have only had it since September last, it has proven out far beyond my expectations. It is an ideal lady's car because of its simplicity in mechanism and shifting." Several writers mentioned that their wives and daughters frequently drove their Dodge Brothers cars. John M. Denis offered the following testimonial: "It is with pleasure that I hereby give you my testimonial of my perfect satisfaction with my 'DODGE.' She sure comes up to my expectations. I have never seen a car that pleases me better. It has never failed to respond to any requirement, and if you have a customer that hesitates about buying a Dodge send him to me, so I can tell him about the superiority of the Dodge over all others." The Reverend Sidney Walker, who would not lie, said: "You have asked for our opinion of the Dodge car. The fact that we have bought two, the second after a hard trial of the first ought to be enough. We find the Dodge car to be in every way as guaranteed and in our judgment superior to any car we have examined and had demonstrated of anything near its price. . . . If I had the money, I would at once buy a Dodge Roadster."[21]

Unsolicited customer endorsements helped spread the Dodge Brothers automobile's reputation for reliability. During the 1916 U.S. expedition in Mexico, war correspondent A.H.E. Beckett reported in *Motor Age* on the use of three Dodge Brothers cars in a surprise raid against the headquarters of a bandit leader, Colonel Julio Cardenas, in Chihuahua. Efforts to capture these bandits with cavalry had failed because horses were too slow. On 14 May, a daring Lieutenant George S. Patton, Jr., led a successful raid using three Dodge Brothers touring cars. They sped over a mile-long approach and surprised the enemy, killing Cardenas and two lieutenants. Patton explained, "We couldn't have done it with horses. The motor car is the modern war horse."

Brigadier General John H. "Black Jack" Pershing, the commander of the American forces in Mexico, had initially requested six Dodge Brothers touring cars for his officers on 31 March 1916. Following Patton's successful raid, Pershing requested 250 Dodge Brothers cars and ordered his staff to use them exclusively. Pershing's officers used many of these until the United States abandoned the Mexican campaign in February 1917. When Pershing took command of the American Expeditionary Force in France in June 1917, he had the remaining Dodge Brothers cars shipped to the battlefront, along with his personal Dodge Brothers car, which he named Daisy. For part of the war, Eddie Rickenbacker, the famous race car driver and flyer, served as the driver of Pershing's personal Dodge Brothers touring car.[22]

Dodge Brothers supplied more motor vehicles and chassis for the U.S. Army during the First World War. According to Konrad Schreier, the army purchased 8,191 touring cars, 175 roadsters, and forty sedans; an additional 2,644 commercial vehicles, mostly screensides; and chassis for more than 1,000 ordnance light

Dodge Brothers touring car in 1916 Mexican campaign. Courtesy of DCHC.

repair trucks, much like a pickup, and perhaps 1,000 ambulances. A Dodge Brothers booklet, *After Five Years* (1919) gives a figure of 12,795 vehicles. Few ambulances and probably no more than one-third of the passenger cars saw service in France, but most screensides and repair trucks did. A *Detroit Free Press* article in early July 1918 shows 50 Dodge Brothers screenside trucks lined up on the test track behind the factory, ready for delivery to the U.S. Army Quartermaster's department. The November 1918 newsletter of the Automobile Club of Southern California ran a brief article and photograph showing Dodge Brothers cars packed in boxes for shipment to France. Dodge Brothers shipped the "boxed cars" from Detroit to the East Coast by truck.[23]

Dodge Brothers claimed that its cars outperformed all others in toughness, durability, and reliable operation. The December 1918 issue of a company advertising newsletter showed pictures of Dodge Brothers cars and ambulances at work at the front in France and featured testimonials offered by American soldiers. One letter from a soldier at the front described the various transportation options available to the troops:

> Up at the front you travel by narrow gauge (railroad), truck, side car, "a pied," or Dodge. The narrow gauge is all right if it doesn't run off the track and you are possessed with an infinite patience and a prospective shower bath. The truck furnished

Dodge Brothers 1918–19 U.S. Army ambulance. Courtesy of DCHC.

a chiropractic sort of experience until it develops gastronomic asthma, or a failing for ditches. The side car makes the hand salute a menace to the right eye, and "a pied" is O.K. if you aren't wearing the socks that mother or sister sent you. But the Dodge—the Dodge. Be it the most debilitated Dodge that ever rattled, it will make even a lieutenant lounge with the comfortable ease of a Q. M. Paymaster Cadillacing south.[24]

By the end of the war, Dodge Brothers and their dealers had received hundreds of testimonial letters from soldiers who used Dodge Brothers cars at the front in France. George H. Phelps created a booklet, *The Good Will of an Army,* in November 1921, using forty of these letters. One surviving copy of the brochure had a second page customized for the dealer who used it, the Brownell Auto Company of Birmingham, Alabama.[25]

Dodge Brothers also received a ringing endorsement of their cars in September 1921 from Major Albert T. Rich, adjutant general for Indiana. The *Indianapolis Star* had offered a prize for the best argument for buying a particular car and Rich, who had served in France during the First World War, submitted a long letter in which he praised what he called the "Unknown" Dodge Brothers touring car he used for eleven months starting in May 1918. It reliably moved through all kinds of difficult roads and battlefield conditions and never needed repairs other than replacing tires punctured by bullets or shrapnel. He added, "In the memory of those who witnessed its services during the World War there is a place set aside for the 'Unknown' Dodge Brothers Touring Car that took the bone in its teeth and chugged along through h—— and high water for eleven hard, car-breaking months when other cars were being laid up for repairs at all times." In responding to Rich's letter, Frederick Haynes commented, "We have always endeavored to build into each Dodge Brothers Car, all the service that we knew how; and never has there been, or will there be, a thought of cost where serviceability is concerned. Dependability must be maintained at any price." Dodge Brothers took Rich's testimonial and Haynes's reply and reprinted them as a pamphlet, *From the Heart of a Soldier,* for distribution throughout its dealer network. George H. Phelps informed his advertising managers and dealers that Dodge Brothers planned to distribute two million copies of the brochure, presumably to Dodge Brothers dealers. He argued that the brochures offered "an excellent opportunity to overcome sales resistence [sic]."[26]

Military sales during the First World War probably made up for the loss of overseas sales that accompanied hostilities. There is little information available on Dodge Brothers foreign sales, with one major exception. Sydney Cheney has provided fascinating details about the wartime experience of Dodge dealers in South Australia and on the rest of that continent. Australia imported about 15,000 cars in 1917, with Model T Fords accounting for 10,000 units; Dodge Brothers cars about 2,300; Buicks another 1,500; and the remainder split among scores of nameplates. On 10 August 1917, Australia's government announced an embargo on the importation of automobile bodies. Cheney convinced Edward Holden, an Adelaide leather manufacturer, to make bodies for Dodge Brothers cars. Three weeks after the embargo announcement, Cheney displayed a Dodge Brothers chassis outfitted with a handsome body from Holden. The demonstration helped Cheney forge an agreement among all the Dodge Brothers dealers in Australia and Holden for Australian-built bodies. Holden built 5,000 bodies during the first year and Dodge Brothers sales leaped ahead of Ford's.[27]

With a supply of bodies assured, Cheney then faced a potential stoppage of chassis deliveries due to the severe shortage of shipping space during the war. The Australian newspaper industry, which was facing a severe shortage of newsprint for the same reason, developed a daring solution. A Melbourne businessman bought a derelict steamship, the *Coolgardie,* which was lying idle, and repaired it enough to make it barely seaworthy. He then used this vessel exclusively to transport newsprint from Vancouver, British Columbia, to Australia. Cheney paid for deck space on the *Coolgardie* to carry Dodge Brothers chassis packed in wooden crates. For each ship passage he had fifty crates, each with two chassis, delivered by rail from Detroit to Vancouver. More than once the chassis arrived in Australia damaged and covered with seawater, but Cheney managed to salvage them for sale. The freighter made the voyage four times a year and carried Dodge Brothers chassis for more than two years, thus providing Cheney with a steady supply.[28]

Wartime Ordnance Contracts

The Dodge brothers took on an important ordnance contract during the First World War that reaffirmed their reputation as innovative, energetic manufacturers. After the war, Cleveland Moffett wrote about this achievement in *McClure's,* but he never specifically named Dodge Brothers. He said that "one of our great automakers who has an immense plant in Detroit" took on this challenge. He then revealed that "his name is John and I take off my hat to him." In fall 1917, U.S. Secretary of War Newton Baker searched for an American manufacturer to produce delicate recoil mechanisms for two French heavy artillery pieces, the 155-millimeter Schneider howitzer and the 155-millimeter Filloux general purpose field gun. French manufacturers, using highly skilled hand craftsmen, produced a total of only five per day. No one had ever manufactured these delicate recoil mechanisms, also known as hydropneumatic recuperators, outside France. According to Benedict Crowell, "It is scarcely fair to a modern hydropneumatic recuperator to say that it must be finished with the precision of a watch. It must be finished with a mechanical nicety comparable only to the finish of such a delicate instrument as a navigator's sextant or the mechanism that adjusts the Lick telescope to the movement of the Earth." Moffett claimed that the Germans captured many of these French guns but were never able to make them in their own factories because they could not duplicate the recoil mechanisms.[29]

John Dodge met in Washington, D.C., with Secretary of War Baker and a delegation of French manufacturers, who offered to send their skilled machinists to Detroit to teach the Dodges how to make the device. John Dodge replied in angry and earthy language that he and Horace needed only blueprints to begin machine production. According to Dodge family lore, Secretary Baker responded, "Look here, Mr. Dodge, I'm not accustomed to being spoken to in that kind of language." John Dodge replied, "The war would be a hell of a lot better off if you were!" John Dodge offered to build and equip the munitions plant and supply fifty of the mechanisms per day, beginning four months later. Dodge Brothers would do the work at cost plus 10 percent (to allow for payments of taxes), provided the U.S. government would agree not to interfere with their efforts. On 27 October 1917, Baker accepted the Dodges' offer.[30]

The Dodge Brothers contract with the U.S. government reveals the details of the arrangement. Dodge Brothers agreed to make 3,120 recoil mechanisms for the 155-millimeter Schneider howitzer and 1,424 recoil mechanisms for the 155-millimeter Filloux general purpose field gun. They were to follow the drawings and specifications attached to the contract. A list attached to the contract shows forty-two sheets of drawings for the howitzer mechanism and seventy-one for the general purpose field gun. The contract specified that Dodge Brothers should build a factory of about 500,000 square feet costing no more than $1,500,000 and buy and install the necessary machinery and tools at an additional cost of no more than $2,000,000. In both cases, the government would pay the Dodges their actual costs, plus 10 percent. For the mechanisms proper, the government would pay the Dodges actual costs of production and a fixed profit of $300 per unit for the howitzer recoil mechanism and $600 per unit for the general purpose field gun mechanism. The contract called for deliveries to begin on 1 March 1918 and end by 1 November 1918. Deliveries were to start at a modest level of 103 units in March, but then reach the peak of 828 units in July. Working six days a week, peak production would reach about thirty-five units a day, not the fifty originally promised by Dodge Brothers.[31]

Within a day of signing the agreement, construction workers begin to prepare the factory site in Detroit on Lynch Road, east of Mount Elliot Avenue. Water, sewer, and electric lines reached the site in a matter of days, and within a week of the contract, structural steel began arriving. The concrete foundations were in place within a month, and 1,800 men were at work on the 578 feet by 818 feet factory. The first machines began working at the start of March 1918. The Detroit architectural firm of Smith, Hinchman & Grylls Associates (SH&G) designed the original buildings and later additions. The SH&G engineers also produced drawings for some parts for the 155-millimeter guns. On 19 November 1917, SH&G gave Dodge Brothers an initial estimate of the cost of the manufacturing building and powerhouse, including boilers and cranes, amounting to $1,378,767. Wartime inflation, however, nearly tripled the original contract price of $3.5 million for the plant and equipment to $10 million.[32]

Horace Dodge developed an entirely new manufacturing system to make the recoil mechanisms and in the process designed 129 brand-new machines with specialized tooling. Fred Lamborn, an experienced machinist who first worked for

Dodge Brothers ordnance factory (plant no. 3). Courtesy NAHC.

Dodge Brothers in 1914, was in charge of preparing the tooling in the ordnance plant. For starters, the Dodges had to convert all the blueprints, which used the metric system, into the American system using inches. The difficulties inherent in this manufacturing process, a pioneer effort, were monumental. They produced the howitzer recoil mechanism from a solid steel forging weighing 3,875 pounds. After all the borings, grinding, and lapping were completed, the finished recoil mechanism weighed 870 pounds. The Mesta Machine Company of Pittsburgh supplied forgings for the howitzer, and the Carnegie Steel Company made the forgings for the general purpose field gun. Neither company delivered forgings to Dodge Brothers until spring 1918.

A nationwide shortage of machinery also hampered the Dodge brothers' efforts to bring their ordnance factory into production. According to Benedict Crowell, assistant secretary of war and director of munitions in 1917–20, federal government agents discovered trainloads of machinery waiting on the docks for shipment to the Russian government. They simply confiscated the machinery and even rescued a giant planer that had fallen overboard in the harbor, sending the badly needed machines to the Dodge Brothers plant and to other arms factories.[33]

Dodge Brothers delivered the first 155-millimeter Schneider howitzer recoil mechanisms in July 1918, seven months after signing the contract. Tests in August revealed some minor defects, which Dodge Brothers promptly fixed. Quantity pro-

155-millimeter Schneider howitzer. Courtesy of Oakland University's Meadow Brook Hall.

duction on the mechanisms began in earnest in October, and they completed a total of 495 in November 1918, nearly twenty-four a day. By late April 1919, when the contract ended, Dodge Brothers had finished a total of 1,601 of the howitzer recoil mechanisms. Production of the recoil mechanism for the Filloux general purpose gun did not get underway until October 1918, and in January 1919 the Dodge Brothers ordnance plant was making only four a day. By the end of April 1919, they finished a total of 881. To be sure, Dodge Brothers never completed fifty recoil mechanisms a day, but their record was nevertheless impressive. They achieved quantity production of a delicate mechanical device using specialized machine tools designed by Horace Dodge.[34]

Despite the efforts of Dodge Brothers to operate this plant with no government interference, they were subject to oversight by the inspector of ordnance, which sometimes generated friction. In mid-May 1918, two ordnance officers, Captain Jeffords and Lieutenant Wilber Van Scoik, made what seemed petty charges against Dodge Brothers. They accused one of the Dodges' drivers, Mr. Jeffers, who drove army ordnance officers to and from the ordnance plant, of impersonating an officer because he wore a military uniform with U.S. Army buttons. Jeffers was in

155-millimeter Filloux general purpose gun. Courtesy of DCHC.

the Home Guard and had the right to wear a uniform, but with different buttons. Further investigation by Howard Bloomer, the Dodges' personal attorney, revealed that after Captain Jeffords had tried to interfere with Dodge Brothers purchases of materials, they had asked for his removal and denied him the use of an ordnance car. Van Scoik and other ordnance officers charged Dodge Brothers with "stonewalling" them when they requested detailed information about purchases. The Dodge brothers resisted these efforts to interfere with their operations and threatened to challenge any prosecution aimed at them all the way to the U.S. Supreme Court. The Ordnance Department apparently resolved these "problems" outside the courts by mid-June.[35]

This work was important to John and Horace Dodge as both a mechanical challenge and an act of patriotic service to the United States. Every year since the introduction of the Dodge Brothers automobile, John and Horace Dodge held an elaborate dinner for about thirty of their top sales executives at the Detroit Athletic Club in downtown Detroit. The 1918 dinner had a decidedly military and patriotic flavor. Guests sat at a circular table enclosing a sunken garden and a large electrically powered fountain. Lieutenant Colonel Frank F. Evans spoke about his experiences with the British Army in France. A young boy dressed as a Yankee soldier emerged from the center of the fountain, under a spotlight in the darkened room, and recited a poem titled "Victory: A Prophesy," which was followed by the "Star-Spangled Banner," sung by a quartet. Two Boy Scouts then raised the American flag.

Liberty bond rally, Dodge Brothers Hamtramck plant, 1917. John and Horace Dodge on podium. Courtesy DCHC.

Menu, Dodge Brothers sales department dinner, Detroit Athletic Club, 23 May 1918.
Courtesy of Dodge Brothers Club Historical Archives.

Table and fountain, Dodge Brothers sales department dinner, 23 May 1918. Courtesy of Dodge Brothers Club Historical Archives.

John Dodge concluded the dinner with a brief speech about the work of the Dodge Brothers ordnance plant. When Detroit turned its traditional Thanksgiving Day parade into a "Victory Parade" in 1918, the Dodge Brothers contingent consisted of the Dodge Brothers Industrial Band and 3,000 Dodge Brothers workers. Instead of pulling floats, U.S. Army tractors pulled a 155-millimeter Schneider howitzer and a 155-millimeter Filloux general purpose field gun, both equipped with Dodge-built recoil mechanisms. Both had seen service in France.[36]

The ordnance plant later became the site for key manufacturing operations for Dodge Brothers and later for the Chrysler Corporation. Dodge Brothers initially offered to buy the plant and much of the machinery from the U.S. government in June 1919 for $1,619,643.37 and bought the plant a year later for $1,400,000. Two decades later, Fred Lamborn, who had worked at the ordnance plant, recalled that Dodge Brothers got the property for about 30 percent of its original cost. The U.S. government shipped the machinery and finished recoil mechanisms to its Rock Island arsenal for storage, and Lamborn saw the recoil mechanisms from 1918 still in storage there in June 1940. Graham Brothers Company and then Dodge Brothers, Inc., used the buildings, found south of Lynch Road and east of the Plymouth Lynch Road Assembly Plant (1928), to assemble trucks until 1938 and then for axle manufacturing.[37]

Dodge Brothers office building decorated for Marshall Foch's visit of 7 November 1921. Courtesy of Oakland University's Meadow Brook Hall.

On 7 November 1921, long after the end of the First World War and the deaths of John and Horace Dodge, Marshall Ferdinand Foch visited the Dodge Brothers factory in Hamtramck and paid tribute to the Dodge brothers' contribution to the war effort. His visit to Detroit was brief and the Dodge Brothers factory was the only auto plant he visited. Dodge Brothers presented Foch and his staff with a booklet, *A Mechanical Triumph,* published in English and French versions, recounting the history of the ordnance plant. George Harrison Phelps devoted most of the 11 November 1921 issue of the Dodge Brothers advertising newsletter to Foch's visit.[38]

Dodge Brothers' Formula for Success

John and Horace Dodge's success as engineers, designers, and manufacturers largely resulted from their complementary talents and their ability to work together. Throughout their careers as independent businessmen, the Dodge brothers made all of their important decisions together. They did, however, have a basic division of labor in their work and maintained separate offices at opposite ends of the administration building at their Hamtramck factory. John Dodge negotiated contracts with suppliers; managed the firm's finances; directed sales, advertising, and public relations; and served as the general administrator for the company. He also served as the vice president of the Ford Motor Company.[39]

John Dodge was particularly effective at developing and nurturing a network of dealerships to sell the Dodge Brothers products. He and Horace Dodge held a convention of Dodge Brothers district representatives every May beginning in 1915. These gatherings usually began on a Tuesday and extended through Saturday. The first three days involved a series of lectures, demonstrations, and tours. Thursday evening, the Dodge brothers held an elaborate banquet for the sales executives at the Detroit Athletic Club (DAC) in Detroit. They played golf and held competitions at the Bloomfield Hills Country Club in suburban Detroit on Fridays and Saturdays.[40]

The banquets at the DAC became increasingly elaborate over time. The fourth annual banquet, mentioned earlier, featured a patriotic theme. To commemorate their five-year anniversary of producing cars, Dodge Brothers held a particularly elaborate banquet on 22 May 1919. Twenty-nine men attended, including all of the top executives and fifteen district sales managers. Ten of the sixteen district sales managers appointed in 1914 were still with Dodge Brothers. Each received a special bound volume, titled *After Five Years,* which contained biographies of all twenty-nine. The DAC converted the ladies dining room into a Hawaiian garden for this occasion. Diners sat at a circular table that surrounded a large pool stocked with fish from the Detroit Aquarium, and the Detroit Institute of Arts supplied decorative statues for the evening. John Dodge was the only speaker. They held their sixth annual banquet (1920) in the DAC gymnasium, which they decorated to look like a roof garden, complete with a simulated New York City skyline. Each guest received a twelve-inch bronze bust of the late John F. Dodge, cast by Tiffany.[41]

Horace Dodge was a mechanical genius who designed the products Dodge Brothers manufactured and many machines used in their operations. He organized and managed production. The shop floor was Horace's domain. He was responsible for the engineering and design of the Dodge Brothers automobile and for the design of scores of machines needed to manufacture the French artillery recoil mechanism during World War I. In describing Horace's mechanical inclinations, one biographer noted:

Dodge Brothers sales department dinner, Detroit Athletic Club, May 22, 1919. Courtesy of Dodge Brothers Club Historical Archives.

His office was literally a museum of parts, past, present and prospective, for Dodge Brothers cars. He was constantly scheming improved details, new processes, new methods and always building new machinery. He never lost the touch of the crafts-man, could never let machinery alone. The atmosphere of the shop, as he entered it, would cause a noticeable change in his bearing. Outside, in the offices, in the places where men gather, even at home, he was quiet, reticent, and could be termed shy. But within the four walls of the shop he was the taciturn yet unquestionable master of the business.[42]

In manufacturing parts and later, complete automobiles, the Dodge brothers were extremely efficient large-scale producers of quality products and were as innovative as the Ford Motor Company in developing and using new machinery. Ford revolutionized the assembly of automobiles by minutely dividing the work into simple tasks and by refining the moving assembly line to produce the Model T on an unprecedented scale. Ford simultaneously used thousands of specialized, single-purpose machines to manufacture Model T components. Historians have written extensively on Henry Ford's accomplishments, to the exclusion of others like the Dodges. This emphasis on Ford reflects in part the vast amount of information generated by contemporary observers and by Henry Ford's efforts at self-promotion. Horace L. Arnold and Fay L. Faurote, in their *Ford Methods and the Ford Shops* (1915), document the operations of the Ford Highland Park plant in great detail.[43]

The Dodge Brothers factory was already a well-equipped, highly efficient factory and the largest automobile parts plant in the United States before the Dodge brothers made their own automobile. A contemporary observer noted, "It takes efficient manufacturing to supply parts like crankshafts, connecting rods, steering gears, transmissions, differentials, and axles to the manufacturer of almost the cheapest car in the world, on which the manufacturer has made millions, and to make millions yourself in selling those parts. That's what Dodge Brothers have done."[44]

The Dodge Brothers Hamtramck factory and the Ford Motor Company Highland Park complex were remarkably similar around 1915, once the Dodge plant expansion was completed. The basic layout of the two complexes shared common features, which is not surprising given Albert Kahn's role in designing both and the Dodge brothers' familiarity with the Ford plant. Both had their offices and power-houses fronting on the main street, Woodward Avenue in Highland Park and Joseph Campau Avenue in Hamtramck. Both used their smokestacks as giant billboards displaying the name of their company and car. Machine shops and assembly buildings were four-story reinforced concrete structures located near the front of both complexes. Foundries, heat-treating plants, and forges were single-story, steel-framed buildings situated at the rear of both factory complexes. Material handling systems were virtually the same at the two plants, with mechanical systems including freight elevators, a monorail system, and overhead traveling cranes. Both still used hundreds of men who delivered materials in hand trucks.[45]

Much of the specialized machinery at the Ford Highland Park plant in 1915 was also in the Dodge Brothers plant that same year. *Ford Methods and the Ford Shops* devotes much space to Ford's multiple-spindle drill presses used in various operations, special-purpose milling machines, and automatic turret lathes. These were all used at the Dodge Brothers plant as well. Much like Ford, the Dodges broke down complex manufacturing processes into discrete operations that their workers did sequentially. Preparation of the cylinder block for the Dodge Brothers motor, for example, involved seventy-three foundry operations and eighteen machine shop operations. At Highland Park, Ford machined his cylinder blocks in twenty-eight distinct operations but used virtually the same machinery as Dodge Brothers. This is not to suggest that the two factories were identical. Photographs of the Dodge Brothers plant in the 1910s do not show machines packed close

Crankshaft and camshaft turning machines, 1915. Courtesy of NAHC.

Upholstery department, 1915. Courtesy of DCHC.

Chassis assembly, 1916. Courtesy of DCHC.

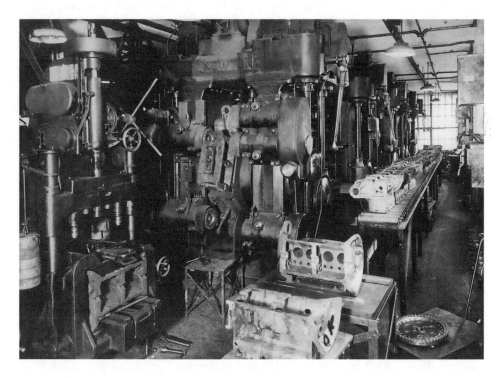

Engine machining department, 1915. Courtesy DCHC.

together, as they were at the Ford plant. Ford's production of the Model T consistently dwarfed the Dodge Brothers output after 1914. In 1917, for example, Dodge Brothers clearly was a large company, with production of 101,270 automobiles. For the year ending 31 July 1917, Ford turned out 730,041 Model T's.[46]

Once the Dodge brothers built their own car, they enjoyed the advantages of vertical integration by manufacturing most of the key components on a single site and assembling the final product there. Henry Ford and the Dodge brothers recognized the economic advantage of vertical integration, so both expanded their operations after their split in 1914. Because they fabricated most of the parts and components needed for their automobiles (with the exception of bodies, tires, glass, batteries, and lights), the Dodge brothers and Henry Ford controlled the cost and quality of components while assuring themselves a reliable supply. Dodge Brothers never achieved the vertical integration Ford Motor Company later enjoyed at the River Rouge plant, which made its own iron, steel, glass, and tires. Walter Chrysler admitted that he bought Dodge Brothers in 1928 in part to free the Chrysler Corporation from outside suppliers.[47]

The Hamtramck factory and the labor force employed there continued to grow substantially from 1915 until the deaths of the Dodge brothers in 1920. The original 1910 plant, which had nearly tripled in size in 1914–15 to 1.4 million square feet, grew to enclose 3.3 million square feet by 1920. Major new construction included a battery building (1916) and an eight-story concrete warehouse (1917). The latter building occupied the space used by the test track, which they moved to an area south of the assembly building.[48] Roy S. Drake, editor of *Automobile Topics,* described the plant around 1916: "Just on the edge of the city limits of Detroit, the Dodge Brothers works is itself almost a city. To tell exactly how big it is, is to be wrong tomorrow, because it is growing so fast."[49]

In May 1919, the Dodge Brothers directors approved an addition to the body plant, costing (with machinery) $1,050,000, and a new assembly building with a price tag of $3,854,000. Dodge Brothers delayed building the new assembly building until 1923. Building projects completed in 1920 included an eight-story construction building housing the offices of Dodge Brothers construction department; an eight-story body building of 950,000 square feet, where bodies were prepared and painted; a four-story addition to the pressed steel shop, which pressed steel body parts; and an enormous new powerhouse (1920). The building program in 1920 alone cost $8 million, with the powerhouse accounting for $3.5 million. Dodge Brothers employment, which stood at more than 7,000 in April 1915, leaped to more than 17,000 by mid-1919. While Dodge Brothers could not match Ford

1919 Dodge Brothers four-door sedans, Dodge Brothers plant, 1919. Courtesy of DCHC.

Motor Company's workforce of 45,000 in 1919, the Dodge Brothers enterprise was large-scale by most definitions.[50]

The Dodge Brothers factory was directly responsible for the rapid growth of the community of Hamtramck north of the plant. This village of roughly 500 residents in 1900 had a population of 2,559 in 1910, but by 1920 had 48,615 residents. Today, Hamtramck is an independent city surrounded by Detroit. Located immediately north of Detroit's "Poletown" community first settled in the 1880s, Hamtramck filled with Polish immigrants who found jobs at Dodge Brothers and other nearby auto plants. By 1920, some 66 percent of Hamtramck's heads of household were born in Poland, and another 4 percent were children of Polish immigrants.[51]

The factory workers who toiled at the Dodge Brothers factory in Hamtramck enjoyed a slower and more humane pace of work than their counterparts at the Ford Highland Park plant. Descriptions of the Dodge Brothers factory in Hamtramck often included comments about the reasonable pace of work at the plant, presumably in contrast to conditions at Ford's factory. The Dodge brothers, themselves mechanics for much of their lives, identified closely with their employees and made special efforts to remain in touch with the shop floor. Horace Dodge had the habit of appearing on the shop floor, rolling up his sleeves, and going to work repairing or adjusting some piece of troublesome machinery. The workers genuinely admired and respected the Dodge brothers. To be sure, they were not trying to manufacture a low-priced car with a low profit margin in large quantities like Henry Ford. Nor were they paying Henry Ford's wage of $5 a day. According to one observer, writing in 1914, "There are tales of thoughtful kindnesses in the plant and out of it, and rumor has it that more than once, on some hot and trying day in the smithy or the forge shop, ice-cold tin pails of some grateful beverage have arrived just in time to make life not so bad after all."[52]

The Detroit Board of Commerce established the Americanization Committee of Detroit (ACD) in 1914 to encourage immigrants to learn English and become U.S. citizens. Early in 1916, the ACD tried to get Dodge Brothers to institute mandatory evening classes in English and citizenship for its "foreign" workers. J. Walton Schmidt, the secretary to the education committee of the ACD, had met with A. L. McMeans, the company secretary, but was unhappy with the company's attitude. In fall 1915, Dodge Brothers had put 3,000 men on the night shift and when the evening school program was announced, hundreds of these workers requested transfers to the day shift so they could attend school. Because of the potential disruptions to production, the firm would not promote the night-school programs and refused to display an ACD poster. The Dodge Brothers employment manager refused to ask the men about their citizenship status or their English skills, as requested by the ACD. The company did finally provide the ACD with information about its workforce sometime before 1 June 1916. Out of a total of 9,400 employees, 3,000 were classified as "foreigners," and only 157 non-English-speaking workers were attending evening school classes. The Dodge brothers were unwilling to adopt the heavy-handed Americanization programs of Henry Ford.[53]

Dodge Brothers was a highly profitable enterprise with John and Horace Dodge at the helm, as illustrated in table 4.2. Dodge Brothers' success in the automobile industry before the deaths of John and Horace Dodge was remarkable on several grounds. With Henry Ford already dominating the low-price segment of the car market and with their desire to produce a higher-quality car, the Dodge brothers entered the highly competitive mid-priced segment of the market. The Dodge Brothers touring car, priced at $785, was more expensive than the Ford Model T touring car, which Ford priced at $490 in August 1914. By 1920, when the Ford Model T touring car sold for $440, the comparable Dodge Brothers model cost $1,085. Their cars were really situated in the lower end of the mid-priced market segment. For example, in 1920, the least-expensive Oldsmobile touring car sold

Table 4.2
Dodge Brothers Performance, 1914–1920

Year Ended	Number of Units Sold	Net Sales	Net Income Before Taxes	Net Income As Share of Sales
30 June 1915	17,959	$11,665,940	$268,939	2.3%
30 June 1916	60,390	39,621,171	6,833,351	17.2
30 June 1917	89,077	61,060,801	9,269,012	15.2
31 Dec. 1918*	135,336	112,477,214	10,824,141	9.6
31 Dec. 1919	121,010	120,970,810	24,196,836	20.0
31 Dec. 1920	145,389	161,002,512	18,190,310	11.3

*Period of eighteen months.

Source: Dodge Brothers, Inc., prospectus for securities issues of 1925, submitted to the State of Michigan, Commerce Department, Securities Bureau, found in the State of Michigan Archives, accession 70–5-A, lot 15, box 135. The sales figures for the entire period from 1914 to 31 December 1920 are remarkably consistent with the figures for factory production presented in table 4.1. Total sales figures were 569,161 and total factory production was a total of 569,548 units. The figures refer to combined automobile and commercial vehicle sales.

for $1,450 and the comparable Buick touring car retailed for $1,495. In 1918, 1919, and 1920, mid-priced cars ($876–$1,375) accounted for 33.5 percent, 27.7 percent, and 25.8 percent, respectively, of U.S. sales. Dodge Brothers was competing with cars at the bottom of the mid-priced automobile market such as Maxwell, Hudson, and Studebaker.[54]

The Dodge Brothers car sold well in the competitive mid-priced market segment because it was well-designed, well-built, and dependable. Chris Sinsabaugh claimed that in the 1910s "it used to be said that whereas the Cadillacs purred and the Fords rattled, the Dodges 'chugged.'" These were practical cars that operated without pretension, with a healthy "chug-chug" sound. In comparing Dodge Brothers cars with others in the same price range, Tad Burness noted that they came with a 12-volt electrical system, rather than the usual 6-volt system, and a starter-generator in a single unit. Despite sporting few cosmetic changes in their appearance over their first seven or eight years on the market, Dodge Brothers cars had a solid reputation and continued to sell well.[55]

Dodge Brothers was in third place in the industry in 1915, the first full year of production, with only one-tenth of Ford's numbers and only half the production of Willys-Overland. This is a deceptive ranking because Dodge Brothers barely edged out Maxwell, Buick, and Studebaker for third place. The following year, Dodge

Brothers fell to fourth place, with an output of 71,400 units versus third-place Buick's 124,834. The popular, low-priced Chevrolet pushed Dodge Brothers back to fifth place in 1917 and 1918. Dodge Brothers' jump in production in 1919 moved it into practically a dead heat with Chevrolet and Buick for the number-two spot, and the following year Dodge was clearly second only to Ford. However, Dodge Brothers' 1920 production of about 141,000 cars was only one-third of Ford's record of nearly 420,000 units. By any standard, John and Horace Dodge's car and their company was an unquestionable success.[56]

Before their premature deaths in 1920, John and Horace Dodge seemed ready to follow Henry Ford's move toward greater vertical integration of his operations at his River Rouge complex. Like Ford, they were going to produce their own iron and steel. In mid-May 1919, the Dodge Brothers board of directors authorized the purchase of 295 acres of land on the Detroit River immediately south of Zug Island and set aside $14,152,784 for that purpose. The same meeting approved spending $5 million for an open hearth furnace and a steel rolling mill with a capacity of 2,000 tons a day, plus $1.5 million for a malleable iron foundry with a capacity of 100 tons a day. The Dodge brothers were intent on entering the iron and steel business in a serious way.[57]

William G. Mather, president of the Cleveland-Cliffs Iron Company, a major Great Lakes iron ore producer, wrote to John Dodge in late December 1919, only three weeks before Dodge's death. H. A. Raymond, Cleveland-Cliffs' ore sales agent, has just returned from meeting with John Dodge, who had confirmed the Dodge brothers' plans to build blast furnaces and a steel mill somewhere on the Detroit River. Mather offered to supply them with iron ore for this new undertaking.[58] The Dodge brothers were closely following Henry Ford's lead in pushing vertical integration at his River Rouge site. Ford began building an iron works there in fall 1919, and the first blast furnace went into service on 17 May 1920. The deaths of John and Horace Dodge in 1920 killed off these plans.

FIVE

The Dodge Brothers
in Perspective

And it was not the mere physical fact of brotherhood that welded
these two, John and Horace Dodge, together. It was a bond that had
in it something of strange depth and purity and fineness—something that transcended the usual brother-bond of good fellowship
by splendor hardly to be guessed by men who have known no such
love, and became a thing richly spiritual and very beautiful. For the
brothers loved each other as friends. They were friends.

Detroit News editorial, 13 December 1920, following the death
of Horace Elgin Dodge

The story of John and Horace Dodge ended tragically in 1920 with their deaths.
Their lives and personalities and identities were more intimately intertwined
than any other pair of brothers I know. Each brother's interests and talents complemented the other's perfectly. Long after becoming extremely wealthy, John and
Horace Dodge felt more comfortable among ordinary shop floor workers in the factory than with Detroit's business and social elites. John's instruction that the pallbearers at his funeral would all be ordinary "shop men" is but one indication of this.
Neither sought publicity, although both gained some notoriety from their private
behavior.

Like most others with newfound wealth, they tried to join Detroit's more established "polite" society. However, it was John and Horace's wives, Matilda Rausch
Dodge and Anna Thomson Dodge, who pushed their husbands to gain social respectability. They built large, tastefully appointed mansions, commissioned some of the
largest yachts Detroit had seen, and made charitable donations to many Detroit
institutions. John Dodge was a member of Detroit's Water Commission and Street
Railway Commission and became a force in the Michigan Republican Party. Horace
was quietly responsible for the development of a world-class symphony orchestra
for Detroit.

John F. Dodge (left) and Horace E. Dodge (right), ca. 1914. Courtesy of NAHC.

John and Horace Dodge are in many respects tragic figures, in part because they died so young. Contemporaries in business and commerce recognized them as manufacturing and automotive giants, as did the informed public. However, their important place in the emerging Michigan automobile industry is not widely recognized today. The Dodge brothers have remained obscure figures in popular history because their tenure as automakers was so short and because they lived in the shadows of self-promoting, dynamic auto industry leaders like Henry Ford and William ("Billy") Durant. John and Horace Dodge's contemporaries, however, did recognize their importance. Their deaths and funerals, discussed below, brought enormous outpourings of public recognition and grief.

The Year of Tragedy and Transition: 1920

On 2 January 1920, John and Horace Dodge left Detroit by train to attend the National Automobile Show, which ran for a week starting 3 January at the Grand Central Palace in New York City. Friends Oscar Marx, Milton Oakman, and Ed Fitzgerald accompanied them to New York, but the Dodges' wives remained in Detroit. By Wednesday, 7 January, when they were supposed to host a Dodge Brothers sales luncheon, John and Horace had contracted influenza, which quickly developed into pneumonia. By December 1919, influenza was beginning to reach epidemic proportions in the United States, although this was not as serious an outbreak as the influenza epidemic of 1918, which killed half a million Americans.[1]

Initially, Horace was much sicker than John. The Dodge brothers brought their personal physician from Detroit, and both wives arrived in New York on 10 January. John's eldest daughters, Winifred and Isabel, came three days later. Early newspaper reports in Detroit were overly optimistic about the medical condition of both brothers. Articles appearing on 11 January and 12 January 1920 in the *Detroit Free Press* reported the brothers recovering and out of danger. The next day all three Detroit papers announced that Horace continued to recover but that John Dodge was critically ill and unconscious. The *Detroit News* then revealed in its afternoon edition of 14 January that John Dodge was improving slightly. Matilda telegrammed her sister Amelia Rausch the morning of 13 January and sounded optimistic about John's prospects: "Just came from seeing John and while he is still very, very ill, he is some[what] better than last night." Horace slowly recovered, but John's pneumonia worsened. Having lungs previously ravaged by tuberculosis only made the struggle more difficult. John Dodge died at 10:30 p.m. on 14 January at the Ritz-Carlton Hotel, with Horace at his side. He was fifty-five years old.[2]

John Dodge's body returned to Detroit in a baggage car on the *Wolverine* train. The rest of the funeral party traveled in the private railroad car *Commonwealth*, which John Dodge had already leased, intending to use it to take his family to Florida after the auto show. Matilda Dodge, herself very ill, daughters Winifred and Isabel, and the three friends (Marx, Oakman, and Fitzgerald) accompanied the coffin. Horace Dodge remained in New York, still too weak to travel. The *Wolverine* arrived at the Michigan Central Railroad station in Detroit on Friday, 16 January, at noon. More than three hundred Dodge workers met the train, and a group of sixteen longtime shopmen from the factory served as pallbearers, following John Dodge's instructions to his family. The men removed the coffin from the baggage car and placed it into a hearse for transport to William Blake's funeral home on Peterboro Street in Detroit. There, they transferred his remains into a bronze casket, which they delivered to the Dodge home at 33 East Boston Boulevard, where visitors could view the body Saturday.[3]

Several thousand people viewed John Dodge's body during the morning and early afternoon of Saturday, 17 January 1920. The funeral was at 2:00 p.m., with burial in the Dodge Mausoleum at Detroit's Woodlawn Cemetery. Matilda Dodge was too ill and distraught to attend the funeral. John Duval Dodge also was unable to return to Detroit from Texas in time for the funeral. The family reduced the number of pallbearers, all Dodge workers, from sixteen to ten for the funeral and burial ceremonies. The initial plan was to have 55 honorary pallbearers, one for each year of John Dodge's life, but the number quickly grew to 107. A cross-section of the Detroit auto industry and political elite, the list included James Couzens, Henry Leland, William Metzger, John C. Lodge, Oscar B. Marx, Robert Oakman, and many others. Notably absent were Henry and Edsel Ford, Ransom E. Olds, Alfred Sloan, and Walter P. Chrysler. Horace Dodge had remained in New York, too sick to attend John's funeral, and asked for one last chance to see his brother. Only after Horace returned to Detroit in mid-February did the family have the casket sealed and placed in the family vault.[4]

Opening the Dodge home for thousands to view John Dodge's body was a concession made to the thousands of factory workers who wanted a chance to pay their last respects to their boss. Upon hearing of John Dodge's death, a delegation of workers asked that the family move the body to the Dodge Brothers factory Friday afternoon to allow all 18,000 workers a chance to view it. The family denied the request since this large number of workers would need more than twelve hours to view the body. Even with the more limited arrangements, workers began lining up on Boston Boulevard at 7:00 a.m. on Saturday, and within the first two hours more than 1,500 had viewed the body. By midmorning, the line of mourners extended for blocks on nearby Woodward Avenue.[5]

The Detroit newspapers noted the numbers of mourners, but more important, the heavy presence of Dodge Brothers factory workers. One noted that "several

Negro workers in the plant were among those who paid tribute."[6] The *Detroit Journal* described the appearance and demeanor of the factory workers:

> At first glance one knew they were not dwellers of this residential neighborhood or of the class usually to be found in such sections.
>
> Their faces, hands, clothes and bearing proclaimed them [to be] of other districts. Their faces, glowing in the extreme cold, showed signs of unusually careful shaving and ablutions. Their square hands, when uncovered, displayed callouses in the palms, traces of grime around the blunt finger tips, or were clothed in gloves and mittens more serviceable than stylish.
>
> Their clothes were neat, indifferent as to style, obviously their "Sunday best." Their carriage was broad-shouldered, stooped, flat-chested, the unconscious loll of the toiler.

The appearance of hundreds of women who worked for Dodge Brothers added "a softer feminine touch" to the stream of mourners.[7]

The Reverend Joseph A. Vance, pastor of the First Presbyterian Church of Detroit, delivered the eulogy. He noted John Dodge's strength as a business executive: "John Dodge had a marvelous virility in his big red-blooded body, and he had a will indomitable, which opposition stimulated instead of discouraged. His great executive ability was natal like the big body it tenanted. These things do not come to man by education, any more than does the genius of these friends of his who are making the music of his requiem." The Reverend Vance went on to talk about John Dodge's private side:

> There is one thing more of which you must let me speak, and that is his devotion to his family and his home. Many of you knew John Dodge only as a great lusty man, who with ripping oath could break into a crowd and get his way. He could do this. He was a masterful man; and never met defeat till he took the count at the hands of the disease which was always his greatest dread. But John Dodge had a wonderful, a beautiful love for his family and his home. He was red-blooded, but no woman could lure him from fidelity to the woman he made his wife; and all his plans grouped around his wife and his children.[8]

The *Detroit Free Press* observed at the time of his death: "This community can ill afford to lose John Dodge. He was a citizen who counted. He was one of the big forces in the making of modern Detroit and there is every reason to believe that if he had lived, the next ten-year period would have been the time of his greatest accomplishment."[9]

John Dodge was the subject of scores of public resolutions praising his contributions as a manufacturer and as a public servant. During the week beginning 15 January 1920, resolutions of remembrance came from the Detroit Board of Commerce, the Common Council of the City of Detroit, and the boards of directors of the Highland Park State Bank, the First and Old Detroit National Bank, the Bank of Detroit, and the Merchants National Bank. The National Automobile Chamber of Commerce did the same on 4 March 1920. Matilda Rausch Dodge saved these resolutions, but also created scrapbooks of newspaper clippings concerning John Dodge's illness, death, and funeral. One of her staff tallied the number of lines of coverage in Detroit's newspapers between 6 January and 29 January 1920. To preserve John Dodge's place in history, she also paid fees to ensure that his biography would appear in various biographical dictionaries. In December 1921, she made a payment of $350 to the S. J. Clarke Publishing Company for a four-page biographical entry (including a portrait) on John F. Dodge in Clarence M. Burton, *The City of Detroit, Michigan, 1701–1922.* She had to pay an additional $65 for a set of Burton's volumes.[10]

The death of John Dodge required a realignment of the top management positions at Dodge Brothers. Horace Dodge became president and continued to serve as treasurer, Howard B. Bloomer became vice president, and Frederick J. Haynes, plant manager since 1912, became a director. At the end of May 1920, the Dodge Brothers directors (Horace Dodge, Haynes, and Bloomer) made Haynes a vice president and general manager at a salary of $100,000 per year. They also named Charles W. Matheson "acting general sales manager," with a salary of $50,000, to replace Arthur I. Philp, who had been ill and incapacitated since September 1919. The board also agreed to pay John Dodge's family his 1920 salary of $350,000. The annual stockholders' meeting in mid-July 1920 confirmed these actions.[11]

In late November 1920, Horace Dodge's continued poor health forced him to leave Detroit for Florida, and the board of directors prepared for his absence. They agreed to expand the board from three to five members and immediately elected John Ballantyne as the fourth director. Horace Dodge foresaw his own death and set into motion a series of decisions that would assure management continuity and the survival of the company bearing his family name. According to the board minutes, Horace Dodge "felt, that in case of his death, various interests throughout the country would try to destroy the organization of the company." He wanted to be certain that his long-term associates, Howard Bloomer, Frederick Haynes, and John Ballantyne, "should be the controlling factors in the business." Bloomer had been a legal advisor to the Dodges for many years and Ballantyne was president of the Merchant's National Bank of Detroit and longtime financial advisor to John and Horace Dodge.[12]

Horace Dodge convinced his board to grant these three men employment contracts to keep them at Dodge Brothers. He formally authorized the board to sign a five-year contract with Haynes to serve as president of Dodge Brothers after his death. In November 1920, the board extended Haynes's contract as general manager at a salary of $150,000 per year and offered Bloomer the position of "directing head" of the company at the same salary. They gave Matheson a one-year contract as sales manager at $50,000 a year and Harry V. Popeney, the secretary, agreed to continue for a $30,000 salary. The dollar figures for these salaries were net of Michigan and U.S. income taxes, that is, these were take-home salaries.[13]

Horace Dodge's concerns about the future of Dodge Brothers were not unfounded. Immediately after his death, *Automotive Industries* predicted that New York financial interests would try to gain control of the firm and would probably succeed. The Dodge brothers had rebuffed earlier offers by New York investment bankers, but the widows were more likely to sell. None of the children of John or Horace Dodge had any interest in running the business or the ability to do so. The factory closed during the first three months of 1921 because of depressed sales, but then reopened in April with Haynes clearly in control.[14]

Horace did not survive the year. Chronically ill with influenza and psychologically devastated by John's death, he saw no reason to live. When the Dodge Brothers midwestern dealers met in Chicago on 27 January 1920, Horace Dodge did not attend, but sent a message explaining that his continued illness ruled out his appearance. He offered additional insight into his state of mind: "The passing of my dear brother, Mr. John F. Dodge, is to me, personally, a loss so great that I hesitate to look forward to the years [ahead] without his companionship, our lives having been, as you all know, practically inseparable since our childhood." On 1 July 1920, Dodge Brothers celebrated the building of its 500,000th automobile, only six years after the company stopped making components for Ford Motor Company. The firm held elaborate ceremonies in the middle of the factory commemorating this achievement. The Dodge Brothers Band played a special concert and general manager Frederick J. Haynes delivered an address. Horace Dodge was notably absent.[15]

Horace Dodge spent most of 1920 in Palm Beach, Florida, hoping that the warmer climate would help him recover. He was there from mid-February until May, when his health had improved enough for him to return to Detroit and resume some work at the factory. After the marriage of his daughter Delphine in June 1920, he attended the 1920 Republican Convention in Chicago in July as a delegate, traveling there with friends on the *Delphine*. He started what was supposed to be a six-week fishing trip on Lake Superior in early August, but suffered a serious relapse that left him bedridden for weeks. After that, he played no active role in his business. Horace Dodge spent the last four months of his life at his Palm Beach ocean-side mansion, Villa Marina, where he died on 10 December 1920 at age fifty-two.[16]

The Detroit newspapers reported that Horace Dodge died of complications from his earlier battles with influenza and pneumonia, with some mention of "hemorrhaging" as well. But articles in the *New York Times* and *Automobile Topics* said that "the immediate cause of death was cirrhosis of the liver." One of Horace's doctors, I. L. Hill from New York City, stated clearly that "Horace Dodge died of liver trouble." The death certificate signed by Hobart E. Warren, M.D., who had attended Horace Dodge for a week before his death, is unambiguous. He listed the cause of death as "atrophic hepatic cirrhosis," with the notation that Horace Dodge had this condition for two years. A secondary, contributing cause of death was "hematemesis" (vomiting of blood), which can occur when enlarged veins in the esophagus (which are a symptom of cirrhosis) burst. The vomiting of blood had lasted seven days and is likely the "hemorrhaging" that the newspapers referred to.[17]

Horace Dodge's body arrived in Detroit by special train at the Michigan Central Railroad station on Monday, 13 December 1920, at 4:00 p.m. and then went to the Blake Chapel (Blake funeral home) on Peterboro Street in Detroit. The family agreed to have Horace's body lie in state at the Blake Chapel from 5:00 to 9:00 p.m. to enable Dodge Brothers workers to view the body. Tuesday morning, they moved the body to Horace's Grosse Pointe mansion, Rose Terrace. In a tribute to Horace Dodge, the Detroit Symphony Orchestra played the funeral march from Beethoven's "Eroica" as the final number of their Sunday evening concert.[18]

The funeral, which began at 2:00 p.m. at Rose Terrace, featured the Detroit Symphony Orchestra playing a funeral dirge. Frank Taft, a New York organist, played music on Horace's pipe organ, and soloist Harold Jarvis sang "Beautiful Isle of Somewhere." Reverend S. H. Forrer, the Presbyterian minister who delivered the eulogy, described Horace Dodge as "a man with a passion for music. . . . a mechanic with the soul of a poet." The fourteen pallbearers consisted of old friends and business associates, including Adolph Vocelle, who had helped Horace in his early boat-building efforts. The Dodge family also named 137 honorary pallbearers, more than John Dodge's 107. These included virtually everyone who had served as pallbearers for John Dodge and many others associated with Horace through the Detroit Symphony Orchestra, including Ossip Gabrilowitsch. Following the funeral, a procession of cars, including the hearse with Horace's body, went from Rose Terrace past the Hamtramck factory to Woodlawn Cemetery, where Horace took his place next to John in the Dodge Mausoleum.[19]

A few days after Horace's death, T. R. Fassett offered a memorial poem to honor him:

Gone from this world of sorrow.
   Gone from all earthly care;
Gone to the grove tomorrow,
   To be with his brother there.

Gone and thousands left weeping,
   Gone to that land so fair;
Gone, not dead—just sleeping,
   To awaken with his brother there.[20]

The Dodge brothers, like others who have achieved considerable fame and notoriety, have been the subject of rumor and speculation over the years. Several authors have viewed the Dodges' deaths as suspicious. Caroline Latham and David Agresta raised the possibility that John and Horace Dodge were poisoned by liquor they drank during the New York Automobile Show in January 1920. Their book, *Dodge Dynasty*, refers to persistent rumors in Detroit that the Dodges were poisoned. They even suggest arsenic as the agent and Henry Ford as the perpetrator. By getting rid of the Dodges, Ford would resolve his bitter hatred of the brothers and eliminate a serious automotive competitor from the field.[21]

This kind of speculation is "tabloid journalism" at its worst. First, this author knows of no one familiar with Dodge or Ford history who has ever heard this rumor, which contradicts all the known historical evidence. Henry Ford did not hold a grudge against the Dodges. Ford was emotionally upset when he heard of John Dodge's death. Both he and Edsel Ford served as honorary pallbearers at Horace Dodge's funeral. Besides, the Dodge Brothers automobile was in no sense a threat to Henry Ford's dominant position in the low-price mass market.

However, there was a contemporary rumor that John and Horace became sick from wood alcohol served at a banquet at the auto show in New York. In a slight variation on the story, Bernard Baruch, who had served as a member of the War Industries Board in the First World War, recalled that John Dodge offered him a drink at the Ritz-Carlton in New York but that he did not have the time to join him.

Baruch claimed that the prohibition liquor John Dodge consumed that day caused his death. This is the rumor that I. L. Hill addressed in an interview he gave the *New York News* in mid-December 1920. He pointed out that John Dodge first became ill (with influenza) two days *after* the banquet. John Dodge died of influenza and pneumonia, which "was aggravated by diabetes from which he had long been a sufferer." Horace died eleven months later from liver trouble. Hill added, "They were both drinking men, but wood alcohol did not cause their deaths."[22]

There is also a persistent myth that the Dodge brothers adopted their unique corporate logo (a six-pointed star or hexagram created with two intertwined triangles) because they were Jewish, or they were forced to do so by Jewish bankers from whom they had borrowed money, or as an insult to the anti-Semitic Henry Ford. There is not one shred of evidence to support any of these theories. John and Horace Dodge grew up as Methodists in Niles, Michigan. Neither man was religious. Their religious affiliation in Detroit after they became wealthy was Presbyterian, mainly because of their wives. John Dodge was a member of the First Presbyterian Church, and Horace attended the Jefferson Avenue Presbyterian Church. Second, Dodge Brothers never borrowed money from banks during the period when it made automobiles. They may have done so briefly in 1903, when they were starting production for Ford.

Ironically, this notion that the Dodges were Jewish may have come from Ford's rabidly anti-Semitic *Dearborn Independent,* which sometimes misidentified people as Jewish. Rumors to that effect must have been swirling around when *Detroit Saturday Night* offered an editorial, "Hebraizing the Dodges," in July 1921. The editor noted that because of the *Dearborn Independent*'s recent work, "the Jewish population of Detroit is receiving some astonishing accretions." The editor also noted sarcastically that Henry Ford never acknowledged his defeat by the (Jewish) Dodges in the lawsuit over dividends. Finally, the editor observed, "Oh, that John and Horace were here to enjoy the fun! Howbeit, the theory that they were Jews is quite as sane as any other we have seen in the anti-Semitic antics of Ford's paper."[23]

Intertwined Lives and Personalities

Despite their distinct personalities, interests, and talents, John and Horace Dodge— partners in work, in play, and in life—were a team. Even the corporate symbol they adopted embodied their utter dependence on each other. The Hindus first used this symbol as a charm against evil, as did ancient Arab peoples who put it on their drinking cups. The Jews later adopted the symbol during the Talmudic period of their history, named it "Solomon's Seal," and used it to ward off evil. During the Middle Ages, the symbol stood for the mystical union of the body and the soul, of truth and beauty, and of other dualisms. The symbol is especially appropriate for John and Horace Dodge, since a triangle represents the fourth letter of the Greek alphabet, delta. On the Dodge Brothers logo, the triangle pointing up is white, supposedly representing the soul, while the triangle pointing down is blue and stands for the body. This is not a Star of David and does not refer to Judaism in any way.

For John and Horace Dodge, the symbol represented the union of the two brothers into one. The intertwined "D" and "B" in the middle of the six-pointed star further emphasized this point. The star and letters appear over the oceans and continents of the world as a background, in blue. Dodge Brothers applied for a trademark for the symbol on 14 August 1921 and the U.S. Patent Office registered the trademark on 10 January 1922, more than two years after Horace's death. The application stated that the firm first used the symbol on 12 November 1914 and had used it continuously since then.[24]

Another indicator of John and Horace Dodge's very close relationship was their decision to build an elaborate mausoleum on their plot in Woodlawn Cemetery in Detroit. They would share this mausoleum in death, much as they had shared many things in life. One Detroit newspaper announced the completion of the Dodge Mausoleum in late January 1915. Lloyd Brothers of Toledo, which had built a monument and grave markers in 1912 for the Dodge family members buried in Niles, also built the mausoleum. Woodlawn Cemetery records show that John Dodge moved the remains of Ivy H. Dodge, originally buried at Woodlawn in October 1901, into the Dodge Mausoleum on 16 December 1914. When completed, this impressive Egyptian Revival building, surrounded by massive columns, featured a pair of stone sphinxes flanking and guarding the bronze entrance door. The entablature decoration over the doorway, including wings and a pair of coiled cobras, is a copy of the one at the Temple of Isis from the third century BC. The stained glass windows on the back wall feature a scene from Egypt, complete with pyramids and palm trees.[25]

The brothers insisted that mail directed to the business be addressed "Dodge Brothers" or they would return it unopened. They would not accept letters sent to either of them as individuals, or mail sent to "Messrs. Dodge," or to "the Dodge Factory." Nor would "Gentlemen" or "Sirs" work either. This practice reflected the fact that they saw themselves as one, at least with respect to their business operations.[26]

Dodge Mausoleum, Woodlawn Cemetery, Detroit. Author's photograph.

They sometimes had disagreements bordering on fights, but a genuine sense of mutual affection and camaraderie always won out. According to one legendary story, the two were drinking at the bar at the Pontchartrain Hotel in Detroit and began to argue about where they would take their jointly owned, $300,000 yacht, the *Nokomis,* for a cruise on the upcoming weekend. John wanted to go north from Detroit, past Port Huron and into Georgian Bay. Horace preferred to cruise south past Toledo into Lake Erie, ending at the Thousand Islands. John proposed that they flip a coin for sole ownership of the yacht and Horace won the coin toss. John conceded that he would now have to go to the Thousand Islands, but Horace insisted that since John was now his guest, he would take his brother to Georgian Bay.[27]

The brothers often showed genuine affection for each other. Horace had long admired a painting that hung in Charles Churchill's saloon on Woodward Avenue in Detroit. The painting portrayed four monks caught drinking and playing cards by their abbot in the cellar of their monastery. Created by the Florentine painter C. Renaldi around 1892, the canvas had been on display at Churchill's saloon since 1893. Many who normally would never visit that establishment, including society women and teetotalers, made special trips there just to view it. Early in 1912, John

Dodge offered Churchill $5,000 for the painting, but Churchill refused to sell. He finally parted with his prize painting for $10,000 and John Dodge had it delivered to Horace that same day as a surprise.[28]

John and Horace Dodge were members of an informal fraternity of Detroit automakers, political leaders, and other entrepreneurs who became friends and companions away from work. This was a group of hardworking, newly successful (male) Detroiters who frequented the same saloons and eventually were admitted into the same clubs, particularly the DAC. In the spirit of camaraderie of the times, a group of Horace Dodge's friends presented him with a sterling silver "loving cup" as a birthday gift. The inscription reads, "On His 41st Birthday, To Horace E. Dodge. A Few Friends Meet to Offer Greetings and This Cup of Loving Remembrance, May 17, 1909." Among the thirty signatures were those of Louis Schneider and Charles Churchill, both saloon owners, John F. Dodge, Oscar Marx (later mayor of Detroit), and brothers Robert and Milton Oakman, both of whom were heavily involved in Detroit real estate and politics.[29]

The Dodge Brothers and Their Employees

Long after they became successful automobile makers and extremely wealthy men, the Dodges continued to use paternalism to help their employees and simultaneously discourage labor unions. Some of their practices directly aided the health and welfare of the employees. They maintained a free clinic at the plant, with a full-time medical staff on duty around the clock. The Dodges established a $5 million trust fund to help needy workers and the dependents of former employees.[30]

Late in 1919, Dodge Brothers purchased a group life insurance policy for all of its employees through the Aetna Life Insurance Company. Each policy included the following statement from Dodge Brothers: "In appreciation of your loyalty and cooperation we present to you this certificate of life insurance, our expression of good will. We assume the entire cost of this insurance and expect only in return that you continue to do your part in maintaining that spirit of loyalty and hearty cooperation, so necessary to our common welfare." The life insurance remained in effect only while the employee worked for Dodge Brothers. The coverage was on a sliding scale depending on the length of continuous service. An employee with between three months and six months of service received a policy with a benefit of $250. An individual with fifteen years or more of service received a policy that paid $2,500 at death. Given the low cost of living (and death) in 1919, these were generous insurance policies. They also reflected the Dodge brothers' progressive thinking regarding their employees.[31]

Dodge Brothers also encouraged activities that enriched their employees' lives. There is photographic evidence of company sponsorship of a Dodge Brothers Bowling League in 1915 and a Dodge Brothers baseball team in the same period. Dodge Brothers sponsored free boat excursions for their employees, including one on 15 July 1916. A booklet, "Count Your Calories," produced by the Dodge Brothers Girls Athletic Association in 1920, is another example of their sponsorship of workers' organizations. The Dodge brothers also created a workshop (the "Playpen"), which provided space, materials, and tools to their small force of retirees who wanted to do craft work. Once, when John and Horace returned from a long trip, they found that the plant superintendent had closed the "Playpen" as an economy measure. They not only reopened it but drove around to the retirees' homes and personally invited them all back.[32]

The company established the Dodge Brothers Industrial Band, also called the Dodge Brothers Concert Band, during the first Liberty Loan drive right after the United States entered the First World War in 1917. Each member of the band worked at the Dodge Brothers automobile factory or ordnance plant and practiced on his own time. It seems likely that they hired men who showed musical talent. The original director was Alessandro Liberati, who conducted the concert band through fall and winter 1918–19, often performing at the Arcadia Auditorium in Detroit. They played at the luncheon for Dodge Brothers eastern dealers at the Ritz-Carlton Hotel in New York on 7 January 1920, but with Arthur Prior as the guest conductor.

A program for a concert they did on 29 March 1920 at the Detroit Armory identified each of the sixty musicians by instrument and by the department that employed them. The band had a new director, William Robert Burnham, and he was still the conductor at the dealers' meeting in New York City in January 1921. During warm weather, the band gave noontime concerts outside the factory, and in May 1920 they gave a Sunday concert for inmates at the Detroit House of Correction.[33]

Dodge Brothers was, along with Ford, one of the first Detroit auto companies to hire African American workers. John Dancy, executive director of the Detroit Urban League, went to the Dodge Brothers offices on the off chance that he might talk to someone in authority about hiring black workers. To Dancy's surprise, John Dodge met with him and offered to hold a luncheon meeting of the National Urban League at the Dodge Brothers plant. Following that meeting (15 November

Dodge Brothers baseball team, ca. 1915. Courtesy of DCHC.

Dodge Brothers Industrial Band playing at a Dodge Brothers company picnic, ca. 1918.
Courtesy of Dodge Brothers Club Historical Archives.

1919), John Dodge gave his employment manager, Charles T. Winegar, the responsibility of increasing black employment at Dodge Brothers. Winegar in turn hired James Bailey from the Detroit Urban League to serve as a liaison between Winegar and the black employees.[34]

We do not know the exact number of African American employees at Dodge Brothers in 1919–20. If Dodge followed the practices of Ford, the only other Detroit automaker to employ African Americans, most of these minority workers held the most difficult and dangerous jobs at the factory, usually in the foundries or paint shops. We also know little about female workers. No detailed payroll records have survived, but some intriguing photographs have survived. A 1920 booklet on the Dodge Brothers plant includes a photograph of the upholstery department staffed entirely by men, but also "a section of the trim shop" with an all-female workforce at sewing machines, with female supervisors. The only other photographic evidence of women working at Dodge Brothers shows a group of (mostly) female employees in front of the office building in the early 1920s, presumably clerks, stenographers, and bookkeepers. By the 1930s, women also commonly worked in the wiring department, preparing wiring harnesses, but there is no evidence that this was the case in the late 1910s or early 1920s.[35]

The various paternalistic practices did not guarantee that all Dodge Brothers workers would love and respect John and Horace. John Olejnik, a thirty-five-year-old employee, faced criminal charges in federal court in April 1918 for sending letters to John Dodge threatening to kill him, Horace, and their families unless Dodge Brothers paid $5 a day for nine hours of work. Before the arrest, private detectives guarded the Dodge families. They convicted Olejnik in July 1918 and sentenced him to a five-year term at Fort Leavenworth prison.[36]

Managing the enormous force of shop workers and office staff at the Hamtramck factory became more difficult as the numbers grew. In mid-December 1919, less than a month before his death, John Dodge (with Horace's approval) issued a series of directives regarding personnel policies to Alfred L. McMeans, the company secretary and a director. All were to take effect on 1 January 1920. The policies included the following: (1) every employee regardless of rank will punch a time clock; (2) employees cannot miss more than 100 hours of work a year and keep their jobs; (3) all Dodge Brothers employees are entitled to a 15 percent discount on a single new Dodge Brothers car per year; (4) the factory garage will no longer service private vehicles of employees, regardless of rank; (5) no employee, regardless of rank, can use a company car for personal business; and (6) employees of Dodge Brothers cannot have any private work done for them by any other employee, even for pay. Taken

Dodge Brothers office staff, early 1920s. Courtesy of DCHC.

as a whole, these directives reflected an attempt to correct disciplinary problems and to forestall corruption within company operations. This was no longer a small intimate company where personal loyalty to John and Horace Dodge created a cooperative spirit and a commitment to the company's success.[37]

The Brothers Dodge and "Polite" Detroit Society

The Dodge brothers, like other newly minted Detroit auto millionaires of the early twentieth century, struggled to adjust to their newfound wealth and to gain acceptance by Detroit's "old money" elite. Much of Detroit's "old wealth" emerged in the nineteenth century from lumbering, mining, railroads, and shipping, and from the manufacture of railroad cars, pharmaceuticals, ships, paint, and stoves. Donald Finlay Davis reminds us that there was a sharp distinction within the early Detroit auto industry between the "gentlemen" automobile manufacturers who were already wealthy when they launched their companies and pioneers like Ford and the Dodges. The first group concentrated on luxury models such as Cadillac, Oldsmobile, Packard, Lozier, Hudson, and Northern, while holding newcomers like Ford and the Dodges in contempt. In time, the Dodge brothers could buy at least a patina of respectability in Detroit polite society. They built elaborate homes, generously supported Detroit charities, and married their children into elite eastern families.[38]

The Dodges did not face prejudice simply because they were manufacturers; they faced a more straightforward class prejudice. Members of the established social elites viewed John and Horace Dodge as rough, crude, boorish, uncultured, and lacking in the social graces of polite society. They gained notoriety for late-night drunken escapades in several of Detroit's roughest saloons long after they were millionaires. Following a meeting of Ford dealers in Detroit, the Dodges and several others went out drinking. John Dodge forced one unfortunate saloon owner to dance on top of his bar by threatening him with a pistol. Dodge applauded the effort by smashing dozens of glasses against the bar mirror. The saloon keeper's attorney threatened to sue John Dodge unless he paid $35,000 for damages. Dodge agreed and the matter ended there.[39]

The stories of drunken escapades were not merely urban myths. George B. Holley, Sr., who sold his carburetors to the Ford Motor Company and became a close friend of Henry Ford's, related some of the details about the drinking habits of the Dodge brothers:

> I'd hear remarks (from Mr. Ford) about the brothers drinking and of course he detested whiskey drinking. John and Ed [Horace] would get down there on Woodward Avenue and get loaded up and break all the bottles. It was in that bar over on Jefferson Avenue, Churchill's.
>
> They would go in there and get tight and smash everything all up and tell them to send them the bill. Mr. Ford knew all about that and he would laughingly talk about it. It did not register well with him, but he respected their ability to produce.

There is no indication, however, that the Dodges went on these drinking binges on a daily or even weekly basis.[40]

John Dodge's intense loyalty to friends, combined with a short temper, sometimes led to violence without the aid of alcohol. In September 1916, he was enjoying dinner at the DAC when he saw an article in the *Detroit Times* criticizing him and some of his political allies. John Dodge interrupted his meal and drove to the home of the paper's owner, James Schermerhorn. Dodge punched him twice, knocking the errant publisher to the ground, and promised to beat him more severely if he ever criticized his friends in print again. John Dodge's penchant for violence became legendary, in part because he was unable to keep the worst incidents out of the local papers.[41]

The ugliest example of John Dodge's temper took place in Louis Schneider's saloon on lower Woodward Avenue in downtown Detroit on 3 January 1911. John Dodge and his friend Robert Oakman, both drunk, viciously attacked a prominent Detroit attorney, Thomas J. Mahon. They knocked Mahon, who had two wooden legs, to the ground, beat him with his cane, and kicked him repeatedly in the face, head, and body. They momentarily felt guilty and offered to help Mahon, but when he refused their aid, they attacked him again. More than two weeks later, while Mahon remained confined to bed, he filed a $25,000 damage suit against Oakman and Dodge. Attorney Edmund Joncas, also a victim of this attack, filed an affidavit supporting Mahon's account. The case never came to trial, suggesting that Dodge and Oakman gave Mahon a large out-of-court settlement to end the dispute. As a direct result of this incident and the publicity it generated, Detroit's prestigious Liggett School threatened to expel John Dodge's daughters if the press reported additional violent episodes.[42]

John Dodge and Robert Oakman were political allies and close friends for much of the 1910s. Oakman, who invested heavily in real estate and other ventures, had asked his bank, the Wayne County and Home Savings, for an additional loan of $250,000. Julius Haass, the bank president, refused the loan because of Oakman's poor track record in his various businesses. When John Dodge heard of this, he stormed into the bank and threatened to withdraw his funds if the bank did not accommodate Oakman. Haass refused to budge, but suggested that John Dodge could sign a note for a loan for Oakman. Dodge signed a bank note, but left the amount blank for Oakman to fill in later that day. Oakman took a line of credit for $500,000 guaranteed by John Dodge and repaid him in full.[43]

Horace Dodge had a slow-burning temper that exploded less frequently than John's. One cold winter night in downtown Detroit, Horace left Charlie Churchill's tavern and tried to crank-start his car. As he struggled and sweated, a passerby made a joking comment about Horace's troubles. Dodge stopped cranking long enough to punch the man in the jaw and knock him halfway across the street.[44]

John and Horace Dodge earned fame as machinists and automobile manufacturers and gained unwanted notoriety because of occasional public drinking and violence. A tiny surviving sample of their correspondence also shows them to have been dutiful parents involved in the details of their children's lives. John Dodge received a letter from the Detroit police commissioner reporting that a vehicle registered in his name was seen speeding on Jefferson Avenue in Detroit. He admitted that this was an electric car used by his two daughters, Winifred (age seventeen) and Isabel (age fifteen). He added, "They have been severely reprimanded and I am sure there will be no cause for further complaint." After daughter Isabel applied for admission to exclusive Wellesley College, John Dodge discovered that she would have to live in a private home near the college if she went there. He wrote to Wellesley, "As I do not approve of this arrangement, I would request that you cancel her application and return the entrance fee."[45]

Horace Dodge took an active interest in Horace E. Dodge, Jr.'s affairs while he was a student at St. John's School in Manlius, New York. The school included military training and young Horace needed a horse for military maneuvers. In October 1911, the elder Horace asked one of the school staff, a Mr. Grigsby, to give his son a horse temporarily. He also asked H. C. Dunston at St. John's for advice. Horace, who was eleven at the time, wanted a large horse, but his father thought a smaller horse would be better. Less than a week later, Horace Sr. informed the school that he had purchased a horse for his son and was shipping it by railway express, but wanted Mr. Grigsby to buy an appropriate saddle and bridle. Horace added, "We believe the horse is very much to his liking and is also very kind and gentle, and I am told is thoroughly broken to military maneuvers and also does not seem to be afraid of anything."[46] Much like their social peers, John and Horace Dodge sent their children to exclusive secondary schools and colleges.

The Dodge brothers eventually won reluctant acceptance from Detroit's establishment, but only after involving themselves in a variety of charitable activities. The elite Detroit Club denied John Dodge admission, while the DAC, with many auto barons among its members, admitted the Dodge brothers. According to Malcolm Bingay, the DAC admitted them "after deep misgivings." Horace unsuccessfully applied for membership in the prestigious Grosse Pointe Country Club in 1906. Angry and humiliated, he bought a large tract next to the club, where he vowed to build an extravagant home that would make the country club "look like a shanty."[47]

There, he built an elaborate red sandstone English Renaissance–style house. Completed in late 1911, it included an enormous pipe organ and extensive rose gardens extending to the banks of the Detroit River (thus the name Rose Terrace). According to one report, a pipe-organ manufacturer who wanted Horace to consider one of his organs for his mansion bought a four-page advertisement in a yachting magazine simply to get Horace Dodge's attention. In mid-July 1911, Horace Dodge insured the pipe organ for $12,000 while it was still sitting unassembled in his garage. He ordered music rolls for the organ in mid-November, suggesting that he did not play particularly well.

Horace also personally ordered many furnishings for the new house. During the second half of 1911, he wrote eighteen letters to Tiffany & Company in New

York ordering rugs, wall coverings, woodwork, furniture, and light fixtures. Horace Dodge and his family moved in sometime in late December, when he ordered the stoppage of electric and gas service at their home at 475 East Grand Boulevard in Detroit. The new mansion had an enormous boathouse and docks for Horace's yachts and speedboats. Building Rose Terrace, however, did not by itself bring Horace Dodge and his family instant acceptance into upper-crust Grosse Pointe society.[48]

Commissioning increasingly larger yachts did, however, bring Horace Dodge some status in Grosse Pointe. The first Dodge speedboats (*Lotus* and *Hornet*), discussed in an earlier chapter, did not impress his wealthy neighbors. However, Horace's 96-foot steam yacht, designed by Peter Studer and also called the *Hornet,* brought grudging recognition. This was a "day yacht," a vessel with dining facilities but with no overnight accommodations. Dodge Brothers designed and built the quadruple-expansion oil-fired engine, rated at 1,000 horsepower, at their machine shop on Monroe Avenue in Detroit. A pair of Deering water-tube boilers provided steam at 600 pounds pressure. This yacht featured a tri-screw design and could reach a speed of 35 miles per hour. After Mrs. Horace Dodge christened the *Hornet* on 6 July 1905, the Detroit Shipbuilding Company plant on Orleans Street in Detroit installed the engines and boilers, and the yacht went into service in 1906. Horace sold the *Hornet* in 1911 to Ora J. Mulford of Detroit, who renamed it the *Viking*.[49]

The Dodge brothers replaced the *Hornet* with the *Hornet II,* an even faster yacht. Maritime engineer Alfred Seymour designed the *Hornet II,* christened on 19 April 1910 by John Dodge's daughter Winifred at the Great Lakes Boat Works in Detroit. This steel-hulled 99-foot vessel had a pair of 1,000 horsepower quadruple expansion steam engines designed by Horace Dodge and could achieve a speed of 41 miles per hour, supposedly the fastest yacht in the world. Although the *Hornet II* was scrapped in 1921, one of its engines has survived in the collections of the Smithsonian Institution. The Detroit Motor Boat Club (Detroit Boat Club) elected Horace Dodge commodore in December 1913, replacing prominent newspaper publisher William Scripps. Horace was also instrumental in organizing the *Miss Detroit* Powerboat Association to build a powerboat to represent Detroit in the Gold Cup Trophy race. *Miss Detroit* won the Gold Cup on 14 August 1915 at Manhasset Bay in Long Island Sound.[50]

John and Horace Dodge also wanted a "cruising yacht," complete with sleeping chambers. They commissioned the New York firm of Gielow & Orr to design a 185-foot vessel that required a crew of thirty. The Robins Dry Dock Company of

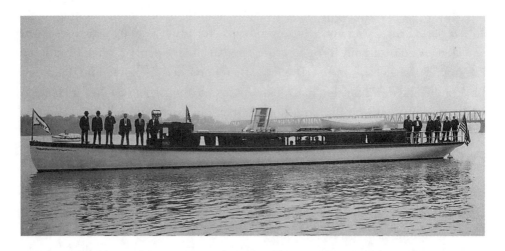

Day yacht *Hornet* (1905). Courtesy of the Dossin Great Lakes Museum, Detroit.

Brooklyn, New York, built the steam yacht *Nokomis,* christened by Horace's daughter Delphine on 20 December 1913. Horace Dodge even received a "Complimentary Frank" from the Marconi Wireless Telegraph Company of America granting him and the *Nokomis* free unlimited service between any of the Marconi Company's ship and shore stations. Its use was restricted to "personal social messages" and could not be used for "business or political communications." When the U.S. Navy requisitioned the *Nokomis* for service in the First World War, the Dodges held a special farewell ceremony at the Detroit docks in May 1917 to see her off. The Dodges produced a farewell booklet and sister Delphine (Della) Dodge wrote an emotional poem, *"Nokomis,* Goodby!" for this occasion:

> The wind is lashing the somber lee,
> And the foam-flecked waves roll high,
> And my heart is stiller like the stormy sea,
> As you sail from the shores of "Used-to-Be"
> Goodby, Nokomis, goodby!
>
> You've served me well in days of yore,
> When the sun shone bright on high,
> Go now and weather the storms of war,
> And make me proud of the name you bore.
> Goodby, old friend, goodby![51]

In December 1917, the U.S. Navy recommissioned the vessel *U.S.S. Kwasid* and it served as a submarine chaser on the East Coast of the United States. Sold at the end of the war, the *Nokomis* finished its life as the *Saelmo* and later as the *Dupont*.[52]

The Dodges quickly commissioned an even bigger yacht, the *Nokomis II,* also designed by Gielow & Orr. The Pusey & Jones Company shipyard in Wilmington, Delaware, completed the vessel in late 1917, but the U.S. Navy requisitioned the ship before it was finished and commissioned it as the *U.S.S. Nokomis* on 3 December 1917. This yacht was 243 feet long, with a beam of 31 feet, and was capable of sixteen knots. With a crew of 103, the *U.S.S. Nokomis* patrolled the Atlantic coast during the war and remained in service with the U.S. Navy for two decades.[53]

Having lost two of his yachts to government service, Horace Dodge bought the yacht *Caroline* (1917) from Edward Ford of Toledo in late 1917. He renamed the 187-foot-long steam yacht the *Delphine* in 1919 after his daughter. Horace had previously owned a 45-foot gasoline-powered launch, also called the *Delphine,* which he bought in 1914. Delphine Dodge and her husband James Cromwell spent their honeymoon in June 1920 on the yacht *Delphine.* After a new yacht of the same name went into service in 1921, Horace's widow, Anna Thomson Dodge, sold the *Delphine/Caroline* to Mrs. Joseph B. Schlotman of Grosse Pointe Shores. She renamed it the *Stellaris* and it remained in active service for another decade. A New York City–based cruise company purchased the vessel in 1941, renaming it the *Sylph II*.[54]

John Dodge commissioned one last large boat before he died. The *Francis,* completed in December 1920, was a 104-foot-long cruiser, powered by four Murray and Tugurtha engines generating 1,600 horsepower combined, driving triple screws. The Great Lakes Boat Building Corporation of Milwaukee built this cruiser, which was intended to have an operating speed of 30 miles per hour. At the first official trials, the *Francis* achieved 31.3 miles per hour.[55]

Construction began in June 1920 at the Great Lakes Engineering Works yards in River Rouge, Michigan, on an enormous yacht, briefly called the *Delphine II* until they sold her namesake. Delphine Dodge Cromwell christened the vessel on 2 April 1921, well after her father's death. Designed by H. J. Gielow, this was the largest private yacht on the Great Lakes, some 258 feet long. It cost $2 million, featured nine staterooms and a $60,000 pipe organ, and required a crew of sixty. It suffered a disastrous fire and sank in September 1926 on the Hudson River. Anna Thomson Dodge, by then Mrs. Hugh Dillman, had the yacht raised and refurbished at a cost of $800,000. The U.S. Navy requisitioned the *Delphine*

Steam yacht *Nokomis* (1913). Courtesy of Oakland University's Meadow Brook Hall.

Farewell to the *Nokomis*, 16 May 1917. Left to right: John F. Dodge, Adolphe Vocelle, Albert Andrich, unidentified naval officer, Robert Oakman, Edward Fitzgerald, Horace E. Dodge, and Mayor Oscar Marx. Courtesy of Walter Reuther Library, *Detroit News* Collection, Negative No. 19993.

in January 1942, renamed it the *U.S.S. Dauntless*, and assigned the vessel to
Admiral Ernest J. King, who used it in the Chesapeake Bay. Mrs. Dodge refurbished the *Delphine* after the war and used it until 1955. This magnificent yacht
has changed hands several times since the early 1960s, but is still sailing in
European waters and is owned by a Belgium industrialist. The *Delphine* underwent a thorough restoration starting in 1997 and was rechristened in 2003 at
Monaco.[56]

Horace's wife Anna was much more interested in joining upper-crust social cir-
cles than was he. The Horace Dodges wintered in Palm Beach, Florida, where
Anna Dodge launched daughter Delphine into social circles more exclusive and
cosmopolitan than upper-crust Detroit society. Horace boosted their status in Palm
Beach by donating $50,000 to the local Good Samaritan Hospital. Delphine met
James H. R. Cromwell, who was from a prominent Philadelphia family, and the
two married in June 1920. More than three thousand members of the Detroit and
Philadelphia elites attended the wedding, which featured ostentatious displays of
Dodge wealth everywhere. Horace presented Anna with a five-strand pearl necklace that had belonged to Russian Empress Catherine the Great and cost $825,000.
Horace gave his daughter, among many expensive presents, a more modest necklace worth $100,000. Following Delphine's wedding, Anna Dodge convinced Hor-
ace to buy a large seaside villa in Palm Beach, appropriately named Villa Marina.
Anna constantly strove to stand on an equal footing with the wealthiest scions who
wintered there.[57]

John Dodge, like his brother Horace, did not always feel comfortable with his
wealth, but he did not refrain from spending it conspicuously. In 1906, he moved
into his new $250,000 home on East Boston Boulevard in Detroit, designed by
Smith, Hinchman & Grylls. This was the last house in which he lived. When he
built the Boston Boulevard house, John Dodge purchased a 320-acre farm in
Rochester, north of Detroit, as a country retreat. With additional parcels, he created the sprawling Meadow Brook estate. At the time of his death, John Dodge
was building an enormous mansion on Lake Shore Drive in Grosse Pointe. John
and Horace Dodge and friends Oscar Marx and Robert Oakman welcomed in
the new year of 1920 at John Dodge's Boston Boulevard home. Ironically, John
told his guests, "This is the last time that my brother and I will ever greet the
New Year in this house."[58]

Smith, Hinchman & Grylls designed John Dodge's Grosse Pointe mansion, to
be finished in fall 1920. This Tudor-style house featured granite from the famous
Weymouth quarries in Massachusetts. About 150 stone cutters who had worked
on Andrew Carnegie's Skibo castle were hard at work on the Dodge house in

Matilda and John Dodge next to a transplanted tree at their unfinished Grosse Pointe mansion, 1919. Courtesy of Oakland University's Meadow Brook Hall.

1919. It would have 110 rooms and 24 baths, a 4,000-square-foot servants' wing, and a swimming pool. John and Matilda planned the grounds as carefully as the house. They moved huge trees hundreds of miles and built enormous flower gardens. The finished estate would include a miniature farm to raise vegetables and livestock, along with sprawling greenhouses. John Dodge spent $4 million on the mansion before he died, but Matilda Dodge never finished this house, which she

John and Matilda Dodge's unfinished Grosse Pointe mansion, 1919. Courtesy of Oakland University's Meadow Brook Hall.

left vacant and subsequently demolished in 1941. She instead built Meadow Brook Hall (1929), which also cost $4 million, in Rochester.[59]

John and Matilda Dodge also spent lavishly on social events to showcase their wealth and to achieve some acceptance in Detroit society. Daughter Winifred's social debut in December 1913 featured an elaborate dinner dance at the Pont-chartrain Hotel in Detroit. Decorators turned the ballroom into a replica of an English garden, complete with plants, flowers, and songbirds hidden in the shrubbery. On 30 October 1916, Winifred married William Gray, Jr., the son of a Detroit banker. One of her bridesmaids was Josephine Clay, the sister of Eleanor Clay, future wife of Edsel Ford. As a wedding present, John Dodge gave the newlyweds a large house at 1723 Iroquois Avenue in Detroit's fashionable Indian Village neighborhood. Still, Matilda Rausch Dodge never sought acceptance by Grosse Pointe society as desperately as Anna Thomson Dodge did.[60]

John and Horace Dodge were not alone in receiving little recognition for their accomplishments. All of the Detroit automakers struggled for social acceptance. An examination of *The Book of Detroiters* (1908), the principal guide to Detroit's elite, speaks to the Dodges' low profile in the community. Thomas J. Mahon, the lawyer John Dodge attacked in a bar fight, had a biographical sketch of seven lines, the same amount of space given to Henry Ford. John Dodge and James Couzens had three lines each, and Horace Dodge was not listed at all. Two automobile executives associated with the Chalmers Motor Car Company, Roy D. Chapin and Howard Coffin, had eleven lines of text and Henry Leland received ten lines.[61]

The pattern remained the same in the revised edition of *The Book of Detroiters,* published in 1914. John Dodge's entry expanded to ten lines and Horace was absent again, probably because he simply refused or neglected to send information to the editor. Henry Ford's entry had grown to eighteen lines, while James Couzens had nineteen lines. Although Henry Leland and Roy D. Chapin were arguably less significant to the automobile industry and to the Detroit community than Ford or Couzens, Leland's entry stood at twenty-three lines and Chapin's at twenty-seven lines of text.[62]

In time, both John and Horace Dodge slowly made their way into most of the clubs of the elite. In the case of the Detroit Club, neither was a member as late as 1913, but they were admitted sometime before 1920. They both became members of the DAC and the Detroit Golf, Yacht, Motor Boat, and Country Clubs. Both belonged to a half-dozen additional golf/country clubs in the metropolitan Detroit area. Horace was more active than brother John, in part because of his serious interests in yachting and music. He belonged to the Larchmont (New York) Yacht Club, the Atlantic Yacht Club, the Chicago Yacht Club, the Chamber Music Society, and the Detroit Symphony Society. Horace was also a member of the New York Athletic Club, Detroit Curling Club, Racquet Club of Philadelphia, and a half-dozen other athletic clubs. John and Horace were members of the Detroit Board of Commerce. By the late 1910s, both had joined a wide variety of prestigious social clubs in Detroit and elsewhere. They were not content, however, to merely enjoy their fortunes and the benefits that came with wealth.[63]

Charitable Contributions, Public Service, and Politics

Both John and Horace Dodge made substantial contributions to Detroit charities, especially in the late 1910s. In John's case, wife Matilda and sister Della Eschbach (Ashbaugh) "steered" his generosity toward their pet causes. While Anna Thomson Dodge did the same with husband Horace, he was more independent when it came to donations than brother John. There is no comprehensive listing of the Dodge brothers' charitable contributions, so the discussion below is necessarily incomplete. Their largest gifts came in 1919, reflecting in part the windfall each received ($12.5 million) from the sale of their Ford Motor Company stock that year. John and Horace made donations to separate charities as well as identical donations to the same worthy causes.

One of the first substantial Dodge donations was a gift of $35,000 from John Dodge to the Detroit Federation of Women's Clubs in 1913, to be used for a club house. John's sister Della was the president of the federation at the time. The federation purchased an existing residence at Hancock and Second Avenue in Detroit, then remodeled the house and built an addition to serve as an auditorium. Matilda Dodge presented the keys to the club house to the federation when the facility was formally dedicated in late January 1916. Expressing their gratitude, the federation published a lengthy tribute to John Dodge following his death. Another charity Della was committed to was the Salvation Army Rescue Home for Girls and Women, which launched a $60,000 fund-raising campaign for a new facility in April 1916. Dodge Brothers made an initial donation of $2,500 to kick off the campaign.[64]

Both Dodge wives did more than simply steer contributions from their husbands to their favorite charities. Anna Thomson Dodge was the chair of the factory committee of the Red Cross Christmas seal campaign of December 1913. Right before Christmas, the committee announced total sales of 130,000 seals, with Mrs. Dodge personally selling 109,000 of the total. Seventy-five percent of the moneys raised went to support poor patients at the Detroit Tuberculosis Sanitarium. Sister-in-law Matilda Rausch Dodge was chair of the committee charged with selling Christmas seals to drug stores. The following February, Anna Thomson Dodge made a donation of $12,000 for an addition to the Detroit Tuberculosis Sanitarium. The gift funded a separate building to house twenty children suffering from this disease.[65]

Horace Dodge became a key promoter of the fledgling Detroit Symphony Orchestra (DSO) in the late 1910s. In 1918, he helped finance the search for a permanent conductor who could give the DSO world-class standing. The DSO hired Ossip Salomonowitsch Gabrilowitsch, a brilliant pianist who was also Mark Twain's son-in-law, in part because Horace and Anna Dodge were partial to pianists. Gabrilowitsch, or "Gabby," as he was known less formally, agreed to come to Detroit only if the DSO had a new concert hall.[66]

Horace Dodge personally contributed at least $100,000 for the construction of a concert hall and led the fund-raising campaign for the rest of the $1 million that was needed. He was a substantial stockholder (250 shares of the total of 2,650) in the corporation established in April 1919 to build the facility and was one of the nine original directors. He was also one of several directors of the Detroit Symphony

Society, which served as the business management team for the DSO and as fund-raisers (the director managed the orchestra) from 30 May 1919 until his death in December 1920. Orchestra Hall, built in a record four months, opened in October 1919 and served as the DSO's home in 1919–39 and from 1989 to the present. Ironically, the DSO played in the Henry and Edsel Ford Auditorium in Detroit's riverfront from the mid-1950s until 1989. Horace Dodge's love for music was renown. At one point, he left a hunting expedition in northern Michigan to catch the performance of a favorite concerto. He supposedly chartered a train to Detroit, arrived at Orchestra Hall just in time, and sat in the back of the concert hall wearing his hunting clothes.[67]

The DSO played at the wedding reception of Horace's daughter Delphine in June 1920 and at Horace's funeral, in recognition of their most important supporter. Upon the death of Horace Dodge, the Detroit Symphony Society offered the following resolution:

> The unfailing sympathy and support given by Mr. Dodge to the Symphony Orchestra have been of inestimable value to the City, as through his generosity the Orchestra has been enabled to reach a higher plane than otherwise would have been possible. While his modesty forbade his taking any prominent part in the affairs of the organization, his appreciation of its excellence, and his ready generosity in helping its development, have been of the highest value to the Society, and an inspiration to those working with him.

After Horace Dodge's death, Victor Herbert composed "The Dodge Brothers March," dedicated to Horace Dodge "in appreciation of his generous efforts towards the advancement of American music." Dodge support for the DSO did not end with Horace Dodge's death. For the entire decade of the 1920s, Anna Thomson Dodge remained a stockholder and director of Orchestra Hall and a director of the Detroit Symphony Society. She made an additional donation of $25,000 in February 1921, only two months after Horace's death.[68]

Both men made large contributions to their own pet charities. John Dodge's 1919 donations included $137,400 to the Salvation Army; $62,597 to the Detroit Federation of Women's Clubs; and $250,000 to the First Presbyterian Church of Detroit, Matilda's church. John's gift to the Presbyterian Church (the First Protestant Society of Detroit) consisted of $150,000 for its endowment fund and $100,000 for a "settlement house" to help new arrivals to industrial Detroit settle into an unfamiliar environment. The Dodge Community House, located at 6201 Farr Avenue in Detroit, not far from the Dodge Brothers factory, finally opened in

November 1925. In early January 1920, before he left Detroit for New York City, John Dodge gave an additional $6,500 for "child welfare work" to the Federation of Women's Clubs to provide "Penny Lunches" for schoolchildren. In 1919 alone, John Dodge made charitable donations amounting to $504,848, including several that were the same as his brother's.[69]

Horace Dodge's contributions to charity in 1919, some $147,971, appear much less generous than John's, but this figure does not include the $100,000 (possibly $150,000) in gifts to the Detroit Symphony Orchestra. His gifts in 1919 included $25,000 to the Protestant Orphan Asylum, $10,000 to the First Presbyterian Church, which John attended, and $54,738 to the Westminster Presbyterian Church. In July and November 1920 he gave an additional $80,000 to the Protestant Orphan Asylum. At Anna Dodge's urging, Horace also donated $50,000 to the Good Samaritan Hospital in Palm Beach in April 1920. Following Horace's death, one Detroit newspaper pointed out that Horace Dodge made numerous donations anonymously. Among other things, he paid for the college education of dozens of young men, without them ever knowing their benefactor. Horace Dodge, wife Anna, and daughter Delphine became members of the Jefferson Avenue Presbyterian Church in 1912 and 1913, but they were probably not large benefactors during Horace's life. Anna Thomson Dodge made a large anonymous donation after Horace's death for a new church building, which opened in 1925. The Horace Dodge Memorial Chapel there acknowledges that donation.[70]

John and Horace Dodge also supported churches that many of their employees attended. In 1919, they each donated $7,500 to the African Methodist Episcopal Church and $2,500 to the Hamtramck Polish Catholic Church (St. Florian's). The brothers often made identical contributions to broad community charities. They donated $25,000 each to the American Red Cross Fund in the second half of 1917. The YMCA War Fund received gifts of $6,500 from John and Horace in March and April 1918. Starting in June 1918, the two brothers made substantial regular gifts to the Detroit Patriotic Fund, an all-purpose community charity that became the Detroit Community Fund in the early 1920s. Between 15 June 1918 and 15 May 1919, John and Horace Dodge each gave $50,000 to the Detroit Patriotic Fund, and an additional $25,000 each on 31 December 1919. Their donations of $150,000 in 1918–20 were the eighth largest overall and fifth among automakers, after Henry Ford, James Couzens, and the owners of Packard Motor Car Company and the Hudson Motor Car Company. Dodge Brothers, the automobile company, donated $50,000 in 1921, 1922, and 1923, continuing the tradition started by John and Horace Dodge.[71]

Unlike brother Horace, John Dodge developed an interest in politics and became a powerful political figure in Detroit in the 1910s. Before Detroit voters elected Hazen S. Pingree (Republican) as mayor in 1890, the Democratic Party machine had dominated Detroit politics. Pingree established Republican control of Detroit government until fall 1918, when a revised city charter went into effect. It replaced a forty-two-member Common Council elected by wards with a nine-member body elected at large. More important, all elections were held on a non-partisan basis starting in 1918, when James Couzens won the mayor's post. In the meantime, active Republicans like John Dodge had considerable influence.[72]

Exactly how John Dodge became active in Republican politics is not clear. George Codd, Detroit's mayor in 1905–06, appointed him to the Detroit Water Commission in 1905 and he served in 1905–10 and briefly in 1913. During much of Dodge's term as water commissioner, he was chairman of the Committee on Extension and Construction, which considered thousands of requests to extend the water lines into new neighborhoods. He served briefly as president of the Board of Water Commissioners in March–June 1910, when he left the commission. John Dodge and fellow commissioner and friend James Wilkie planned a new water pumping plant to serve the needs of the rapidly expanding city. Wilkie, appointed to the board in 1908 at the suggestion of John Dodge, was the chief mechanical engineer for Parke, Davis and Company, the pharmaceutical firm. Construction began in July 1909 but was not completed until five years later.[73]

The work of the water commissioners was largely apolitical. Although John Dodge was in the (Republican) minority at the time, his one request for the appointment of a man to a job (inspector) was approved. That man, J. G. Everson, wrote to Dodge in June 1911 complaining that he had been fired by the water board because of his politics, despite his impeccable work record. A long newspaper feature on John Dodge in the *Detroit News* (20 October 1915) pointed out that when the new pumping plant was being planned, John Dodge and the other commissioners often met three nights a week. This was all unpaid public service on their part. The improvements to the Detroit water system that resulted from John Dodge's work were impressive. With the completion of the new pumping station, the water works plant was valued at $15 million, with less than $2 million in bonded debt. Detroit had one of the most modern urban water systems in the United States and among the lowest water rates. When John Dodge's political crony Oscar B. Marx became mayor of Detroit in January 1913, he reappointed John Dodge to the Board of Water Commissioners.[74]

John Dodge also served as a member of Detroit's Board of Street Railway Commissioners, a far more politicized and controversial job than that of water commissioner. The privately owned streetcar lines serving Detroit had been the subject of severe criticism from the public and from political leaders since the 1890s. Poor service, high fares, and the failure to extend lines into new neighborhoods were the main complaints. The Detroit United Railway (DUR) had a monopoly over streetcar service within the city since 1900, operating under a franchise from the Detroit Common Council. The Michigan state legislature empowered Detroit, through the Verdier Act of March 1913, to form a commission to purchase and operate a street railway system in the city.[75]

In late May 1913, Oscar B. Marx, Detroit's mayor in 1913–18, announced the first Detroit Street Railway Commission, which included Joseph S. Stringham, John F. Dodge, and William D. Mahon, the president of the Amalgamated Association of Street and Electric Railway Employees of America. Stringham declined the appointment and Marx took nearly two months to find the third commissioner—James Couzens, a major stockholder in the Ford Motor Company, as well as its vice president and business manager. Couzens, with encouragement from Henry Ford, accepted the appointment in late July. John Dodge was named president of the commission at its first meeting.[76]

A curious subplot developed before John Dodge began any official work on the commission. He had spent three months in Europe, mostly a pleasure trip, and returned to Detroit in early July 1913. He had publicly announced his intent to study carefully public ownership of streetcar systems in Europe while touring, but upon his return, revealed that he had done little except to observe them in operation. He was unwilling at first to say anything about his European experiences. Less than three weeks later, after long discussions with Oscar Marx and his advisors, John Dodge declared European streetcar systems a great success and strongly urged Detroiters to push for municipal ownership. He claimed that he had carefully "studied" the systems in Glasgow, Liverpool, and Sheffield, all of which were successful.[77]

One of the first acts of the new commission was to force the DUR in early August 1913 to rescind a threatened fare increase and to keep the 3-cent fare offered during "workingmen's hours" on all of their lines. If the DUR carried out a threatened shutdown of part of their system, Henry Ford (at the urging of Couzens and Dodge) threatened to provide the city with 1,000 Ford automobiles to replace the streetcars. Couzens, Dodge, and Mahon strongly advocated Municipal Ownership (M.O.) of Detroit's street railways, but Mayor Marx no longer supported the idea. The Street Railway Commission made an offer to the DUR later in summer 1913, which the DUR rejected, claiming that it would not even cover their bonded debt. The DUR and the Street Railway Commission agreed to submit the question of M.O. to the voters in a special election in November 1915. If the voters approved, then the Circuit Court of Wayne County would determine the price, which would be binding on both parties.[78]

William Mahon suddenly quit the Street Railway Commission in mid-April 1914, marking the start of conflicts within the commission and between some members of the commission and Mayor Marx. Mahon claimed that he quit out of frustration over the lack of significant movement toward M.O. He blamed the political machine of Oscar Marx for preventing the commission from doing any significant work. Mahon argued that the Marx machine did not support M.O. and had held a series of secret meetings with the DUR to sabotage the efforts for M.O. He further complained that James Couzens had been in California most of the time since his appointment and that John Dodge refused to share commission documents with him. Several newspapers articles reporting his resignation pointed out that Mahon had also seldom been available for commission meetings, making it impossible for the group to function. Two days after Mahon's resignation, Mayor Marx named Water Commissioner James Wilkie to fill Mahon's seat.[79]

Internal bickering and public disputes raged on. In mid-May 1914, the *Detroit Journal* claimed that Marx's political machine was angry with James Couzens because he was "stealing the glory" from John Dodge regarding the work of the Detroit Street Railway Commission. Dodge, who was the chairman of the Board of Street Railway Commissioners in 1914, had developed a plan for a subway to relieve downtown surface congestion, but Couzens adopted the plan as his own. At the same time, Mayor Marx hosted a ground-breaking for the construction of a new sixteen-mile belt line for the DUR, essentially killing off M.O in the mind of his critics. Marx and his political machine had pushed approval of this line through the Detroit Common Council. James Couzens roundly criticized this new line and Marx's support for the DUR. In mid-October 1914, John Dodge temporarily derailed the DUR's cross-town line by refusing to grant them permission to complete a key junction.[80]

Despite the dangers inherent in this political minefield, John Dodge remained a strong advocate of M.O. He also worked hard to keep the system operating well while the issue was being decided. In May 1915, the street railway workers went on strike after the DUR fired Motorman Peter J. Whaling. They shut down the entire system for a day. William Mahon turned down a compromise offered by the

Street Railway Commission and planned to ask the union members to endorse a continuing strike. John Dodge attacked Mahon, first by saying, "You have been spoiling for a fight all day. Now you are going to get it." Dodge argued that while he was friend of the workers, including the street railway workers, and was not sympathetic to the DUR, he strongly believed that the union had no right to deny workingmen all over Detroit the right to get to work. John Dodge attended the union meeting the following morning and directly appealed to the men to approve binding arbitration to settle the dispute. He delivered a powerful speech that won the men's approval:

> I'm looking forward to the day when there won't be any D.U.R. You help get us possession of the car lines for you, and the trouble between you and your employers will end. I say this because I know all you want is a square deal. . . .
>
> Boys, I had 8,000 men who walked to work yesterday morning. Those fellows are workingmen, just like you and I. Some of them walked seven miles to the shop, and did it without a murmur. We hauled them home the best way we could last night, but a lot of them walked again today.
>
> After all, these men and you are all part of one big corporation. We're all part of the city of Detroit. That's why municipal ownership of the street railways will succeed. You'll be working for yourself and for the men you haul on the cars.

The workers voted unanimously in favor of arbitration. James Couzens was named the third arbitrator, along with the state labor commissioner and a representative from the DUR. They ruled in favor of the union and the DUR reinstated Whaling.[81]

John Dodge inevitably got caught up in the political mudslinging that became part of the M.O. controversy. Opponents argued that because the Dodge Brothers factory was in Hamtramck and the Ford factory in Highland Park, both outside of Detroit, neither Dodge nor Couzens had to worry about the tax ramifications of a Detroit takeover of the streetcars. John Dodge fired back by reprinting his check for his July 1915 taxes to Detroit (more than $18,000) in the *Detroit News*. Remarkably, he missed much of his daughter Winifred's wedding reception in order to speak in favor of municipal ownership at a mass public meeting at the Detroit Armory at the end of October.[82]

Municipal Ownership lost in a referendum vote in November 1915, in large part because the public did not know the price tag for acquiring the DUR system. Journalist William Lutz argued that the referendum would have passed if Couzens and Dodge had followed Police Commissioner Gillespie's suggestion that they give the saloon owners $5,000 to ensure passage. Donald Davis claims that in the aftermath of that defeat, John Dodge dropped his public support for Municipal Ownership, while Couzens became even stronger in his advocacy.[83]

John Dodge attended his last meeting of the Board of Street Railway Commissioners on 9 July 1918 and resigned by the end of 1918. James Couzens decided to run for mayor in 1918 and no one gave him any chance of winning. John Dodge claimed that Couzens could not get elected dogcatcher or coroner. In early August 1918, three weeks before the primary election, Couzens pulled off a magnificent publicity stunt. The DUR had recently raised fares on some lines from five to six cents and Couzens refused to pay the higher fare. He also refused to get off the car and when news of his action spread, hundreds of other riders followed suit and the DUR briefly shut down their lines, leading to sporadic rioting around the city. The DUR rescinded the fare increase and the voters rewarded Couzens by electing him mayor in November 1918. Yet another referendum approving city purchase of the DUR, this time with a price of $31.5 million attached, also went down in defeat in April 1919. James Couzens served as mayor of Detroit in 1919–22, kept pushing for Municipal Ownership, and, in 1922, finally achieved it.[84]

John Dodge became a major supporter of Oscar Marx's political machine right after Marx became mayor of Detroit in 1913. Norman Beasley and George W. Stark, longtime Detroit newspaper reporters, claimed that John Dodge spent a fortune bankrolling Marx in the 1910s. Marx enjoyed his friendship and support, while John Dodge did not ask for specific favors or privileges. Rather than political power, Dodge wanted political influence, which Marx gladly granted him.[85]

The triumvirate of John Dodge, Robert Oakman, and Oscar B. Marx, who served as mayor of Detroit in 1913–18, controlled the Republican Party in the Detroit area throughout the 1910s. John Dodge urged Marx to name James Couzens to the Detroit Street Railway Commission in July 1913. When Marx attempted to salvage his mayoral reelection campaign in September 1916 by appointing James Couzens as police commissioner, he consulted with John Dodge about the decision. John Dodge was among the seven largest Michigan contributors to the national Republican Party in 1916 and was one of thirty Michigan delegates sent to the June 1916 Republican National Convention in Chicago. Charles Evans Hughes, the Republican presidential nominee in 1916, visited the Dodge Brothers factory as a guest of John Dodge on 7 August 1916. John Wanamaker, a prominent Philadelphia Republican, asked John Dodge in late October 1916 to place Republican political advertisements in Michigan papers for the presidential election. Dodge responded, "Personally, I feel I have done all I can afford to do and it is useless in my case to ask either our City or County Committee [to contribute] as they are both bankrupt. Affairs in Michigan appear to have been badly handled." John Dodge became the chair of the Michigan Republican Party Finance Committee in 1918. In a "political letter" addressed to prominent Michigan Republican Thomas H Newberry, Cameron Currie made the following observation about John Dodge's political power: "John, I think, is the unquestioned 'Warwick' of the present dominant section of the local Republican interest, and can have them do his will by a mere word." Many of his Republican friends wanted him to run for the U.S. Senate when William Alden Smith retired in 1918, but he refused. In March 1918, he denied rumors he would run for the Senate and then further denied in July 1918 that he was interested in any public office. On the eve of John Dodge's death in January 1920, Frank O. Lowden, the governor of Illinois and a presidential candidate, tried to arrange a meeting with him in Detroit, but Dodge's illness intervened.[86]

Detroit's newspapers accused John and Horace Dodge of enjoying special treatment from police and judges because of their personal and political ties to Oscar Marx and his political machine. In late August 1913, Police Commissioner John Gillespie denied that he had provided Dodge with four police officers to guard his Boston Boulevard home. He admitted, however, that he had assigned a single officer to stand guard there because Dodge reported some unsavory characters lurking around the neighborhood.[87]

A more serious incident took place in early October 1913. John Dodge was at the wheel of his car with Oscar Marx on board when he smashed into a Hupmobile on Jefferson Avenue in Grosse Pointe. Dodge, who was driving at least 45 miles per hour at the time, never stopped, but the accident was witnessed by a motorcycle officer who caught up with the Dodge car. John Dodge reportedly said, "That'll teach them to keep to the right." The *Detroit Journal,* which doggedly pursued this story, asked Oscar Marx why he and Dodge told different accounts of this incident. Mayor Marx went into a rage and nearly assaulted the reporter. The officer filed charges against Dodge, who then pleaded guilty to speeding and was fined $50. The "trial" took place secretly in the private home of Grosse Pointe Village Judge Robert Trombley, at John Dodge's convenience. The criminal justice system evidently offered special privileges to well-connected millionaires.[88]

The same can be said for brother Horace. The *Detroit News* reported in early November 1916 that Horace Dodge had failed to report in police court to face charges of speeding filed two weeks earlier. The next month, Wayne County Sheriff-Elect Edward F. Stein announced the appointment of Horace E. Dodge as undersheriff effective January 1917. Horace apparently enjoyed the role of millionaire undersheriff. He agreed to accompany Sheriff Stein and pal Robert Oakman in transporting four murderers from Detroit to the state prison in Marquette, in the central part of Michigan's Upper Peninsula, in February 1918. They rented a private rail car for the occasion, at a cost of $1,000. Dodge and Oakman flipped a quarter to decide who would pay for the car and Dodge lost. They reportedly got stuck temporarily in a serious snowstorm in St. Ignace, just north of the Straits of Mackinac. The prisoners did not seem to mind the delay.[89]

These incidents aside, John and Horace Dodge were a powerful force in Detroit society throughout the 1910s, participating significantly in politics, civic affairs, and charitable endeavors. They were not content to simply enjoy the benefits of their success as automotive suppliers to Ransom Olds and Henry Ford and as manufacturers of their popular nameplate. The company John and Horace Dodge founded survived their deaths, first as an independent producer until 1928, then as a key division of the Chrysler Corporation in 1928–98, and finally as a significant nameplate among the vehicles sold by DaimlerChrysler since 1998.

SIX

Dodge Brothers under Frederick J. Haynes, 1920–1925

Dodge Brothers offers to the business public of America an entirely new principle in Coupe body construction.

It is the first all-steel closed car ever marketed. The design anticipates every possible requirement of commercial travel. It insures unique quietness—unusual grace—unusual stamina.

Motor World, June 1922

Dodge Brothers survived without its founders and continued to produce cars and trucks profitably through most of the 1920s. Top executives seasoned during the 1910s and groomed to run the firm provided management stability and continuity. With Horace Dodge absent, the Dodge Brothers board of directors put Frederick J. Haynes in charge in May 1920, and he served as president through April 1926. After suffering a severe drop in sales and profits in 1921, as did the rest of the auto industry, Dodge Brothers recovered and enjoyed considerable success.

Dodge Brothers was the first American automaker to introduce all-steel closed bodies for some of its 1923 models. The company entered the truck business in a major way through a sales partnership in 1921 with Graham Brothers, a manufacturer of medium and heavy-duty trucks. The most significant change came when Matilda Rausch Dodge and Anna Thomson Dodge sold the company to the investment banking firm of Dillon, Read & Company in April 1925. The sale marked the end of any direct Dodge family involvement in the company that John and Horace founded in 1900.

The Frederick Haynes Era

On 13 January 1921, after Horace Dodge's death, the Dodge directors (Howard B. Bloomer, Frederick J. Haynes, and John Ballantyne) named Frederick J. Haynes president and elected Arthur T. Waterfall as its fourth member, but only after consulting with the two Dodge widows. They named Harry V. Popeney, who had served as secretary, as the fifth board member in July 1921. The Dodge Brothers directors signed a five-year contract with Haynes in October 1921 to serve as "active executive head" (president) of Dodge Brothers for five years at an annual salary of $150,000 net of taxes.

Howard Bloomer had initially turned down the opportunity to become chairman of the board at Dodge Brothers, mainly because he was advising both widows on the management of their estates and felt uncomfortable wearing both hats. In late February 1922, Bloomer agreed to serve, but did so only after getting two strong endorsements from both widows. He also signed a five-year contract dated 15 March 1922 for the same salary paid to Haynes.[1]

In March 1922, the Dodge Brothers directors also agreed to spend up to $350,000 to purchase lands to donate to the State of Michigan to create parks in memory of John and Horace Dodge and to create favorable publicity for the company. In fall 1922, the company announced the donation of eleven park sites totaling 627 acres. This gift created the first permanent memorial for the two brothers.[2]

Around 1914, John Dodge had purchased real estate some fifteen miles east of Pickford in the far eastern end of the Upper Peninsula to give himself, Horace, and friends an enjoyable place to hunt and fish. He originally built a spacious main lodge and a caretaker's dwelling, and then added five guest cabins shortly thereafter. He named this retreat the Munuskong Hunting and Fishing Club and invited his friends to become members. The club members probably bought the property from John Dodge's estate following his death. In mid-December 1924 the Dodge Brothers board of directors approved the purchase of this property for $55,000, and turned it over to the State of Michigan for a state park. Dodge Brothers claimed the property was worth $80,000 when the firm transferred it to the state in March 1925.[3]

A listing of Michigan state parks in 1926 showed a total of only ten Dodge Brothers parks (numbers 2–10 and Munuskong). Seven were in Oakland County, north of Detroit, while Monroe, Macomb, and Chippewa Counties had one each. Three of the ten were still "undeveloped," while two were under development in 1926. A 1931 listing in the *Michigan Gazetteer* listed the same three parks

Frederick J. Haynes, 1927. Courtesy of NAHC.

(numbers 3, 7, and Munuskong) as undeveloped. By 1939, Dodge Park No. 1, on Island Lake in Livingston County, was also open for visitors and campers.[4]

Dodge Brothers was in many respects controlled by the ghosts of the Dodge brothers until the property changed hands in 1925. John and Horace Dodge's widows continued to influence the Dodge Brothers operations. The directors declared a special dividend of 120 percent ($12,000,000) at the end of 1921 to help the two estates pay heavy federal and state inheritance taxes that were due. John Dodge's estate also needed cash to fight John Duval Dodge's lawsuit contesting his father's will.[5]

Interactions between the Dodge Brothers management and the two (largely absent) widows were not always pleasant. Anna Thomson Dodge was particularly troublesome. In late 1922, the Dodge Brothers board of directors pledged $50,000 for the Detroit Community Fund (formerly the Detroit Patriotic Fund) for 1923, and the Dodge Brothers employees pledged an additional $15,000. They had earlier made identical donations for 1921 and 1922. Anna Thomson Dodge criticized their gift as overgenerous and suggested they reconsider the commitment. The board agreed only to explain their reasoning to her, but had no intention of withdrawing the pledge, fearing a public relations disaster. At the same board meeting, they revealed that Dodge Brothers had lent Anna Thomson Dodge $1,150,000 by depositing funds in her bank account at her request. The board resolved to stop advancing funds to her and to insist that she repay the existing loans promptly. In mid-December 1923, she also demanded, through a letter from her attorney, that the Dodge Brothers board of directors obtain her approval before starting negotiations to sell the business or its stock. She also objected to any employment contracts with anyone outside the company unless approved by Frederick Haynes and John Ballantyne.[6]

Such interference was unusual and of little import, primarily because the Dodge widows trusted Frederick Haynes's managerial ability, and with good reason. Haynes and the others whom the Dodge brothers groomed to take over the firm provided conservative leadership during the five years following their deaths. The firm weathered the severe recession of 1921, introduced a variety of new models, and enjoyed moderate to robust profits.

Dodge Brothers management was usually cautious and conservative. The firm faced a serious staffing crisis during the first half of 1922, when many workers began quitting, largely because Dodge Brothers had not granted a pay raise in more than a year and the cost of living was rising sharply. Instead of granting an across-the-board permanent pay raise, the Dodge Brothers board of directors instead introduced a system of "bonus payments" based on an employee's length of service. They awarded a 10 percent increase for the first half of 1922 for employees with five years of continuous service and to all managers down to assistant foremen. A sliding scale applied to everyone else—those with four years of service received an 8 percent increase, while the bonuses were only 2 percent for those with one year of service. They awarded similar bonuses for the second half of the year.[7]

Dodge Brothers' policies regarding factory labor underwent some changes after the passing of John and Horace Dodge. In an interview with B. C. Forbes in 1925, Frederick Haynes stated clearly, "We don't have strikes. We treat all of our people so fairly that they have no reason or desire to strike." He also stated his general view of labor relations: "Give workers the right conditions. After a man is through with his work, let him be his own master. He-men don't want paternalism." When the Dodge Brothers workers initiated something on their own, such as a gun club or a bowling team, the company would support their efforts, but it did not initiate any programs. According to *The Dodge Dollar* (1925), "Dodge Brothers have never had any labor troubles. Their men are unusually well paid." This booklet revealed that Dodge Brothers followed standard labor practices of contemporary automobile manufacturers—they ran the plant as an "open shop" and paid all workers on a piecework basis.[8]

The Dodge Brothers' stockholders, at the urging of the board of directors, increased the capital stock of the firm from $10,000,000 to $50,000,000 in December 1922 by issuing 400,000 shares of stock with a par value of $100 per share. The new stock was fully paid up common stock that they simply credited to the existing stockholders. They each received four additional shares for each share they already owned. This was in essence a dividend paid in shares, not in cash, but it did not bring new capital into the firm. Instead, the Dodge Brothers management merely shifted $40,000,000 of the $52,000,000 in reserves to the capital account.

In February 1924, the board of directors negotiated with the M. A. Hanna Company, a Cleveland-based steel company, for the sale of the Dodge Brothers property on the Detroit River. They were seeking $16,000 per acre for a parcel of 219 acres, or a total of about $3,500,000. They probably wanted to sell real estate they no longer needed and convert it into cash, but the deal fell through. Dodge Brothers still owned the parcel in December 1925, when the Detroit Common Council accepted a consultant's recommendation that the city acquire the property to use for a sewage disposal plant. In mid-October 1927, the Detroit Common Council voted to acquire the Dodge Brothers parcel by condemnation, but faced legal barriers under state law. In January 1930, the City of Detroit dropped any further interest in the parcel.[9]

The top officials at Dodge Brothers in early 1924 were the same men installed in 1921. Frederick J. Haynes was president and general manager; A. T. Waterfall was vice president; John Ballantyne served as treasurer; Harry V. Popeney was secretary; and Howard B. Bloomer served as director. The five made up the board of directors. Richard Hoff replaced Bloomer in late 1924, but the management team was essentially the one that Horace Dodge put in place before his death.[10]

However, the firm had some changes in management in the early 1920s. George Harrison Phelps, who had been the Dodge Brothers director of advertising since 1915, resigned effective 30 March 1922 to establish his own independent advertising agency. The company eliminated its advertising department in the same stroke. Dodge Brothers agreed to have Phelps manage the firm's advertising through his new agency, claiming that this arrangement would save Dodge Brothers considerable money. Dodge Brothers lent Phelps $25,000 (at 6 percent interest) to enable him to establish his own company. As part of the realignment, Dodge Brothers promoted Charles W. Matheson from general sales manager to vice president in charge of sales. The automaker named John A. Nichols, Jr., general sales manager in place of Matheson.[11]

Charles W. Matheson (1876–1940) was an important figure in the Dodge Brothers sales operations for nearly a decade. Matheson and his brother Frank formed the Matheson Motor Car Company in Battle Creek, Michigan, in 1903, moved their factory to Holyoke, Massachusetts, and then to Wilkes Barre, Pennsylvania, in 1906. Matheson's firm manufactured the Matheson automobile, a luxury model, from 1903 to 1913. Dodge Brothers named him their New York district sales representative in 1914 and then appointed him service manager for the entire company in May 1915. Matheson became the assistant sales manager, and finally general sales manager in 1920. As vice president in charge of sales (1922–24), Matheson focused on long-term sales strategies. The Dodge Brothers sales operations became unraveled under Matheson. During a board meeting in late February 1924, "President Haynes outlined to the Board of Directors a situation existing in the Sales Department which he considered detrimental to the best interests of Dodge Brothers, in that there was a lack of harmony and cooperative effort." The board of directors accepted the immediate resignation of Charles W. Matheson, the vice president in charge of sales; H. M. Roberts, director of foreign sales; and A. E. Houghton, the director of sales districts. John A. Nichols, Jr., remained on board as the general sales manager.[12]

On the heels of Matheson's resignation from Dodge Brothers, Walter P. Chrysler, then chairman of the board of the Maxwell Motor Corporation making Chalmers, Maxwell, and Chrysler automobiles, asked Leo Butzel about Matheson's availability for a position. Butzel apparently knew Matheson and was trying to help him find work. Matheson instead took a position in March 1924 as assistant to Alfred P. Sloan, president of General Motors Corporation, and served as vice president and sales director for the Oakland (later Pontiac) Motor Car Company starting in September 1924. He resigned from Oakland in December 1926 and then served as vice president and sales director for the Kelvinator Corporation.

In April 1928, before Chrysler Corporation's purchase of Dodge Brothers, Walter Chrysler appointed Matheson vice president in charge of sales for the new DeSoto Motor Corporation. Later that year, in mid-December, Mrs. Alfred G. Wilson, the former Matilda Rausch Dodge, sent Matheson a very informal letter addressed "Dear Charlie" and signed "Matilder," suggesting their long friendship. She wrote, "It all seems like a night mare to think you are back after five years in the office which I was at one time so fond of visiting." On 28 October 1930, Matheson left DeSoto to take the position of general sales manager for the Graham-Paige Motors Corporation, the last automobile company where he worked.[13]

Following the precepts laid down by John and Horace Dodge, Haynes promoted engineering improvements in the Dodge Brothers cars, rather than mere cosmetic changes. Dodge Brothers' introduction of the all-steel closed car in the 1923 model year was a good example of Haynes's willingness to innovate. Dodge Brothers and others had produced closed cars for some years, but they still used composite (steel and wood) construction. The closed car was growing in popularity in the early 1920s and would continue to do so. In a single year, from fall 1921 to fall 1922, the share of closed cars in the Dodge Brothers production "mix" jumped from 13 percent to 35 percent. With the approval of the Dodge Brothers board of directors, Haynes and Edward G. Budd jointly developed the new models.[14]

The 1923 model of the Dodge Brothers business coupe, introduced in June 1922, was the first all-steel closed car in the automobile industry. A meeting of the Dodge Brothers board of directors on 15 December 1921 approved the new model, which they described as "a type of enclosed roadster designed to meet the needs of doctors, salesmen, collectors and all persons needing an inexpensive enclosed car carrying two passengers." An all-steel four-door sedan followed in fall 1922. The all-steel body used a steel frame and steel panels and was lighter and stronger than the composite wood and steel bodies of the time.

1921 Dodge Brothers three-passenger coupe, with composite body. Courtesy of NAHC.

1924 Dodge Brothers two-passenger business coupe, with all-steel body. Courtesy of NAHC.

One great advantage of the steel body was that it allowed Dodge Brothers to use baked enamel finishes on its closed vehicles. The Dodge Brothers wood-framed sedan body required eighteen coats of hand-rubbed paint and took thirty days to build, while the all-steel sedan body could be finished in five days with only one coat of paint. Strictly speaking, the "all-steel" bodies were not "all-steel" when delivered to customers. Once the painting was completed, wood strips were added to the interior to allow for the tacking of the upholstery and interior trim.[15]

Other than the all-steel closed body, the Dodge Brothers' automobile offerings did not change very much in appearance from 1921 through 1925. The 1921 models offered heaters for the first time. The original drive train dating back to 1914 underwent some minor changes for the 1922 models. Dodge Brothers altered the roof and hood lines for 1922 and equipped the cars with semi-floating rear axles. The automaker introduced slightly redesigned commercial vehicles (screenside delivery and panel delivery) in late May 1922 for the 1923 model year. The commercial cars sold in the 1924 and 1925 model years were substantially changed. They had a longer wheelbase of 116 inches and a higher three-quarter-ton payload rating. Commercial car production continued to grow as a share of combined output. In 1925, commercial cars accounted for 21 percent of the total, up from 10.8 percent in 1920. Dodge Brothers extended the wheelbase for all 1924 models from 114 to 116 inches and introduced the Special Series, which were their regular models with deluxe equipment or appointments. The company showcased two new models at the New York Automobile Show in January 1925, a two-door sedan and a special coach. Still, the continuity of the basic components of Dodge Brothers cars stands out.[16]

Sales Strategies, Dealer Relations, and Business Practices

Dodge Brothers did not make changes in the appearance of their cars for the sake of stimulating sales, but relied instead on the car's reputation for dependable service. This is not to suggest that the company did not advertise extensively in national publications like the *Saturday Evening Post.* Nor was the company averse to making emotional appeals to potential Dodge Brothers car buyers. On the heels of Horace Dodge's death, composer Victor Herbert wrote the music for the *Dodge Brothers March,* a tribute to Horace Dodge for his work in promoting American music. Herbert used lyrics written by Maxwell I. Pitkin, who was on staff at

Cosmopolitan, but who had previously worked in the Dodge Brothers advertising department. Dodge Brothers made the piano score available to its dealers for only five cents a copy and a phonographic record of the music for 60 cents each. According to Pitrone and Elwart, Dodge Brothers distributed 100,000 copies of the music. In May 1921, the firm offered its dealers an assortment of match boxes, watch fobs, and lapel buttons inscribed with either the "DB" monogram or the Dodge Brothers trademark logo to give away as goodwill souvenirs.[17]

Dodge Brothers followed the same basic manufacturing and marketing philosophy of its founders throughout the Frederick Haynes era. A Dodge Brothers sales brochure for the 1924 models used the slogan, "Constantly Improved—But No Yearly Models," while showing a lineup of touring cars from 1914 through 1924, all looking essentially the same. The brochure added, "Dodge Brothers policy of retaining the same basic design year after year without making radical annual changes to stimulate sales through the appeal of a new model has very definite advantages for owners." The major advantages were the savings in manufacturing costs, which they passed on to the customer, and the higher values of used Dodge Brothers automobiles. Dodge Brothers, along with Ford Motor Company, did not change models every year, a practice initiated at General Motors under Alfred Sloan. Dodge Brothers advertising instead emphasized the durability and reliability of its vehicles. A *Saturday Evening Post* advertisement of May 1926 claimed that more than 90 percent of all Dodge Brothers motor cars built during the firm's first eleven years were still in service.[18]

This is not to suggest that Dodge Brothers vehicles remained unchanged. The company's listing of significant improvements in vehicle design, compiled in 1926, showed only four changes of any note in 1921, but then double-digit numbers for 1922 (12), 1923 (11), 1924 (10), and 1925 (13). As in 1914–20, the overwhelming majority of these changes were to the mechanical components of the vehicle. Typical changes included improved radiators, a stronger frame, better rear springs, upgrades to wheel bearings, stronger axles, and all-steel closed bodies. These "constant improvements" included more "appearance and comfort items" than in the early years. The addition of a heater, improved seats and upholstery, windshield visors, windshield wipers, rubber mats, improved door window regulators, one-piece windshields, and lacquer finishes were not functional improvements. Over time, Dodge Brothers cars became more comfortable, more attractive, and easier to drive.[19]

Dodge Brothers received an unusual but welcome endorsement of their cars when the explorer and archaeologist Roy Chapman Andrews used Dodge Brothers

DODGE BROTHERS
MARCH

MUSIC BY
VICTOR HERBERT
LYRIC BY
MAXWELL I. PITKIN

DEDICATED BY MR. HERBERT TO THE LATE
MR. HORACE E. DODGE IN RESPECTFUL
APPRECIATION OF HIS GENEROUS
EFFORTS TOWARDS THE
ADVANCEMENT OF
AMERICAN MUSIC

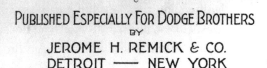

PUBLISHED ESPECIALLY FOR DODGE BROTHERS
BY
JEROME H. REMICK & CO.
DETROIT —— NEW YORK

Dodge Brothers March sheet music cover page, 1921. Courtesy of Oakland University's Meadow Brook Hall.

cars during his Central Asiatic Expeditions in Mongolia and China in 1922, 1923, 1925, 1926, and 1928. The expeditions, sponsored by the American Museum of Natural History, went into the Gobi Desert and through other difficult terrain in search of prehistoric remains of humans and animals. Andrews decided to use motorized vehicles for the explorers/archaeologists, while using camels to transport food, gasoline, and other supplies. After studying the past performance of other cars along the old caravan routes in Mongolia, he concluded that Fords were not sturdy enough but that Dodge Brothers touring cars were ideal for the task: "For travel in the Gobi, a car must be light, have a high clearance, great durability, a flexible chassis and not less than a twenty-eight horsepower engine. The Dodge Brothers cars fulfilled these specifications to the letter." Andrews used three Dodge Brothers touring cars and two one-ton Fulton trucks for the initial expeditions in 1922 and 1923. All gave excellent service, but the trucks proved too heavy for the desert surfaces. He reported that the Dodge Brothers cars accumulated more than 10,000 miles each, with no significant mechanical problems. The world-renowned explorer later noted, "The record speaks for itself and all the men on the expedition are as proud of the cars as though we had manufactured them." He later sold them to a Chinese company involved in importing furs and wool from Mongolia and they continued in service for several more years.[20]

In his autobiography, *Under a Lucky Star,* Andrews recounts that he was in New York City, probably sometime in 1924, raising funds for his next expedition when a Dodge Brothers representative approached him, proposing an advertising "deal." Dodge Brothers would give him free cars for use in his work in return for his endorsement of their durability. Andrews said he would accept the offer as long as Dodge Brothers would furnish him with eight cars modified to his specifications. He went to Detroit and called on Frederick Haynes, who assured him that Dodge Brothers could customize their cars as needed. Andrews notes, "This was the beginning of one of the most satisfactory business associations I ever have had. . . . Their advertising was always dignified and thousands of cars were sold because of our endorsement. It saved the expedition about fifty thousand dollars."[21]

Later sources, including Andrews, suggest that Dodge Brothers did not provide all eight cars at once. They gave him five modified Dodge Brothers cars for his 1925 expedition. Four were screenside commercial cars equipped with air cleaners, extra-heavy springs, twenty-one-gallon gas tanks, and special heavy-duty hooks welded to the frame to make towing easier. The fifth was a touring car. A photograph of the 1925 expedition shows a convoy of five Dodge Brothers cars and two Fulton trucks. Dodge Brothers then supplied four new cars for the 1926 expedition, and Andrews operated a "fleet" of eight in 1926 and again in 1928, probably the same vehicles.[22]

When possible, Dodge Brothers promoted stories about the ruggedness or durability of its vehicles to enhance sales. In mid-December 1923, an admirer of Calvin Coolidge delivered a pair of bears to the White House in a Dodge Brothers screenside commercial car. "Colonel Idaho Bill" Pearson captured these bruins in the mountains of Mexico and drove them 4,000 miles to Washington, D.C. He had driven Dodge Brothers cars more than 100,000 miles on hunting trips into the wilderness areas of the western United States and Mexico. Apparently impressed by Dodge Brothers' reputation, the Republican National Committee chose two Dodge Brothers sedans for a cross-country publicity campaign for Coolidge's reelection campaign. They drove from Plymouth, New Hampshire, to San Francisco, put 6,500 miles on the cars, often over very rough roads, and reported that they suffered no mechanical problems, burned no oil, and delivered between 17 and 20 miles per gallon.[23]

The Dodge Brothers executives never missed an opportunity to remind potential customers of their vehicle's reputation for ruggedness and dependability. When Dodge Brothers produced its one-millionth vehicle in December 1923, a company spokesman claimed that 90 percent of Dodge Brothers cars ever produced were still in service. Given the numbers of cars wrecked in accidents or destroyed by fire, and the habitual abuse of Dodge Brothers cars by their owners, this survival rate was a remarkable tribute.[24]

The Dodge brothers developed a powerful and effective sales organization, especially the dealer body, when they first manufactured their own cars, and the company carefully maintained their network of sales outlets. Dating from January 1915, the first New York Automobile Show in which they showed Dodge Brothers cars, the Dodge Brothers sales organization and the dealers would meet during the show. At the Ninth Annual Meeting of Dodge Brothers Dealers in New York on 9 January 1923, more than one thousand attended, representing a total of 677 dealerships. They witnessed a competition between two factory teams to assemble a Dodge Brothers car in the shortest time, a special display of Graham Brothers trucks, and a variety of entertainment. This was an annual ritual to encourage better communication between the Dodge Brothers management and the dealer body and to build up the morale of the dealers. Dodge Brothers would also hold a series of regional annual meetings for dealers between February and June.[25]

Dodge Brothers established general principles of operation to protect the reputation of the manufacturer while ensuring reasonable profits for the dealers.

Dodge Brothers promoted what it felt were "sound business practices" from its dealers while fostering a cooperative, mutually beneficial relationship. Some documentation exists for various policies that remained in effect in 1920–25 and were probably in effect right from the beginning of Dodge Brothers' retail sales. As a result, the relationship between the company and its dealers and among dealers was generally cooperative rather than adversarial. Frederick Haynes could boast in 1925 that 60 percent of Dodge Brothers original dealers from 1914 were still with the company.[26]

The record from the tumultuous years of 1920–22 illustrates these relationships. During the sales depression of 1921, when combined sales of cars and trucks fell by 36 percent from the 1920 record, only one Dodge Brothers dealer went out of business. The sales drop for Dodge Brothers was much greater than the industry-wide decline of 25 percent. When sales rebounded in 1922 to a record level of more than 164,000 units, Dodge Brothers could not supply enough cars to satisfy its dealers. Its sales in 1922 were 77 percent higher than in 1921, versus an industry-wide increase of 60 percent. To help some smaller dealers who had barely survived the sales slump of 1920–21, Dodge Brothers suggested that larger dealers sacrifice some of their 1922 allotments and the large dealers supported this suggestion. Several dealers volunteered to give up even more cars than the number requested.[27]

The automaker required its dealers to submit standard accounting reports relating to sales, inventories of cars and parts, and profits. The precise date when Dodge Brothers initiated this policy is not known, but the third edition of a manual explaining the system appeared in March 1926. The sample balance sheets used as illustrations cover 1922 and 1923, suggesting that the system was in place by then. Dealers had to submit quarterly financial statements, with the added requirement that one of these be a sworn statement. Dodge Brothers also required monthly statements of profits or loss by department, using a uniform accounting system. By knowing exactly what profits the dealers were making, Dodge Brothers could help dealers improve their operations to earn reasonable profits. The parent company also required all U.S. and Canadian dealers to submit a weekly report on sales and inventories of both new and used cars. Dodge Brothers could then be certain that each dealer had an appropriate inventory on hand.[28]

Unlike many automakers, Dodge Brothers did not force its dealers to take unwanted cars. Right after the announcement of the Dillon, Read purchase of Dodge Brothers, Frederick Haynes explained: "A company may get some temporary advantage for a month or so by shipping to dealers cars which they can't sell. But it doesn't mean anything. The manufacturing economies achieved through high production during the months of such shipments is more than eaten up in the ill-will and merchandising inefficiencies generated in the field."[29] Dodge Brothers thus avoided much of the friction that often dominated the relationship between automobile manufacturers and their dealers.

Dodge Brothers consistently discouraged their dealers from engaging in the used car trade as a way to expand new car sales. Charles W. Matheson suggested to dealers that they follow the practices of the Henshaw Motor Company of Boston regarding used cars. Henshaw would not accept a used car in trade, but would sell the customer's used car for him and, if necessary, advance 75 percent of the asking price to the owner. In a 1922 letter to Dodge Brothers dealers, George H. Phelps warned of the dangers of "curbside dealers," unscrupulous businessmen who sold used Dodge Brothers cars and misrepresented their age and condition. He supplied the legitimate dealers with a list of serial numbers to enable them to date Dodge Brothers cars. The firm also issued a "Stolen Car Bulletin" periodically to its dealers so that they would not take a stolen car in trade. In selling new cars, Dodge Brothers urged its dealers to insist on a large down payment and to avoid accepting time payments longer than a year.[30]

A dealer's agreement between Dodge Brothers and a Georgia dealer, Stewart B. Maxcy, signed in June 1920 points out several key features of this relationship. Dodge Brothers gave Maxcy the exclusive right to sell their cars in Thomas and Grady Counties. Dodge Brothers would supply him with cars at a discount from list price ranging from 15 percent to 17 percent and repair parts at a 25 percent discount. The dealer had to keep an inventory of at least $3,750 in repair parts. For the terms of the agreement (July 1921–June 1922), the dealer agreed to a schedule for the delivery of a total of seventy vehicles from Dodge Brothers (forty-nine touring cars, seven roadsters, five sedans, two coupes, four screensides, and three panel business cars). The dealer also agreed to establish "Dodge Brothers Service Stations" and could supply repair parts at 15 percent above list price. The three-page agreement also showed the Dodge Brothers ninety-day new car warranty on its vehicles. The agreement ended with a policy statement: "There are certain fundamental principles in business which should be observed by both the manufacturer and the dealer to insure permanent success. It is not the intention of the manufacturer to attempt to force the observance of these principles on the part of the dealer by virtue of this dealer's agreement, but rather to work with the dealer in an effort to bring about results mutually beneficial."[31]

A customer order form for a new Dodge Brothers car from a Chicago dealer in September 1921 illustrates how Dodge Brothers dealers typically sold new cars. The purchaser, James War, agreed to take delivery of a new touring car on 15 September 1921. The dealer gave the buyer an allowance of $200 on a 1916 Ford touring car in trade, subject to an appraisal at the time of delivery. Following the general policy of Dodge Brothers, the dealer, Dashiell Motor Company, insisted on a cash payment of 40 percent of the price at the time of delivery, with the balance due in eight monthly installments, with the loan carrying interest of 7 percent.

The Dodge Brothers car delivered from the factory was a very basic car, with few "extras." Dodge Brothers gave the customer a six-page price list for various accessories, including bumpers, heaters, and a rearview mirror. Since the car came with a spare wheel, but no spare tire, Mr. War opted to buy a tire casing (nonskid fabric) for $29.50 and an inner tube for $4.45. He also purchased a "Johnson transmission lock" for $15.00 in an attempt to protect his new car from thieves. Then as now, the availability of dealer-installed options gave the dealer an opportunity to boost his profits.[32]

The sale of a Dodge Brothers touring car by E. J. Ellis & Company of Rochester, New York, to Otto F. Wusnick on 17 May 1922 shows similar practices. The car itself cost $955, but the buyer added a tire and tube ($32.50), a front bumper ($10.50), and a stoplight ($5.50), paid his license fee ($9.61), and bought twelve gallons of gasoline at 23 cents a gallon. The buyer had put down a $50 deposit on the car and paid the balance in cash.[33]

Dodge Brothers had an aggressive advertising program since introducing the first Dodge Brothers car, much to the benefit of the dealers. When Dillon, Read & Company bought Dodge Brothers in 1925, they boasted about their advertising efforts. The parent company paid for national advertising in sixty-three magazines with a combined circulation of twenty-five million. Of the national magazines, thirty-five (circulation of 6.5 million) were aimed at farmers. Dodge Brothers used outdoor advertising (billboards and smaller signs) in 625 cities. The automaker paid half the cost of local advertising, mostly in local newspapers. Dodge Brothers ads ran in 1,500 local papers with a circulation of thirty million. Standard practice was to spend 1.2 percent of gross sales on advertising.[34]

Starting in 1923, Dodge Brothers gave their customers information that would allow them to verify service charges made by their dealers and by "Approved Service Stations," an industry first. They informed customers of the maximum labor time allowed by Dodge Brothers for common service and repairs, with thirty-five pages of the *Book of Information* (owners' manual) devoted to this information. This policy probably helped dealers in explaining repair bills to disgruntled customers, while also serving to the keep dealers honest.[35]

Another business practice peculiar to Dodge Brothers involved the firm's relationship with its suppliers. Dodge Brothers insisted that suppliers allow the automaker to examine their books, including profit and loss statements, as a condition for doing business with them. Dodge Brothers would increase prices they paid for components to guarantee the supplier a profit, but would expect price reductions when the supplier's costs fell. This arrangement reduced risk to the supplier, but eliminated any possibility that a supplier could earn large profits on a supply contract. Because the overall automotive supplier industry remained competitive, Dodge Brothers enjoyed competitive prices. This system, which had its origins in the Dodge Brothers–Edward G. Budd Company relationship starting in 1914, applied to all suppliers by 1925. There is no clear evidence, however, of exactly when this became standard practice.[36]

Dodge Brothers often developed long-term relationships with suppliers that benefited everyone involved over the long term. Frederick Haynes explained the relationship: "We never take a contract away from a parts maker who has been serving us well just because some other fellow comes along and offers us the same thing for a few cents less. It doesn't pay. It's not fair to go back on a company that has been giving you good service for a number of years and with which you have built up real good-will."[37]

The advertising and sales strategies developed largely by John Dodge in the early years of Dodge Brothers production of cars continued under Haynes in the 1920s with additional refinements. While both the styling of Dodge Brothers cars and Frederick Haynes's management style were conservative in the 1920s, the company was not stagnant or backward looking. The significant (and gradual) movement into the production of medium- and heavy-duty trucks is one important example of innovation.

Graham Brothers Brings Trucks to Dodge Brothers

Frederick Haynes's most important business decision during his tenure as president of Dodge Brothers was an alliance with Graham Brothers, Inc., a manufacturer of medium- and heavy-duty trucks, which led to Dodge Brothers' outright purchase of the firm. The Graham brothers (Joseph B., Robert C., and Ray A.), sons of a successful Indiana farmer, began their industrial careers in glass bottle manufacturing in Indiana in the early twentieth century. Their father, Ziba Foote Graham, had invested heavily in the Lythgoe Bottle Company in Loogootee,

Indiana, became president of the firm in 1901, and brought in his oldest son, Joseph, as secretary and treasurer. Father and son bought the company outright in 1905, renaming it Southern Indiana Glass Company. Robert Graham went to work at the enterprise in 1907, when they renamed it the Graham Glass Company, and Ray joined the firm the next year. By then, Joseph Graham had improved early automatic bottle-making machines enough to give Graham Glass Company a competitive advantage.[38]

The Grahams bought a glass bottle plant in Evansville, Indiana, in 1912, equipped it with Graham Automatic Bottle-Making Machines, and within a year employed 300 men there. By late 1915, when the Evansville factory produced more beer and soda bottles than any other plant in the United States, the Grahams had just opened two new glass bottle plants in Oklahoma. Two other successful glass manufacturers, Michael Owens and Edward Libbey, who specialized in sheet glass, merged their companies in spring 1916 to form the Libbey-Owens Sheet Glass Company of Toledo. Libbey-Owens bought Graham Glass and the patents on the bottle-making machine from the Grahams in June 1916. The Graham firm retained its name, and Joseph Graham served as president of the subsidiary for another eight years.[39]

Leaving the glass industry opened the door for the Grahams to enter the motor vehicle industry. They launched Graham Brothers, Inc., in 1917 with a factory in Evansville, Indiana, to produce farm tractors and kits that converted standard automobile chassis into light-duty trucks. They were not leaping from the glass bottle industry into unknown waters. Joseph Graham had patched together his own homemade one-cylinder automobile in 1904, the first seen in Washington, Indiana. While running Graham Farms, in 1910 Ray Graham introduced the first tractor in southern Indiana powered by a four-cylinder engine. He became an early promoter of gasoline-powered tractors and light-duty trucks for farm use. Ray invented a special rear axle and telescoping frame system that allowed the conversion of a standard Model T Ford chassis into a one-ton stake truck. The Graham Brothers operation in Evansville initially manufactured truck conversion units.[40]

The original Articles of Association for Graham Brothers, dated 15 January 1917, showed Ziba, Joseph, and Robert Graham each owning 100 shares of stock, Ray Graham with ninety-nine shares, and Howard W. Harrington with a single share. The original Charter of Incorporation, dated 12 January 1917, showed a total capital stock of $10,000. At the first shareholders' meeting, held on 15 January 1917, the new firm canceled a contract the brothers had signed earlier with the Parrett Tractor Company of Chicago, relieving the Chicago firm of any obligation.

Graham brothers, ca. 1930, left to right: Robert, Joseph, Ray. Courtesy of NAHC.

Instead, they confirmed a contract with the Hercules Tractor Company to deliver "truck units" in 1917. The remaining surviving records are sketchy, but new corporate charters issued by the State of Indiana document an increase in the capital stock to $100,000 on 22 May 1917 and then to $1 million on 6 May 1919, including $500,000 in preferred stock.[41]

Graham Brothers initially specialized in producing conversion units to turn a Model T Ford chassis into a one-ton capacity truck. Graham provided the extended frame and chain-drive rear wheels, a cab, and either a stake or "express" body, all for $350. Later in 1917, Graham Brothers renamed their conversion kit the "Graham Brothers Truck Builder" and claimed that the customer could use the kit with almost any motor car model. This also permitted them to offer conversions of up to three-ton capacity. By late 1919, the Grahams were assembling their own complete truck, the so-called Graham Speed Truck of one-and-a-half-ton capacity. When the Grahams found that Dodge Brothers engines and transmissions were the most durable they could buy, they used them almost exclusively. They bought so many Dodge engines through an Indiana dealership that Haynes became suspicious and discovered their operation and their reliance on Dodge engines.[42]

In April 1921, Dodge Brothers and Graham Brothers announced a partnership agreement between the two firms. Dodge Brothers would have exclusive rights to sell and service Graham trucks through their dealer organization, while Graham Brothers would use Dodge Brothers engines and transmissions exclusively in their trucks. This was a good deal for both parties. Dodge Brothers could offer its customers a full line of trucks ranging from their own half-ton commercial cars to

1924 Graham Brothers trucks. Courtesy of DCHC.

Graham Brothers trucks rated up to two-ton capacity. Graham could sell its trucks through the Dodge Brothers dealer network, which by 1924 boasted 3,500 outlets nationwide. With increased demand coming from this new arrangement, Graham Brothers opened an assembly plant early in 1922 on Meldrum Avenue in Detroit.[43]

The figures for Dodge Brothers and Graham Brothers trucks shipped in 1925 show how the two partners' products complemented each other, with some overlap. For that year, Dodge Brothers shipped 22,293 commercial cars and another 186 trucks with under a one-ton capacity rating, probably their three-quarter-ton pickup. The rest of their shipments were Graham-built vehicles—7,395 trucks of one-ton capacity, 15,926 with a one-and-one-half-ton rating, and 735 buses. In addition to the total of 46,534 commercial vehicles, Dodge Brothers sold 13,347 chassis, for a total of 59,881 units other than automobiles and nearly one-quarter of all sales.[44]

As table 6.1 shows, the number of Graham Brothers trucks sold through Dodge Brothers grew substantially in the early 1920s. The Meldrum plant (13,000 square feet) was unable to satisfy the growing demand for Graham trucks, so the company bought a 60,000-square-foot factory, formerly used by the King Motor Car Company, on Conant Avenue in Detroit in late 1922. Two additions in 1923 enlarged the Conant plant by 86,000 square feet, but this was still not adequate

Table 6.1
Graham Brothers Truck Sales, All Types, 1921–1926

Year	Sales
1921	1,212
1922	3,403
1923	6,971
1924	10,744
1925	24,298
1926	37,463

Sources: Dodge Brothers, Inc., *Annual Report to the Stockholders for the Year Ended* [sic] *December 31, 1925*, 8; *Annual Report to the Stockholders for the Year Ended* [sic] *December 31, 1926*, 8. Details of the product mix (by capacity) for 1922–26 are found in Graham Brothers annual reports to the National Automobile Chamber of Commerce, Graham Brothers corporate files, NAHC. Starting in 1926, Graham Brothers sales and/or delivery figures are included in the Dodge Brothers totals for trucks.

for the increased demand for Graham trucks. The following year, Graham Brothers bought the former Dodge Brothers ordnance plant on Lynch Road in Detroit, providing nearly 500,000 square feet of additional manufacturing space. Graham Brothers also opened assembly plants in Stockton, California, and in Toronto in 1925. By 1926, they were the largest exclusive producer of trucks in the world.[45]

Dodge Brothers Performance and the Sale of the Company

Dodge Brothers suffered through the recession of 1921 but recovered quickly in 1922, as shown in table 6.2. After beginning as the number-two producer behind Ford but well ahead of Chevrolet in 1920 (141,000 versus 122,000 units), Dodge Brothers slipped to third place in 1921, well behind Ford, but only 2,000 units behind Buick. Dodge Brothers held third place in 1922, only 66,000 units behind second-place Chevrolet. In 1923, Dodge Brothers fell to sixth place in terms of production but then rebounded to a strong number-three position in 1924. Taking into account that 1923 was an excellent year for Dodge Brothers and for the American automobile industry, Dodge Brothers' performance in 1924 was remarkable.

Automobile production alone was 42 percent higher in 1924 than in 1923. Production increased slightly in 1925, but Dodge Brothers slipped to fifth place in the industry. Dodge Brothers' last prosperous year as an independent automaker

Table 6.2
Dodge Brothers Performance: Calendar Year Factory Production, 1920–1924,
Factory Sales, 1925–1927, and Financial Results, 1920–1927*

Year Ending Dec. 31	Cars	Commercial Cars and Trucks*	Total	Exports as a Share of Sales (%)
1920	129,191	16,198	145,389	—
1921	80,659	11,817	92,476	2.9
1922	142,041	21,996	164,037	6.9
1923	136,006	43,499	179,505	9.4
1924	194,341	27,894	222,236	10.2
1925	200,086	59,881	259,967	12.0
1926	264,471	67,293	331,764	—
1927	146,527	58,733	205,260	—

Year Ending Dec. 31	Net Sales	Net Earnings**	Net Earnings as Share of of Sales (%)	Dividends
1920	$161,002,512	$12,798,127	7.9	—
1921	83,666,284	2,375,726	2.8	$16,000,000
1922	130,625,774	16,874,722	12.9	$46,000,000
1923	141,332,685	10,195,730	7.2	—
1924	191,652,446	17,520,221	9.1	7,000,000
1925	219,520,842	13,746,657	6.3	9,904,687
1926	252,997,484	21,591,920	8.5	21,591,919
1927	173,581,526	9,641,427	5.6	9,641,426

*Includes chassis and buses. Graham Brothers trucks are included starting in 1925. The production figures for 1922–24 and factory sales figures for 1925–26 are those reported by Dodge Brothers to the National Automobile Chamber of Commerce, found in Dodge Brothers corporate files, NAHC.
**Earnings net of depreciation, interest, and taxes.
Sources: Dodge Brothers, Inc., Prospectus for securities issues of 1925, submitted to the State of Michigan, Commerce Department, Securities Bureau, found in the State of Michigan Archives, accession 70–5-A, lot 15, box 135; Dodge Brothers, Inc., *Annual Report to the Stockholders for the Year Ended* [sic] *December 31, 1925; Annual Report to the Stockholders for the Year Ended* [sic] *December 31, 1926; Annual Report to the Stockholders for the Year Ended* [sic] *December 31, 1927.* Dividends for 1925, 1926, and 1927 are the totals paid on preferred and common stock.

was 1926, when its production of 331,764 put it firmly in third place, with less than a quarter of Ford or General Motors production, but well ahead of the fourth-place automaker, the Hudson Motor Car Company, with 244,667 units.[46]

Sharp cyclical swings in demand for mid-priced cars, Dodge Brothers' market segment, brought sharp swings in Dodge sales. In the depressed sales year of 1921, for example, cars priced between $876 and $1,375 captured only 10.3 percent of the market versus 25.8 percent in 1920. The market share recovered to 20.4 percent in 1922, but then slipped sharply to only 13.2 percent the following year. Over the period 1917–26, sales in the mid-price market segment fluctuated more widely than sales of both low-priced and luxury automobiles. Dodge Brothers faced increasing competition in the 1920s from attractive cars in the same price range. In 1921, for example, when the Dodge Brothers touring car sold for $1,285, the General Motors "lineup" included the six-cylinder Oakland starting at $1,395, a four-cylinder Oldsmobile ($1,445), and a six-cylinder Buick ($1,795). A 1923 analysis of the automobile industry in the *American Economic Review* emphasizes the extreme competition in the medium-priced segment of the automobile market. Dodge Brothers was in direct competition with Buick, Oldsmobile, Oakland, Studebaker, Hudson, Essex, Chalmers, Reo, Willys-Knight, Jordan, Reo, Hupmobile, Chandler, and others.[47]

The growth of the Dodge Main plant did not end with the completion of the $8 million expansion of 1920–21 but continued through 1925 and beyond. In July 1922, the Dodge Brothers board of directors agreed to finish construction of the body building at a cost of $700,000. In September 1922, they broke ground for a second eight-story body plant costing $1.5 million. Dodge Brothers was struggling to supply its dealers with enough cars to meet the current demand mainly because of a shortage of bodies. In addition, the directors stated, "It is felt that the future will create a very increased demand for closed body cars and that this company should provide facilities for building all steel closed bodies as well as all steel open bodies in its own plant as a provision against the danger of stoppage of production in the plants from which bodies are now procured by the company." Less than a year later, in April 1923, the directors agreed to add two more stories to the four-story Assembly Building No. 2 already under construction, at an additional cost of $160,000. In October 1924, the directors approved another six-story addition to this building (some 170 feet long) at a cost of $330,000. At that same meeting, they approved an additional $2 million for two forge shops, a heat treat building, and a die shop.[48]

The figures in table 6.2 show the growing importance of overseas sales to the success of Dodge Brothers in the 1920s. Unfortunately, there is little surviving material that sheds light on the overseas operations. One exception is Sydney Cheney's book, *From Horses to Horsepower,* which provides much detail about Dodge Brothers in Australia. Dodge Brothers (Canada) Limited legally dates from 1917, although operations did not begin until June 1921 in Windsor, Ontario. Initially, the Canadian subsidiary served as a gateway to ship Dodge Brothers cars to the British empire. In time, however, more Canadian-built components were included in the vehicles, such as batteries, wheels, and tires, forcing Dodge Brothers (Canada) to open a larger factory in nearby Walkerville in February 1924. A year later, the Dodge Brothers subsidiary opened a new plant in Toronto, providing 250,000 square feet and costing $1.75 million.[49]

Fortunately, a detailed statement of export shipments of Dodge Brothers cars and Graham Brothers trucks for 1925 has survived. Summarized in table 6.3, the figures illustrate the global presence of Dodge Brothers and Graham Brothers vehicles. A large proportion of the shipments went to parts of the British empire. More than two-thirds of the vehicles shipped (23,383 out of 35,152) were equipped with right-hand-drive. Two-thirds of all shipments to Africa, for example, went to South Africa. In the case of the Far East, one-third of the shipments went to India and another third to China. For Australasia, the largest single market, two-thirds of the vehicles went to Australia. Argentina accounted for two-thirds of the sales to South America. The Caribbean sales district, however, has a misleading name because the district includes Mexico, Colombia, and Venezuela, along with the Caribbean islands. Dodge Brothers and Graham Brothers vehicles were sold in every corner of the globe.

Despite Frederick Haynes's successful managerial record at Dodge Brothers and an apparent bright future for the company, the Dodge widows, Matilda Rausch Dodge and Anna Thomson Dodge, decided to sell the enterprise sometime in early 1925. Why they did so will remain a mystery, as neither offered any public explanation and the surviving records are silent. Perhaps they fully appreciated the vagaries of the automobile industry and decided to sell while the company and the industry were prospering. They may have simply wanted to convert their assets into a more liquid form. Perhaps the time had come finally to break with their dead husbands' industrial legacy and move on with their own lives. The fact that none of their sons had any aptitude for or interest in managing Dodge Brothers probably made their decision easier.

Although Frederick Haynes remained with Dodge Brothers until July 1928, he was no longer in control after the sale to Dillon, Read & Company. Assessing Haynes's contribution to the success of Dodge Brothers is difficult. From 1912

Table 6.3
Export Shipments, Dodge Brothers Cars and Graham Brothers Trucks, 1925

Destination	Units Shipped
British Isles	1,887
Europe	2,441
Near East	614
Africa	3,400
Far East	4,042
Australasia	9,919
South America	3,119
Caribbean	3,884
Canada	3,396
Warehouses	2,440
TOTAL	35,152

Source: "Summary of Export Shipments, 1925," in "Dodge Overseas" collection, NAHC.

through 1920, he operated in the shadows of John and Horace Dodge. When he was in control of the automaker starting in 1921, Haynes was a modest, almost shy executive who preferred to operate quietly with calm and cautious deliberation. This researcher could find only two extensive interviews with Haynes, by W.A.P. John for *Motor* in 1922 and a second with B. C. Forbes in 1925 for *Forbes Magazine.* In describing his managerial style to both interviewers he repeated a statement attributed to John Dodge: "When you've got to decide a thing in a hurry, don't decide it at all." He believed that everyone should work for the benefit of the "Dodge organization" and would not tolerate politics in decision making. Haynes also did not tolerate "yes-men" and preferred spirited debates about company policies and practices. At a brief glance, Haynes seemed to have had the ideal personality to instill a spirit of cooperation and teamwork within the automaker. He seemed like the ideal executive to manage Dodge Brothers following the deaths of the founders.[50]

Once the Dodge widows decided to sell the company, the Dodge Brothers' directors hired an outside firm, the Manufacturers' Appraisal Company, to put a dollar value on the physical assets. Manufacturers' report, issued on 31 March 1925, included the following commentary: "In all our appraisal experience we have never reviewed a more substantial group of buildings, they are not particularly elaborate or ornate in the common sense of the word but are constructed of the best materials obtainable applied in the best known art of the trade and are in keeping with the Dodge Brothers instance [*sic*] on perfection." Their appraisal included buildings, machinery, equipment, tools, dies, and fixtures, but not inventories of raw materials, parts, or automobiles. The "cost of reproduction" (replacement cost) for all the Dodge Brothers plants came to $54,687,352, but the "sound valuation" (depreciated value) was $40,823,601. The Dodge Main plant accounted for $37,175,024 of the latter figure.[51]

The *New York Times* reported that when the Dodge widows informally put the company on the market in January 1925, more than a dozen offers came in. The Dodge families rejected most of these as inadequate or simply because they did not like the potential buyer. Two serious finalists remained at the end. General Motors, acting through its banking house of J. P. Morgan & Company, offered $124,000,000 in cash or a combination of $50,000,000 in cash and $90,00,000 in notes. They would pay the notes in installments of $10,000,000 over nine years, but would not pay interest. The New York investment banking house of Dillon, Read & Company made a more generous offer of $146,000,000 in cash.[52]

The two parties carried out serious negotiations in Detroit, with the Dodge interests meeting at the Merchants National Bank and the Dillon, Read interests at the Book-Cadillac Hotel. The bankers' representatives included E. G. Wilmer, president of the Goodyear Tire and Rubber Company, S. W. Howland, and A. C. Schwartz, all partners in Dillon, Read. John Ballantyne, chairman of the Merchants National Bank and trustee for the Horace Dodge estate, represented the Dodge family's interests, with Charles P. Spicer, vice president of the Detroit Trust Company, and family members John Duval Dodge and Wesson Seyburn. One account credits Schwartz for making the deal possible. In addition to being a partner in Dillon, Read, he had known both Dodge families for some time and had earned their trust.[53]

The widows accepted the Dillon, Read offer, which included a $50,000,000 valuation for "good will," which Dodge Brothers had always carried on its books at $1. Matilda Rausch Dodge and Anna Thomson Dodge attended the meeting of the stockholders on 7 April 1925 that approved the sale. A subsequent unanimous vote of the stockholders on 30 April 1925 ratified the earlier actions. Each of the Dodge widows held or controlled 249,995 shares of stock (out of 500,000), with five others holding two shares each. The deal was consummated on 1 May, when Dillon, Read & Company delivered a certified check for $146,000,000, the purchase price. Business historians have claimed that this was the largest cash transaction in history up to that time.[54]

Details of the actual transfer of the property can be reconstructed through newspaper articles and by examining the original check. Simultaneous meetings were held at the offices of Dillon, Read in New York and in an office of the Detroit

Trust Company in Detroit, with a long-distance telephone line linking the two groups of men. In New York, Dillon, Reed, & Company issued a check written on their account at the Central Union Trust Company in the amount of $146 million, payable to "Dodge Brothers." The check was endorsed by "Charles P. Spicer, Attorney-in-fact," for deposit to the Dodge Brothers' account at the Hanover National Bank, also in New York City. Spicer was a vice president of the Detroit Trust Company and represented the Dodge Brothers stockholders. Once the check was in his hand, Spicer informed John Ballantyne in Detroit of the fact, and Ballantyne then handed over the deed to the property to A. M. Barnes, one of Dillon, Read's representatives in Detroit. S. W. Howland, an attorney for the investment banker, was also at the Detroit meeting, along with Arthur Waterfall, representing the old Dodge Brothers firm, and Harry V. Popeney, secretary of Dodge Brothers.[55]

A few days before the sale was completed, John Duval Dodge, John F. Dodge's eldest son, unsuccessfully tried to block it. In his will, John F. Dodge had provided John Duval Dodge with an allowance of merely $150 a month. The younger Dodge had successfully challenged the will and in 1921 won a settlement of $1.6 million from the remaining heirs. On 4 April 1925, on the eve of the sale to Dillon, Read, he asked the Wayne County Circuit Court to issue an injunction to stop the sale, naming Matilda Rausch Dodge as a defendant. He claimed that he was entitled to one-fifth of the estate of his half-sister, Anna Margaret Dodge, who had died a year earlier, and that this sale affected her estate, which consisted of shares of Dodge Brothers stock. The court dismissed the case four days later, arguing that the sale involved the physical assets and good will of Dodge Brothers, not the stock.[56]

Six months after the sale, the *New York Evening Post* financial columnist reported that at the time of the Dodge Brothers sale, "Wall Street literally stood aghast when it became known that the bankers had paid, all in cash, $152,000,000 less dividends for the property." The columnist went on to argue that this was not an unreasonable price, considering the healthy condition of the firm. Sound business relationships, especially with the Dodge Brothers dealers, resulted in Dodge Brothers having only $33,000 in bad debts. The company's product line was strong as well, with closed bodies making up more than half of all production and the Dodge Brothers three-quarter-ton commercial cars accounting for one-fifth of all the Dodge Brothers business. Dodge Brothers had a strong dealer network, with roughly 6,000 outlets worldwide.[57] The sale of the company to Dillon, Read in 1925 ended not only a quarter century of Dodge family ownership of the business but also the management continuity the firm enjoyed under Frederick Haynes for more than four years after Horace Dodge's death. Dillon, Read brought in its own management team and quickly replaced many of the old Dodge Brothers executives. Edward G. Wilmer replaced Haynes as president in April 1926. Haynes was appointed chairman of the board, a largely ceremonial position. The investment banking firm was ill-prepared to operate a large company like Dodge Brothers in an industry that it did not really understand. The new owners did not neglect their automotive property and invested heavily in new plant and new products, but they made a series of poor decisions that turned Dodge Brothers into a struggling concern by 1927. A little more than three years after Dillon, Read bought Dodge Brothers, the investment banking firm sold the automotive property to the Chrysler Corporation.

SEVEN

The Dillon, Read Years and the Merger with the Chrysler Corporation, 1925–1928

> Buying the Dodge [Brothers, Inc.] was one of the soundest acts of my life. I say sincerely that nothing we have done for the organization compares with that transaction. We had, before the merger, an intensely sharp spearhead in the Chrysler Corporation, but when we put behind it all of Dodge our spearhead had a weighty shaft and had become a potent thing.
>
> Walter P. Chrysler, *Life of an American Workman* (1937)

During the three years the investment banking house of Dillon, Read & Company owned Dodge Brothers, the automaker's performance suffered. Neither Clarence Dillon nor his handpicked manager, Edward G. Wilmer, had any experience in the automobile industry. They turned what had been a growing, profitable company in 1925 into an automaker struggling to sell its products in 1927. Declining profits and falling stock prices led Clarence Dillon to sell Dodge Brothers, Inc., to the Chrysler Corporation at the end of May 1928.

Under Wilmer, Dodge Brothers bought Graham Brothers Company outright and introduced a series of entirely new cars starting with the Senior Six line, which appeared in May 1927, as a 1928 model. A new line of four-cylinder cars appeared in June 1927, followed by the Victory Six line in January 1928 and the Standard Six line in March. The new models were more expensive than the cars they replaced. Only the Victory Six line offered distinctive styling and innovative features. Overall, the new models sold poorly, depressing sales, profits, and share prices.[1]

Dodge Brothers under Dillon, Read Management

Immediately after buying Dodge Brothers, Dillon, Read & Company created a new legal entity, Dodge Brothers, Inc. (chartered in Maryland), to take over the assets of Dodge Brothers, a Michigan corporation. Dillon, Read restructured Dodge Brothers' long-term finances in a way that left the investment banking house firmly in control while making a quick profit. They offered $75,000,000 in Dodge Brothers bonds and $85,000,000 in Dodge Brothers nonvoting preferred stock (850,000 shares) to the public, which quickly snapped up the offerings. Dillon, Read thus received $160,000,000 in cash, turning a quick profit of $14,000,000 on their Dodge Brothers purchase. They also gave owners of preferred stock an equal number of shares of (nonvoting) Class A common stock. Dillon, Read also issued 500,000 shares of Class B common stock, which carried voting rights, but they kept most of those shares and thus had complete control of Dodge Brothers.[2]

After selling Dodge Brothers to the investment bankers, Anna Thomson Dodge bought large blocks of stock in the company. She participated in a syndicate run by Dillon, Read that bought and sold Dodge Brothers, Inc. preferred stock. Before she sold her holdings in early July 1925, Anna Thomson Dodge owned 82,000 shares (of 850,000 shares issued), which brought her $6.3 million upon sale. At the end of June 1925, she also bought substantial quantities of common stock. In mid-October, she still held 66,500 shares of Class A common stock and 15,500 shares of Class B common stock.[3]

Dillon, Read changed the Dodge–Graham Brothers partnership by purchasing Graham Brothers outright. The Dodge Brothers directors decided in August 1924 to secure an option on 51 percent of the Graham Brothers stock and to work more closely with the firm. When Dodge Brothers exercised its stock option on 1 October 1925, it paid $3 million for the 51 percent interest, but also took an option to purchase the remaining 49 percent for $10 million and additional payments based on Graham Brothers profits. Dodge Brothers did not announce the purchase until late November. An appraisal of the Graham Brothers' factories, dated 31 December 1925, included plants in Evansville, Indiana; Detroit; Stockton, California; and Toronto. The "sound valuation" (depreciated value) of all four was $2,328,452, with the Evansville plant accounting for $1,942,452 of the total.[4]

In mid-December 1925, the three Graham brothers became directors of Dodge Brothers, Inc., and received important management positions—Ray became general manager; Joseph took over as vice president in charge of manufacturing; and Robert became vice president and general sales manager. They had bought Dodge

Brothers shares with the proceeds from their sale of Graham Brothers stock and together became the largest Dodge Brothers stockholders. Only four months later, in mid-April 1926, Dodge Brothers paid nearly $13 million for the remaining 49 percent of the Graham Brothers stock, and the three Grahams severed all connections with Dodge Brothers. The Dodge Brothers directors later revealed that they had paid a total of $15,946,660 for the Graham Brothers stock, some $7,926,325 *above* the value of the firm's tangible assets.[5]

The departure of the Graham brothers from Dodge Brothers came only a year after Dillon, Read & Company purchased Dodge Brothers. Their departure, after they had served as directors and vice presidents for less than four months, remains shrouded in mystery. They may have had fundamental disagreements with Wilmer over the new product lines. It is more likely that they recognized they would never run Dodge Brothers and that their business associate and friend Frederick J. Haynes would have little authority under the new owners. Haynes remained president of Dodge Brothers until April 1926, when Wilmer took his position and named him chairman. The Grahams had long wanted to build their own car but needed capital and independence to pursue that goal. Once they had the proceeds from the sale of Graham Brothers in hand, they began looking for an automobile company to acquire. They first focused their attention on the Paige–Detroit Motor Car Company in September 1926 and bought a controlling interest in June 1927. The Grahams reorganized the firm as the Graham–Paige Motors Corporation, and produced cars for the next two decades.[6]

After taking over Dodge Brothers, Dillon, Read gradually replaced the top managers with their own men. At the end of 1925, only a few members of the "old guard" were still in place, namely Haynes as president; Arthur T. Waterfall as vice president; and Harry V. Popeney as secretary and treasurer. New faces included Arthur Z. Mitchell, vice president (purchasing); Herbert H. Springford, vice president (finance); and the Graham brothers. By December 1925, the board of directors had grown to seventeen members, with Edward G. Wilmer serving as chairman. Clarence Dillon and Horace E. Dodge, Jr., were among the new members. With rare exceptions, they held the Dodge Brothers directors' meetings beginning in May 1925 at the Dillon, Read offices at 28 Nassau Street in New York City.[7]

Dillon, Read substantially changed the Dodge Brothers managerial team when the Graham brothers left Dodge in April 1926. Edward G. Wilmer became president and Haynes was "bumped upstairs" to become chairman of the board. He remained in that largely ceremonial post until Chrysler purchased Dodge Brothers in July 1928, when he resigned. Haynes briefly served as president of Durant

Motors, Inc., starting in January 1929, but then rejoined the Franklin Automobile
Company in November 1930 as general manager and vice president.[8]

Arthur T. Waterfall continued to serve as a vice president at Dodge Brothers, the
only holdover from the pre–Dillon, Read days. Herbert H. Springford and Arthur Z.
Mitchell continued as vice presidents. Raymond P. Fohey became secretary and
treasurer, replacing Harry V. Popeney. Dillon, Read paid Wilmer, who served as
president until the sale of Dodge Brothers to Walter P. Chrysler, a base salary of
$250,000 annually, 1 percent of Dodge Brothers profits between $15,000,000 and
$20,000,000, and 2 percent of all profits above $20,000,000. The board of directors
also gave him $50,000 to cover the expenses of moving his family from New York
City to Detroit. In 1926, when Dodge Brothers earned nearly $27,800,000, Wilmer
earned an additional $200,000 under his contract.[9]

Edward G. Wilmer became president of Dodge Brothers, Inc., at age thirty-
nine. Originally trained as a lawyer, he worked in several executive positions in the
1910s with the Milwaukee Coke and Gas Company, the Newport Mining
Company, and the Steel & Tube Company of America. When Clarence Dillon refi-
nanced and reorganized the troubled Goodyear Tire & Rubber Company in 1921,
he asked Wilmer to direct the efforts. Wilmer led a dramatic financial turnaround
at Goodyear, where he served as president during 1921–23 and then as chairman
of the board until 1926, when he became president of Dodge Brothers.[10]

Wilmer granted an extensive interview to *Automotive Industries* in mid-April
1926, in which he discussed his plans for Dodge Brothers. The previous Dodge
Brothers' management had been competent, but conservative, and Wilmer
intended to be more aggressive in expanding the business. He argued that the complete consolidation of Graham Brothers and Dodge Brothers operations would
bring greater efficiency. Wilmer, however, said nothing about new products. Shortly
after the Dillon, Read takeover, the Dodge Brothers directors had approved a plan
to expand production from 1,100 cars per day to 1,500 and to spend $5,873,400
on new plants and equipment. Major elements included a new forge and heat treat
plant ($2,123,635), storage buildings ($1,780,400), additional enameling capacity for closed bodies ($1,500,000), and machine shop equipment ($1,030,000).[11]

Plant expansion got under way in mid-August 1925, with a projected completion date of 1 January 1926 at an estimated cost of $8 million. Construction of a
new complex on Lynch Road next to the former Dodge Brothers ordnance plant
included three large steel and glass buildings to house the heat treatment plant, a
heavy hammer shop, and a light hammer shop. The Lynch Road construction
included a die shop and a new power plant. At the main plant (Dodge Main), the

Edward G. Wilmer, 1927. Courtesy of NAHC.

largest project was a six-story addition to the assembly building, measuring 100 by 462 feet and providing an additional 282,000 square feet of floor space. Other major additions there included a five-story machining and storage building, measuring 75 feet by 475 feet, and a five-story warehouse, 100 feet by 205 feet. The Dodge Brothers construction department managed these building projects, employing 1,000 men during the second half of 1925 to complete the work.[12]

By the end of 1926, Wilmer transferred the production of Dodge Brothers three-quarter-ton screenside and panel commercial vehicles to the Graham Brothers' facilities in Detroit, and Dodge Brothers manufactured passenger cars exclusively. By then, Dodge Brothers owned Graham Brothers and ran it as an operating division of the larger concern. In 1926, Graham also produced one-ton, one-and-a-half-ton, and two-ton capacity chassis, with a variety of bodies, all sold as Graham Brothers trucks and buses. Overall production in 1926 (331,764 units) was 27.6 percent higher than that of 1925, probably a result of the shake-up in the model lineup from the previous year.[13]

Edward Wilmer and vice president for sales Robert C. Graham launched several initiatives in early 1926 to improve sales. Dodge Brothers held a national convention for its dealers and sales representatives, some 2,500 in total, in Detroit in early January 1926. Besides "wining and dining" their dealers and salespeople, Dodge Brothers held plant tours of the Dodge and Graham factories, created special exhibits, and organized scores of meetings. More important, the firm announced price reductions for all models of cars, commercial cars, and trucks ranging from $60 on the roadster to $205 on the Type A Special sedan. At the end of the meetings, Clarence Dillon revealed his plan to appoint two Dodge Brothers dealers to the Dodge Brothers board of directors, an unprecedented move in the automobile industry. Two months later, Wilmer announced the two new directors, both Dodge Brothers dealers since 1914—C. M. Bishop of Brooklyn, New York, and F. S. Albertson of Los Angeles.[14]

The new Dodge Brothers models that began appearing in early 1926 included a new commercial car, redesigned with a completely closed cab and offered in the popular screenside and panel body styles of the past. The all-steel sedan was two inches lower than its predecessor and came equipped with a one-piece windshield. New models included "sports" versions of the roaster and rumble-seat roadster introduced in January 1926 and a "sports" touring car that appeared later in the year. Dodge Brothers, Inc., also announced in January 1926 that it was adopting the standard SAE gearshift pattern, finally eliminating the pattern peculiar to Dodge Brothers.[15]

Dodge Brothers plant, Hamtramck, 1960. Courtesy of DCHC.

The 1926 models incorporated a series of important mechanical improvements. Dodge Brothers introduced a new four-cylinder engine with a five-bearing crankshaft, replacing the engine with a three-bearing crankshaft in use since 1922. The new engine provided vibration-free power at fifty miles per hour and above. Additional mechanical improvements for 1926 included the introduction of an air cleaner as standard equipment; improvements to the steering gear; better spark, throttle, and carburetor controls; and an improved (6-volt instead of 12-volt) electrical system.[16]

The new owners were willing to spend significant sums to promote Dodge Brothers products. When Curtis Publishing Company revealed the leading automotive advertisers in its magazines for 1926, Dodge Brothers, Inc., ranked third ($963,820), trailing only Chrysler Sales Corporation ($1,043,145) and Willys-Overland, Inc. ($1,014,730). Buick Motor Company held fourth place ($855,625) and Chevrolet Motor Company fifth place ($841,203). Dodge Brothers had twice the advertising expenditures of Ford Motor Company, Nash Motors Company, and the Hudson Motor Car Company.[17]

Beginning in May 1927, Dodge Brothers, Inc., introduced an entirely new lineup of passenger cars, the first major shake-up of Dodge Brothers products since

1914. Besides an entirely new line of four-cylinder cars, Dodge Brothers introduced three new lines of six-cylinder automobiles for the 1928 model year—the Senior Six, the Victory Six, and the Standard Six. The introduction of six-cylinder models in 1927 reveals how out-of-date Dodge Brothers cars had become by then. When the first Dodge Brothers car appeared in 1914, four-cylinder cars accounted for 77 percent of the American market. In 1926, sales of six-cylinder models accounted for 55 percent of the market in the United States and four-cylinder cars 42 percent, with Ford accounting for much of the four-cylinder sales. Dodge Brothers had repeated the same mistake Henry Ford made in sticking with the Model T Ford too long. Unfortunately for Dodge Brothers, the new models introduced in 1927 were not very successful.[18]

We can only speculate as to who made the decisions regarding the new models, particularly their size, styling, engines, and price. Edward Wilmer was clearly in command starting in May 1925. The departure of the Graham brothers in April 1926, when Wilmer also replaced Haynes as president, further solidified his control.

The rationale behind the introduction of the new models was never clearly explained. Wilmer may have believed that Dodge Brothers needed to imitate General Motors if it hoped to prosper in an increasingly competitive automobile market. By expanding the offerings from a single line of cars to three, with a much wider price range than before, Dodge Brothers could imitate GM's "ladder marketing" approach. Dodge Brothers would go "up-market" and focus on six-cylinder automobiles. In a letter to the stockholders (dated 26 January 1928) that introduced the annual report to the stockholders for 1927, Wilmer explained his thinking. Advances in design and manufacturing in the auto industry meant that by 1926 and later, competitors would be selling six-cylinder cars in the same price category as the traditional Dodge Brothers four. So Dodge Brothers needed to produce a four-cylinder car that would be lighter and faster than its traditional four and would sell at a lower price. Dodge Brothers would simultaneously introduce "two lines of superior six cylinder motor cars," one to sell in the $1,000 range and the other in the $1,500 price class. Rather than disrupt the factory organization and the dealers, the company introduced the new models piecemeal.[19]

The first new introduction, the Senior Six line, appeared in early May 1927 and was the most expensive new model, with prices ranging from $1,495 (two-door coupe) to $1,595 (four-door sedan). A completely reworked four-cylinder car, called the Fast Four (base price of $855) went into production in August 1927. Dodge Brothers produced 55,000 of these before the end of the calendar year. The company then introduced the mid-priced Victory Six in January 1928, with a base

1928 Dodge Brothers Senior Six sport cabriolet. Courtesy NAHC.

price of $1,045, but with the price of some models as high as $1,295. Finally, in March 1928, Dodge Brothers announced the Standard Six (also known as the Light Six), priced at $875–$970, to replace the Fast Four, which was less than a year old.[20]

Wilmer used the occasion of the twelfth annual Dodge Brothers' dealers' convention, held in Detroit in early January 1927, to announce the Senior Six line. Wilmer showed the dealers a single prototype but would not reveal if it had a six- or an eight-cylinder engine; he simply informed them that it would be in production by July. It is conceivable that the Dodge Brothers management had not yet decided whether it would be a six or an eight. In at least one sense, it did not matter because Continental Motors, not Dodge Brothers, built the engine. Dodge Brothers built a 560,000-square-foot building on Lynch Road in Detroit to assemble the new car. The plant, which cost $4,500,000 and was finished by early April 1927, included a new one-mile concrete oval test track with banked curves for road testing the new models.[21]

The Senior Six, with four-wheel hydraulic brakes and a seven-bearing crankshaft, was technologically up-to-date in most respects. Reviewers described it as handsome, with good handling characteristics and a reasonable price. The company began designing the Dodge Brothers Senior line less than two years before production began. This was an "all-new" car built in an "all-new" factory. Production of 100 cars a day started in May 1927, with plans to increase that to 300 per day in June. The Senior line never caught the public fancy, however, and by the end of 1927 Dodge Brothers had manufactured only 15,000 Senior Sixes.[22]

The Senior Six was a sales disaster, in part because it differed greatly from previous Dodge Brothers models. By going "up-market" with a more expensive car with a six-cylinder engine, the company forced its dealers to appeal to a different class of customers than traditional Dodge Brothers buyers. Several ads included chauffeurs, while others showed Senior Six owners playing polo, sailing a yacht, or attending formal affairs. With a price range of $1,495–$1,595, the Senior Six was priced well above the entire line of Oldsmobiles, which ranged in price between $925 and $1,205 for the 1928 model year. Even Buick, between Oldsmobile and Cadillac in the General Motors pecking order, offered models less costly than the Dodge Brothers Senior. The Buick Standard Series models for 1928, with a wheelbase of 114.5 inches versus 116 inches for the Senior Six, sold for between $1,195 and $1,375. Even the Buick Masters Series, on a wheelbase of 120 inches, offered six models priced between $1,465 and $1,575. Convincing customers to buy the Senior Six must have been difficult for Dodge Brothers dealers.[23]

Ever since their first cars came off the assembly line in Hamtramck, Dodge Brothers boasted of their all-steel bodies and overall high quality because they built the components in-house according to rigid Dodge Brothers specifications. The Senior Six, however, had a composite steel and wood body supplied by Briggs Manufacturing Company and Murray Body Company and an engine made by Continental Motors. Dodge Brothers provided the specifications to Continental, which received the nod because they could make the engine cheaper than could Dodge Brothers. The Senior Six looked to many customers much like the "assembled cars" that Dodge Brothers salesmen had always ridiculed. After arguing for more than a decade about the superiority of all-steel bodies over composite bodies, the Senior Six was a "hard sell" for Dodge Brothers dealers.[24]

The company touted the new Dodge Brothers four introduced in August 1927 as "the fastest four-cylinder car in America," capable of sixty miles per hour, a speed normally reserved for more expensive models. Four body styles were available at base prices ranging from the coupe ($855) to the cabriolet roadster ($955). The line used the new Dodge Brothers four-cylinder engine with a five-bearing crankshaft, which reduced engine vibration and made higher speeds possible. In addition, the new models had shorter wheelbases and weighed 300 pounds less than

$1495

SEDAN F.O.B. DETROIT

1928 Dodge Brothers Senior Six four-door sedan. Courtesy of NAHC.

those of the previous line. Dodge Brothers also built the Fast Four lower to the ground, giving it a more "sporty" look. Initial sales were encouraging, and Dodge Brothers assembled 55,000 units by the end of the calendar year. This Dodge Brothers model was not much better in terms of style and comfort than the new Model A Ford, which began appearing in showrooms in December 1927 and had a retail price of $495–$570. The Standard Six introduced in March 1928 replaced the Fast Four after only eight months of production.[25]

Wilmer admitted in a letter to stockholders in January 1928 that the introduction of the new models was botched. He explained why longtime Dodge Brothers customers were confused:

> During the early stages of this development, sales of four cylinder passenger cars were somewhat affected by frequent changes in product and in the absence of authentic publicity concerning the company's future plans, many unfounded adverse rumors found ready reception.

Six - Cylinder Performance
Refreshingly New . . . .

DODGE
BROTHERS
Senior Line

WIELDERS of the polo mallet, hunters of moose, hard hitters from the tee—are enthusiastic about this car.

For them its virility and boundless eagerness to go have irresistible appeal.

A car that makes you regret the shortness of a mile—or half a thousand miles.

Owners who have not dared to open the throttle wide report better than seventy miles per hour. Acceleration that masters traffic. Vast reservoirs of power.

1928 Dodge Brothers Senior line advertisement. Author's collection.

1928 Dodge Brothers Fast Four. Courtesy of NAHC.

This uncertainty, which could not be dispelled without prematurely divulging the full program and so working permanent injury to current business, reached perhaps its most difficult stage during 1927.

Of course, "the absence of authentic publicity concerning the company's future plans" was the result of Wilmer's indecisive management style and entirely his fault. Not announcing and possibly not knowing the engine that would power the Senior line six months before the line would go into production is just one example of Wilmer's incompetence. Wilmer, however, did not recognize the other problems that plagued these new Dodge Brothers lines. Except for the Victory Six line, these new models were undistinguished, overpriced, or both.[26]

The Victory Six line, introduced in January 1928, had an innovative body-frame design. A. F. Denham, writing in *Automotive Industries,* described this as a "fish-belly" frame, with the body and seats attached directly to the frame. This allowed the body to be lowered two inches without reducing interior headroom, lowering the center of gravity and improving handling as a result. This body-frame design also saved 175 pounds in overall weight. A similar description in *Automobile Topics* in early January 1928 focuses on the fact that they built the floor and seats of the car right into the chassis frame instead of bolted into body sills, which was the previous practice. A correspondent for *Automobile Topics* took a Dodge Victory Six on a daylong test drive and reported in April 1928 that the car was quiet, comfortable, easy to handle, and had good acceleration and overall performance.[27]

The DeLuxe Sedan

Women show keen interest in Victory performance

The way women have received Dodge Brothers New Victory Six proves that they *are* interested in something besides vanity cases, upholstery and appointments.

Quite as much as men, they express keen interest in the Victory's supreme ability to accelerate more swiftly and maintain a higher speed than any other motor car in its price class. They appreciate, too, the Victory's unruffled comfort over rough pavement—especially when there are small children on the seats.

They are *not* quite so interested, conceivably, in the new facts and features of Victory engineering: more power per pound than any car in the Victory price class—revolutionary new body-construction and body-mounting, etc.—but they are captivated by the thrilling *results* of these features.

And they are gratified to discover that in the business of creating a new and better kind of performance, Dodge Brothers engineers have not overlooked those niceties of style and appointment that capture feminine fancy.

The VICTORY SIX
BY DODGE BROTHERS

TOURING CAR $995 · · ROADSTER $995 · · COUPE $1045 · · 4-DOOR SEDAN $1095 · · DELUXE SEDAN $1170
DELUXE 4-PASSENGER COUPE $1170 · · SPORT SEDAN $1295 · · *f. o. b. Detroit*

1928 Dodge Brothers Victory Six advertisement in *The House Beautiful*, August 1928. Author's collection.

John Bittence has argued convincingly that most of the contemporary auto-mobile industry publications and automotive historians alike have missed the most important innovative feature of the Victory Six—its monopiece or unit body design. The Edward G. Budd Company developed new machinery and electric welding techniques that allowed it to produce the Victory Six body as eight large steel stamp-ings that they shipped to the Dodge Brothers factory for assembly (by welding) into an all-steel body without a network of rails, sills, and braces to support the body panels. Dodge Brothers then added a roof insert (wood-framed, with rubberized cloth), hood, doors, and a few other parts to produce the completed body. Dodge Brothers spent about $10 million to develop the Victory Six, with a substantial part of the investment going to help Budd solve the manufacturing problems inherent in this innovative design. Strangely, automobile writers touted Budd's innovative larger stampings without mentioning Dodge Brothers or the Victory Six.[28]

The Victory Six was the first American production car with a unit body design, which resulted in a stronger and more rigid car, saved weight, and produced a lower center of gravity and improved road handling. E. E. Thum, writing in *Automotive Industries* in September 1928, recognized the significance of the Victory Six mono-piece body design, but he was the only automotive writer who did. Dodge Brothers informed its dealers of the pathbreaking nature of the unit body and the advan-tages car buyers would enjoy in its sales magazine, *The Dotted Line,* but this had little positive impact on sales. When the Budd Company touted its work in devel-oping unit bodies, it did not mention Dodge Brothers. As a result, automotive his-torians have mistakenly identified the 1934 Chrysler/DeSoto Airflow as the first production car with a unit body design.[29]

As a hasty replacement for the failed Fast Four, the company introduced the Dodge Brothers Standard ("Light") Six in March 1928 in four body styles with list prices ranging from $875 to $970. *Automotive Industries* reported that the Standard Six had "a number of features not usually found in cars in the lower price range, such as completely-machined combustion chambers, a fully-machined crankshaft, Nelson-type aluminum alloy pistons, an AC oil filter and ball bearings throughout the transmission gear and the rear axle." This was the same engine used in the Victory Six. The Dodge Brothers Standard Six was a reasonably priced six that sold much better than the four it replaced. The demise of the Fast Four also marked the end of the four-cylinder engine in Dodge Brothers cars until the 1978 Dodge Omni.[30]

The lineup of Graham Brothers trucks also changed and expanded in 1927 and 1928. The distinctive one-ton capacity G-Boy chassis (126-inch wheelbase)

1928 Dodge Brothers Victory Six at Edward G. Budd Company exhibit. Courtesy of NAHC.

appeared as a 1927 model and could be fitted with pickup, canopy, and stake truck bodies. Early in the 1928 model year, Graham Brothers for the first time offered trucks with six-cylinder engines on its two-ton and three-ton capacity trucks. A Graham Brothers catalog issued in September 1928 reveals the broad range of commercial car, truck, and bus chassis and bodies manufactured by Dodge Brothers. Graham Brothers sold chassis ranging from three-quarter-ton to three-ton capacity and with wheelbases ranging from 110 inches to 185 inches, including 12-, 16-, and 21-passenger motor coach chassis. Customers could buy chassis fitted with merchants express panel, canopy, screen, express (pickup), stake, farm box, high rack, dump, tractor, motor coach, and school bus bodies.[31]

The new car and truck models did not bring the expected jump in sales—just the opposite. Combined sales of cars and trucks fell sharply from 331,764 units in 1926 to 205,260 in 1927, a decline of 38 percent. Earnings, which had been respectable in 1925 and 1926, dropped disastrously in 1927. Part of the downturn

1928 Graham Brothers panel delivery trucks. Courtesy of NAHC.

reflected the inherent production difficulties of simultaneously introducing so many "all-new" lines of cars. The new models, which were markedly more expensive than the old Dodge Brothers four-cylinder cars, did not catch the public's fancy. In going "up-market," Dodge Brothers abandoned its longtime customers. By any standard, 1927 was a disaster for Dodge Brothers, Inc. Sales fell from nearly

1928 Graham Brothers stake truck. Courtesy of NAHC.

$253,000,000 in 1926 to $173,581,526 in 1927, and net earnings dropped from $21,591,920 to only $9,641,427. In a single year, the company lost one-third of its sales revenues and more than half its profits.

One positive sales trend that Wilmer continued was Dodge Brothers' expanded sales in foreign markets. The automaker's overseas sales, a minuscule 2.9 percent of total sales in 1921, grew to a healthy 12 percent (30,566 units) in 1925. Dodge Brothers hired Percy Owen as its director of foreign sales on 1 October 1925. Born in Oswego, New York, Owen opened the first gasoline automobile dealership in New York City in 1899, selling Winton automobiles. He worked for Winton in various capacities until 1912, when he became the general sales manager for Chalmers Motor Car Company in Detroit. Owen then served as vice president of the Saxon Motor Car Company in 1915 and was president of the Liberty Motor Car Company of Detroit from 1916 until 1924. He took a position in 1924 with the U.S. Department of Commerce as the chief of its automotive division and conducted several studies of the European automobile market on behalf of the U.S. automobile industry.[32]

Hired by Dodge Brothers because of his knowledge of European automobile markets, Percy Owen resigned his position on 1 August 1926, only ten months later. Neither Owen nor the automaker offered an explanation for his departure. He said simply, "Now I am going fishing." He did not leave because foreign sales had plummeted; just the opposite was the case. Dodge Brothers overseas sales for the first nine months of 1926 were 22.7 percent higher than for the first nine months of the previous year.[33]

Sometime in 1927 Wilmer commissioned R. Carl Hicks and George D. Babcock to conduct a study of the world automobile market, focusing mainly on Europe. On 28 May 1927, they submitted a report to Wilmer in which they offered a series of recommendations for improving Dodge Brothers sales in Europe. They collected detailed data on automobile ownership and sales in Europe by make and interviewed Dodge Brothers dealers there to get a better sense of demand. They concluded that neither the Dodge Brothers four nor any of the various Dodge Brothers sixes would sell very well anywhere in Europe because of the high price of gasoline and high taxes based on horsepower. Germany might become a good market for Dodge Brothers vehicles once its economy recovered.[34]

Success in foreign markets, however did not counterbalance the sales declines the company suffered under Wilmer. The financial value of Dodge Brothers, Inc., stock also declined and this alone convinced Dillon, Read & Company to consider unloading the company when the opportunity arose. Dodge Brothers profits per vehicle fell from $65 in 1926 to $48 in 1927, on a much smaller volume in the later year. More striking was the decline in net profits per share of common stock—$6.46 to $1.43. The stock prices began to reflect the drop in earnings. Between 1 January 1927 and 1 January 1928, Dodge Brothers preferred stock fell from $82 a share to $74 a share, while common stock prices dropped from $25 to $23 per share. The combined stock value of Dodge Brothers, Inc., fell from $190,000,000 to $176,000,000 over the same year. This decline was particularly striking in a year when the prices of automobile stocks increased approximately 50 percent for the shares of twenty-three major automakers.[35]

According to testimony given before the New York State Supreme Court in late June 1928, Edward Wilmer approached the Dillon, Read partners in April 1928 and practically begged them to find someone to buy Dodge Brothers, Inc. He conceded that after spending close to $15,000,000 converting the Dodge Brothers plants for the new six-cylinder models, they had produced new cars they could not sell. These were the circumstances that first led Clarence Dillon to approach Walter P. Chrysler regarding the sale of Dodge Brothers. Fortunately, Chrysler was more than simply amenable to this prospect; he was almost desperate to buy Dodge Brothers.[36]

Merger of Chrysler Corporation and Dodge Brothers

Walter Chrysler wanted the Dodge Brothers property by early 1928. The Chrysler line of cars was popular and profitable, but the company was hard-pressed to increase production and reduce costs. It needed to do both to survive in an increasingly competitive industry. Neither of its two major plants—the former Maxwell facility in Highland Park nor the former Chalmers plant in Detroit—had significant casting or forging capacities. Chrysler admitted that his company bought far too much of the finished car from outside suppliers because Chrysler lacked foundries and forge shops. Dodge Brothers, Inc., had the large, modern, and efficient foundries and forges that Chrysler needed.

Walter Chrysler did his homework before deciding to buy Dodge Brothers. He also considered a merger with Willys-Overland and prepared an operating statement comparing the performance of Chrysler and Willys-Overland for 1927 and the first quarter of 1928. The "tale of the tape" reveals why Walter Chrysler shied away from Willys. Chrysler's sales in 1927 were higher than Willys (192,083 units versus 187,776), but Chrysler's net profits were more than three times those of Willys ($19,485,000 versus $5,529,000). Chrysler earned 11.31 percent profits on sales versus Willys' anemic 3.49 percent. Although Willys shipped 43 percent more cars in the first quarter of 1928 (74,578 versus 52,326 for Chrysler), its projected profits for the year were still less than half those of Chrysler.[37]

Someone in the Chrysler organization compiled similar comparative data for Dodge Brothers and Chrysler for 1927 and the first quarter of 1928. Although Dodge Brothers passenger car sales in 1927 were down substantially from 1926 (146,527 versus 264,471), the analyst projected that they would rebound to about 200,000 units in 1928, roughly the same level as Chrysler's sales. The analyst also compiled detailed comparisons of retail prices and sales volumes of the various Chrysler and Dodge Brothers models, recognizing that the firms had a good deal of overlapping product.[38]

Strategic thinking about the long-term future of the Chrysler Corporation led to the merger with Dodge Brothers, not the narrow calculations of likely sales and profit margins. A three-page summary of the advantages of a Dodge Brothers merger for Chrysler Corporation includes a long list of the advantages the new entity would enjoy by virtue of its larger size and sales volume. In brief, Chrysler could be more like General Motors—it could operate an export company to promote overseas sales and a finance company to finance dealers' inventories and consumer installment purchases, much like General Motors Acceptance Corporation. It could make a greater share of its own parts, especially starting and lighting equipment. Larger size would bring economies in research, engineering, and purchasing. Gaining a truck business was another significant benefit. The most significant overriding benefit was simple: "The combination will result in a strengthened company, better able to finance its requirements for development and expansion and better able to withstand the competition of the dominant factor in the motor industry, General Motors Corporation."[39] Long-term survival was at stake, and long-term success was not likely unless Chrysler Corporation became a lot bigger.

Walter Chrysler desperately needed more manufacturing capacity because of his well-advanced plans to expand his automobile offerings. Before the announcement of the Chrysler–Dodge Brothers merger on 1 June 1928, Chrysler had already started manufacturing two new models, the low-priced Plymouth and the mid-priced DeSoto. The "official announcements" of the new models took place on 7 July and 4 August 1928, respectively, but both were already in production in June. Walter Chrysler began planning for the DeSoto in 1926 and a separate DeSoto Division was already in place before Chrysler bought Dodge Brothers.

Walter Chrysler intended to use DeSoto to force Dillon, Read to sell Dodge Brothers since DeSoto and Dodge were in the same price class. Chrysler later conceded that without the Dodge Brothers factory, he could not have produced the

Plymouth. He needed a lot more manufacturing capacity but could not build it quickly or cheaply. Chrysler estimated that the Dodge Brothers plant, if built from scratch, would cost $75,000,000 and he would need to borrow the money. He would perhaps need a year to build equivalent plant capacity and another year to become efficient in operating it. For Walter Chrysler, the Dodge Brothers merger had two key attractions—he received modern, efficient manufacturing capacity and needed no cash to complete the deal.[40]

Another feature of the Dodge Brothers business that appealed to Walter Chrysler was its large, efficient systems of dealers and distributors, generally viewed as one of the best in the industry. To produce the low-priced Plymouth and compete with Ford and Chevrolet without an extensive dealer system already in place would have been a daunting challenge. Various sources have offered widely different estimates of the number of Dodge Brothers dealerships Chrysler gained in 1928. A *Fortune* article of 1935 offered a precise figure of 3,160, but automotive writer Walter Boynton estimated that Chrysler and Dodge Brothers each had about 4,600 dealers in 1928. Other contemporary reports on the 1928 merger suggest a combined U.S. dealership network of about 9,000 outlets, with Chrysler and Dodge Brothers having about the same number. The higher figure seems most accurate. We know that Chrysler began with about 2,000 (converted Maxwell) dealerships in 1924 and by fall 1925 had approximately 3,800 dealers. This number grew rapidly in 1925–28 with the extraordinary success of the Chrysler line of cars. By late 1929, after Plymouth and DeSoto were well-established brands, the combined Chrysler dealer network had about 12,000 outlets in the United States, 2,600 in Canada, and 3,800 overseas.[41]

In reporting the merger, *Automotive Daily News* offered the following analysis:

> Exactly what is the gain in the whole transaction? The Chrysler, one of the strongest organizations in the industry, acquires an extremely efficient and well-located plant, capable of a higher production, even, than its past records prove it can give. The most important gain that Chrysler makes is unquestionably increased representation. It costs much time and money to build a dealer organization, and by this merger Chrysler is taking over a full-fledged and powerful merchandizing army.[42]

The story of how the Chrysler–Dodge Brothers merger took place is an often-repeated epochal tale based almost entirely on Walter Chrysler's account laid out in his autobiography. Clarence Dillon approached Chrysler in mid-April 1928 and initiated discussions about buying Dodge Brothers. Dillon's move came fresh on the heels of Chrysler's announcement of the new DeSoto line of cars, priced to compete head-to-head with Dodge Brothers. Chrysler feigned a lack of interest while trying to depress the asking price. After more than a month of thrusts and counterthrusts, the two men rented adjoining suites at the Ritz in New York City, where they engaged in marathon negotiations for five days along with their financial experts and attorneys. They reached an agreement, which both men submitted to their respective boards of directors on 29 May for approval. Walter Chrysler also received a legal opinion that the proposed merger would not violate the Clayton (antitrust) Act.[43]

It was vital to Walter P. Chrysler that the merger involve no cash, because he had none. Instead, the Chrysler Corporation issued new shares of common stock, with a market value of about $170,000,000, to exchange for the existing Dodge Brothers shares. Dodge Brothers stockholders would receive one share of Chrysler common stock in exchange for one share of Dodge Brothers preferred stock, five shares of Dodge Brothers common stock Class A (nonvoting), or ten shares of Dodge Brothers common stock Class B (voting). Chrysler Corporation assumed the existing debts of Dodge Brothers, approximately $60,000,000, including $57,276,000 of debenture bonds. One element of the financial restructuring brought by this merger usually ignored by historians was Chrysler Corporation's decision to retire all of its preferred stock at a cost of about $25,000,000. A contemporary article in *The Magazine of Wall Street* examined the merger in terms of the financial interests of all categories of Dodge Brothers and Chrysler stockholders and concluded that the merger was a good deal for everyone.

The key precondition of this deal was a requirement that Dillon, Read get the owners of 90 percent of all three types of stock to agree to the merger by 1 July 1928. Walter Chrysler did not want to become embroiled with minority stockholders challenging the merger in court, as Chalmers stockholders had done in the early 1920s. Chrysler extended the deadline to 31 July, and even then Clarence Dillon barely produced the required amount of stock. Late that afternoon, Chrysler's executives took over the Dodge Brothers plants and posted signs that read, "Dodge Division, Chrysler Corporation."[44]

The stockholder suit that Chrysler feared happened anyway. Calvin Hooker Goddard, an owner of Dodge Brothers preferred stock, sued in the Supreme Court of New York State on 25 June 1928 to prevent the merger from going forward. Acting for fellow shareholders, he demanded $105 in cash for his shares, rather than Chrysler stock, because he was entitled to cash under the Dodge Brothers charter because they were dissolving the company. The judge issued a temporary restraining order against Dodge Brothers, Inc., and on 29 June ordered the company to post a bond that guaranteed they would pay cash to the stockholders. Once done, the court lifted the injunction. Chrysler Corporation "solved" the problem by selling additional Chrysler shares in the open market and using the proceeds to buy out the remaining Dodge Brothers shareholders with cash. By the end of November, only 6.8 percent of the preferred shares were still outstanding and less than 2 percent of the other types of stock. By then, owners of outstanding Dodge Brothers stock received only cash, much less than the market price of the Chrysler shares they could have had.[45]

One major task Walter Chrysler faced after taking over Dodge Brothers was the revival of Dodge Brothers sales, which had plummeted in 1927 and early 1928. Immediately following the merger, Chrysler Sales Manager Joseph Fields informed Chrysler dealers that Chrysler Corporation had no intention of dropping the Dodge Brothers nameplate and that rumors to that effect were false. Chrysler tried to boost the confidence of Dodge Brothers dealers and customers. When 2,000 Dodge Brothers dealers met in Detroit in mid-December 1928, Walter Chrysler and the other top Chrysler officials outlined their plans to improve the Dodge Brothers cars and reassured the dealers that they had a bright future.[46]

If words alone were not convincing, the actions of the Chrysler Corporation in remaking the Dodge Brothers car lines were proof that the Dodge Brothers nameplate would survive. Some changes to the cars were already under way before Chrysler officially took control of Dodge Brothers on 31 July 1928. The Victory Six interior space, including headroom, was too small for full-sized adults and generated many complaints. As a temporary fix, Dodge Brothers raised the head liner in the closed Victory models in January 1928 and offered an adjustable front seat starting in March 1928. Dodge Brothers then introduced larger sedan bodies on 13 June 1928 and larger coupe bodies on 13 July 1928, thus solving the problem. In September 1928, the Dodge Division of Chrysler Corporation announced a new Senior line, with a longer wheelbase, a more powerful engine, more interior room, and a variety of additional mechanical improvements.[47]

To bolster customer confidence and sales, Walter P. Chrysler personally endorsed the Dodge Brothers line of cars in a statement that appeared in the *Literary Digest* and elsewhere in October 1928. He reported that his engineering chief, Fred M. Zeder, confirmed that the new Dodge Brothers cars were "basically as sound as motor cars can be built." The new Dodge Brothers lines proved that "Dodge ruggedness and Dodge dependability can be successfully expressed in terms of flashing performance and advanced style." Chrysler confirmed that the

Dodge Brothers nameplate, sold exclusively by Dodge Brothers dealers, would continue well into the future. These efforts stopped the sales slide and resulted in an increase in car and truck sales from 205,260 units in 1927 to 231,384 in 1928, an impressive gain.[48]

Walter Chrysler continued the effort to boost Dodge Brothers sales in 1929 as well. In August, Dodge Brothers introduced a new one-ton truck, available in eight body styles. This greatly improved truck sold at a base price of $745, some $250 below the price of the model it replaced. In mid-September 1929, Chrysler addressed the top Dodge Brothers managers and outlined his efforts to restore the prestige of the Dodge Brothers name, damaged during the years of Dillon, Read management. He would lead a return to the manufacturing principles and standards pioneered by John and Horace Dodge.

As part of this return to the past, Walter Chrysler revived the Dodge Brothers nameplate and emblem on all Dodge Brothers products, including trucks. The 1928 models did not include the full name on the radiator emblem. They renamed the new Victory Six line the Dodge Brothers Six, and it was a great success. They called the eight-cylinder Dodge Brothers line introduced in 1930 the Dodge Brothers Eight. Chrysler first used the ram's head as a hood ornament on the 1931 model Dodge Brothers cars. Fred Zeder had decided to add a hood ornament that was "distinctive, attractive, and totally American." Since the Rocky Mountain Big Horn Ram was an American species known for its strength and agility, it was a perfect symbol for Dodge. For most of the 1930s, Dodge vehicles used both the ram's head and the intertwined deltas as symbols. Not until 1939 did Chrysler Corporation entirely drop the Dodge Brothers nomenclature and geometric symbol.[49]

All of the contemporary reports of the merger recognized that the Chrysler Corporation had emerged as a very large automaker, behind only General Motors and Ford in sales and manufacturing capacity and clearly well ahead of the remaining firms in the industry. With the successful introduction of the DeSoto and Plymouth lines of cars in 1928, production, sales, and profits soared at Chrysler. Following the merger announcement, *Automotive Daily News* ran an editorial titled simply, "The Big Three," noting, "With this merger completed, the automobile manufacturing field is now dominated by a 'big three,' composed of General Motors, Ford, and Chrysler-Dodge. On their present production schedules . . . these three companies will account for nearly 75 percent of the passenger car manufacturing in this country today." This was the first publication to use that expression.[50]

Retrospective: The Dodge Brothers— The Men, the Motor Cars, and the Legacy

Placing the lives and careers of the Dodge brothers in perspective can be accomplished by comparing them with contemporary auto industry pioneers and leaders. Their management style in running Dodge Brothers was quite distinct from that of contemporary auto industry giants such as Henry Ford (1863–1947), William C. ("Billy") Durant (1861–1947), and Alfred P. Sloan, Jr. (1875–1966). Their management style reflected their equal partnership in the venture and the relatively simple nature of their enterprise. Unlike Ford, Durant, and Sloan, the Dodges enjoyed full ownership of Dodge Brothers from the beginning, never borrowed from banks, and never had to consider stockholders or a board of directors in making business decisions. Henry Ford did not free himself from his stockholders until 1918 and from banks until 1920.

Managing the Dodge Brothers operations was in many respects simpler than at the competitive firms. Production involved only one factory after 1910, the giant plant in Hamtramck. Even the ordnance plant used to manufacture recoil mechanisms and some later Dodge models was nearly adjacent to Dodge Main. In contrast, Ford Motor Company's operations by the late 1910s included two major manufacturing facilities, at Highland Park and at River Rouge in Dearborn, and as early as 1914, fourteen branch assembly plants. The constantly evolving General Motors Corporation under Billy Durant and later, Alfred P. Sloan, included hundreds of manufacturing and assembly plants spread all over North America.[1]

Overseeing and directing Dodge Brothers was a cooperative and rational venture while the Dodge brothers were alive and continued after their deaths. By dividing up the tasks and the responsibilities for those tasks, John and Horace Dodge in one sense "stayed out of each other's way" and thus avoided duplication of efforts and conflict. They genuinely liked and loved each other as brothers sometimes do. John Dodge concentrated on the business side of the operations, taking care of contracts, sales and advertising, relations with the dealers, and general public relations. Horace Dodge managed the manufacturing operations, including toolmaking and plant layout, and the design of most of the components made in-house. Neither was autocratic in the fashion of Henry Ford. They hired middle managers, like Frederick

Haynes, whom they trusted, paid well, and gave a good deal of autonomy. Yet, they remained hands-on managers. John and Horace maintained permanent homes in Detroit and except for hunting trips in northern Michigan and excursions on Horace's yachts, they spent little time outside of Detroit except on business.

Their management style contrasted sharply with that of Henry Ford, Billy Durant, and Alfred Sloan. Henry Ford, particularly after he gained complete ownership of Ford Motor Company, became increasingly autocratic. Even the more sympathetic observers of Ford concede that he became increasingly inflexible, unpredictable, secretive, paranoid, and even irrational in running Ford Motor Company. By the early 1920s, Henry Ford seemed no longer interested in his company's profits but was instead pursuing a variety of political and social interests unrelated to automobiles. Over time, he drove away all of his lieutenants who made him successful, including James Couzens, William S. Knudsen, Charles Sorensen, and his son, Edsel. Henry Ford's decision to give control of the Ford Motor Company to Harry Bennett instead of Edsel demonstrates his state of mind.[2]

The contrast between the management styles of John and Horace Dodge and that of Billy Durant could not be greater. Durant was mainly a financial tycoon, a freewheeling manipulator of stock and companies who combined scores of automobile, truck, and components manufacturers in 1908 to form General Motors. He was the penultimate deal maker who seemed indifferent to the profitability or efficiency of his creations. He had no interest in the day-to-day management of General Motors. His "field of dreams" was not found on the floor of the Buick assembly plant in Flint, Michigan, but on the floor of the New York Stock Exchange. He rarely visited Detroit or Flint, preferring New York City. But Durant also was unwilling to allow competent managers like Walter P. Chrysler to run General Motors without interference. Chrysler left Durant's employ in disgust, and in 1920 Durant permanently lost control of the company he founded. General Motors remained a large but inefficient and unprofitable firm under Durant's leadership.[3]

Alfred P. Sloan, Jr., an engineer by training, began working at General Motors in 1918 and served as its president from 1923 to 1941. He reorganized the giant automaker's administrative structure by decentralizing much of the decision making, eliminating duplication, and creating a system of central financial management and control. Much like Durant, Sloan lived in New York City and managed General Motors from corporate offices there. Sloan also introduced a strategy for selling cars in a saturated market, which was later labeled "Sloanism." It included the creation of a clear "step ladder" of GM car models by size and price; the annual model changeover based on styling changes; the availability of expensive options for cars; the used-car trade-in; and installment buying. Under Sloan, General

Motors focused on making money and not on merely making cars. These strategies worked. By the late 1920s, General Motors was an efficient and profitable automaker and took over first place in the industry from Ford.[4]

During the brief time that John and Horace Dodge manufactured automobiles, Dodge Brothers followed a marketing strategy summed up by the phrase, "constant improvements, but no annual model changes." Dodge Brothers continued the same policy though 1925. Their approach was far more flexible than Henry Ford's policy of leaving the Model T essentially unchanged from 1908 to 1927. At the same time, they did not adopt Alfred Sloan's successful marketing strategy at General Motors, whereby models were changed in appearance every year and older models were made obsolete as a result.[5]

Had John and Horace Dodge never produced their own automobile, they nevertheless would deserve a place in the pantheon of Detroit's automotive industry notables. They played a vital role in the success of Ransom E. Olds during the brief time his company manufactured cars in Detroit. They played an even more critical role in the early success of the Ford Motor Company and in the remarkable growth and prosperity the firm achieved with the Model T. A successful Ford Motor Company without Dodge Brothers is inconceivable.

John and Horace Dodge's accomplishments as manufacturers of the Dodge Brothers automobiles and commercial cars should be recognized as having the same importance as the achievements of Ransom Olds, Henry Leland, and Walter Chrysler. Their production and marketing strategy set Dodge Brothers apart from the two dominant forces in the early Michigan automobile industry, the Ford Motor Company and General Motors. Dodge Brothers employed unique and progressive policies for working with their dealers and suppliers.

John and Horace Dodge were also "pillars of the community," each in his own unique way. John Dodge was involved in civic affairs through his service on the Detroit Water Commission and the Detroit Street Railway Commission, as well as through his involvement with state and city politics. Horace Dodge deserves much of the credit for creating a world-class Detroit Symphony Orchestra, which his family continued to support long after his death. John and Horace Dodge together had a greater involvement in Detroit's civic, cultural, and charitable arenas than other Detroit automakers, including Henry Ford. For all of these reasons, they deserve a more prominent place in the hall of automotive history than they have received to date.

Despite their remarkable accomplishments in the early Detroit automobile industry and their civic, cultural, and charitable contributions to Detroit in the early twentieth century, John and Horace Dodge remain obscure figures among historians and the general public alike. The Dodge name is widely recognized only because of the millions of automobiles and trucks that have carried the moniker. The general public knows nothing of the brothers and their work. Had their company and their widows not made the effort to memorialize them, they would be almost entirely forgotten. This writer could find no schools or highways named in their memory. Only three Michigan state parks have kept the "Dodge Brothers" name. Both brothers are members of the Automotive Hall of Fame (Dearborn, Michigan), inducted separately, Horace in 1981 and John in 1997.

John and Horace Dodge's descendants have taken some measures to ensure that they are remembered. In January 1946, their families made a gift of $130,000 to the Detroit Historical Commission to underwrite a "Dodge Hall of Industrial History" in the projected new Detroit Historical Museum. The museum followed the Dodge family's wishes when the new building opened in July 1951. Dodge Hall now serves as the home for the permanent "Motor City Exhibition," which tells the story of the automobile industry and its influence on Detroit.[6]

In October 1971, a year after Anna Thomson Dodge died, the Detroit City Council approved a plan for a $2 million "Horace E. Dodge and Son Memorial Fountain," to be built in the Philip Hart Plaza on the Detroit River and designed by the Japanese American sculptor Isamu Noguchi. The City of Detroit completed the project and dedicated the fountain on 24 July 1976. The Dodge Fountain plaque reads: "The Horace E. Dodge and Son Memorial Fountain. An Engine of Water at the Gateway to A Great City. Bequested to the City of Detroit by Anna Thomson Dodge in Memory of Her Husband and Son, Pioneer Automobile Industrialists." Unfortunately, the plaque is not found anywhere near the fountain, at least at the time this author was preparing this book. The Dodge Fountain has never worked properly and is so poorly maintained that it seldom works at all. It symbolizes the general neglect of the memory and achievements of these two red-haired brothers.[7]

APPENDIX:
EARLY DODGE FAMILY
HISTORY IN AMERICA

William Dodge (ca. 1604–ca. 1690), a native of Somersetshire, in England's West Country, came to America on the *Fleet,* landing in Salem, Massachusetts, some fifteen miles northeast of Boston, on 10 July 1629. The next four generations of this Dodge family line remained in the northeast coast of Massachusetts, living in Salem, Wenham, Beverly, and Ipswich.

The bare-bones family genealogy runs as follows: William Dodge moved six miles northeast of Salem to Wenham, where his second child, Captain William Dodge (1640–1720), spent his entire life. Captain William Dodge's seventh child, Robert Dodge (1686–1764), fathered ten children, the last of which was William Dodge (1732–1807), the fourth generation of this Dodge line in America. William Dodge was born in Beverly, but died in Newbury, New Hampshire, northwest of Concord, New Hampshire, and about seventy miles northwest of Beverly. Ezekiel Dodge (1782–1869), the tenth of twelve children of William Dodge, was born in Beverly, married Anna Cleves, born in Hamilton, Massachusetts, and appears in Ipswich in the 1840 census.[1]

Sometime in the 1840s, Ezekiel Dodge, the fifth generation of Dodges in America and the grandfather of John and Horace Dodge, moved from Ipswich to Newbury. Ezekiel and Anna Cleves Dodge (1783–1866) had thirteen children. Daniel Rugg Dodge (1819–1897), the father of John and Horace, was the eleventh. All of the New England Dodges were farmers.[2]

Ezekiel Dodge (age 69) appears in the U.S. Census of 1850 living in Newbury and married to Anna Cleves Dodge (age 68). His son Daniel Rugg Dodge (age 30) and his wife Lorinda Dodge (age 35) lived under his roof. The U.S. Census of 1860 shows Ezekiel (age 79) in Niles, Michigan, with his wife Anna (age 78). Living with Ezekiel was his son Daniel Rugg Dodge (age 40), the father of John and Horace Dodge, along with two of his minor children, Charles F. (age 5) and Laura Belle Dodge (age 3). Both children were born in New Hampshire, and Daniel was a widower. The date of Lorinda Dodge's death is not known, but the fact that her family did not bury her in any of the Niles cemeteries (Daniel Rugg Dodge and his second wife are buried in Niles) suggests that she died in New Hampshire. Her death may have prompted Daniel Dodge and the rest of his family to move from New Hampshire to Michigan.[3]

The precise timing of the arrival of the Dodge family in Niles is unknown, but by 1860 Daniel Dodge's older brother, Edwin A. Dodge (age 52), an older sister, Harriet C. Dodge (age 47), and a (slightly) younger brother, Caleb Kimball Dodge (age 38), were also in Niles. Edwin apparently left New Hampshire much earlier because in 1860, he had a son, Albert C. (age 22), and a daughter, Mary E. Dodge (age 11), both born in New York State. Caleb, on the other hand, in 1860 had a daughter, Marinetta Dodge (age 5), born in New Hampshire, but his son, Frank L. (age 1), was born in Michigan. It is possible that Ezekiel and son Daniel moved to Niles to join Ezekiel's other sons, who were already there. Both Edwin and Caleb Dodge listed their occupation as "machinist," as did Edwin's son Albert (age 22).

Ezekiel Dodge died in Niles on 11 March 1869 (age 87), more than two years after his wife Anna Cleves Dodge died on 24 November 1866. The cause of death listed for Ezekiel was "old age." His burial took place two days later in Silverbrook Cemetery in Niles. Ezekiel's sons remained in Niles until the early 1880s. In the 1870 census, Edwin A. Dodge (age 62) listed his occupation as "carpenter." He died on 15 December 1871 at age sixty-three, a victim of pneumonia. According to the census reports for 1870 and 1880, Caleb Kimball Dodge (1820–1882) remained in Niles, and in 1880 the census listed his occupation as "stand pipe and machinery." Apparently his first wife (Emily) died sometime before December 1866, when Caleb (age 46) married Mary R. Grant (age 24) of Niles. The 1880 census no longer listed Mary Grant Dodge or any of her children, but Caleb's sister, Harriet C. Dodge (age 67), was living with him. Caleb Kimball Dodge died in Niles on 4 July 1882 at age sixty-one, with "apoplexy" listed as the cause of death. Edwin Dodge and brother Caleb Kimball Dodge are found in Silverbrook Cemetery as well.[4]

NOTES

Chapter One

1. There are three book-length studies of the Dodge family: Jean Maddern Pitrone and Joan Potter Elwart, *The Dodges: The Auto Family Fortune and Misfortune* (South Bend, IN: Icarus, 1981); Jean Maddern Pitrone, *Tangled Web: Legacy of Auto Pioneer John F. Dodge* (Hamtramck, MI: Avenue, 1989); and Caroline Latham and David Agresta, *Dodge Dynasty: The Car and the Family That Rocked Detroit* (New York: Harcourt Brace Jovanovich, 1989). None of these authors is a professional historian, and their books lack scholarly documentation. In addition to their work on the Dodges, Jean Pitrone and Caroline Latham collectively have published a dozen books, mainly biographies, all nonscholarly in nature. David Agresta is an actor who became a Dodge family aficionado. All three books focus on the lives and often-scandalous behavior of the descendants of John and Horace Dodge. None of these books features the automotive history and accomplishments of the two brothers. The erroneous information on Ezekiel Dodge is in Latham and Agresta, *Dodge Dynasty*, 9–10.

2. U.S. Census of Population, 1860, Michigan, Berrien County, Niles City, pp. 251, 259; U.S. Census of Population, 1870, Michigan, Berrien County, Niles City, p. 286R; and U.S. Census of Population, 1880, Michigan, Berrien County, Niles City, p. 269. Latham and Agresta, *Dodge Dynasty*, 10–11, make several egregious errors in their discussion of the marriage between Daniel Dodge and Maria Casto. They claim that Maria was three years his junior, when she was really sixteen years younger. They also state that she married Daniel Dodge shortly after both her parents died in 1859, but they were both listed in the U.S. Census of 1860 as still alive. Daniel Dodge appears in the 1860 census as unmarried. Indie Casto's middle name appears on her headstone at Silverbrook Cemetery in Niles as "Duvall," and the death dates for her and her husband William Casto are given as 1860 on their headstones. I have not been able to find any record of the marriage of Daniel Rugg Dodge to Maria Casto. Since the 1860 census was completed in July, if they married in 1860, it was later in the year.

3. Pitrone and Elwart, *The Dodges*, 3, 6; Latham and Agresta, *Dodge Dynasty*, 10; *Michigan State Gazetteer and Business Directory for 1867–8* (Detroit: Detroit Post, 1867), 318; *Michigan State Business Directory, 1870–71* (Detroit: Tribune Printing, 1870), 290; Ed. B. Cowles, comp., *Berrien County Directory and History, 1871* (Niles, MI: Ed. B. Cowles, Compiler and Publisher, 1871), 84; *Directory of Niles and the Principal Villages in Berrien County, 1874–75* (Detroit: Burch, Montgomery, 1874), 30; *Michigan State Gazetteer and Business Directory for 1875* (Detroit: Tribune Printing, 1875), 586; *Michigan State Gazetteer and Business Directory for 1877* (Detroit: R. L. Polk, 1867), 318; and *Michigan State Gazetteer and Business Directory, 1879* (Detroit: R. L. Polk, 1879), 848.

4. *Michigan State Gazetteer and Business Directory, 1881* (Detroit: R. L. Polk, 1881), 878; and *Michigan State Gazetteer and Business Directory, 1883* (Detroit: R. L. Polk, 1883), 1169.

5. Sanborn Map and Publishing Company, *Insurance Maps of Niles, Michigan* (New York: Sanborn Map and Publishing, 1884, 1889, 1900); *Michigan State Gazetteer and Business Directory,*

1885 (Detroit: R. L. Polk, 1885), 1254; and *Niles, Mich., 1889* (bird's-eye drawing), drawn and published by C. J. Pauli & Company, 726 Central Avenue, Milwaukee.

6. "Former Niles Men Made Good: John and H. E. Dodge Now of Detroit Worth $50,000,000," *Niles Daily Star,* 9 August 1913, 1; and "Mayor Bonine Summons City Officials to Do Honor to Memory of the Late John Dodge," typescript found in the vertical file "Dodge Brothers," Niles Community Library.

7. A unique perspective on Henry Ford's childhood is recounted by his sister Margaret Ford Ruddiman in "Memories of My Brother Henry Ford," *Michigan History* 37 (September 1953): 225–75. The quote is from "Former Niles Men Made Good."

8. Pitrone and Elwart, *The Dodges,* 3, 6; and Latham and Agresta, *Dodge Dynasty,* 8, 11, 14.

9. U.S. Census of Population, 1860, Michigan, Berrien County, Niles City, Second Ward, p. 262; U.S. Census of Population, 1870, Michigan, Berrien County, Niles City, Second Ward, p. 298; U.S. Census of Population, 1880, Michigan, Berrien County, Niles City, p. 31; and Pitrone and Elwart, *The Dodges,* 4–5. Pitrone and Elwart misidentify the wealthy man as John S. Tuttle; Joseph S. is correct.

10. Pitrone and Elwart, *The Dodges,* 4; *Directory of Niles and the Principal Villages in Berrien County, 1874–75,* 49; "A School Incident," in typescript, "Mayor Bonine Summons City Officials," n.p.; and "Johnny Dodge in '76 Tussled with His Arithmetic," *Niles Daily Star,* 24 March 1936.

11. U.S. Census of Population, 1880, Michigan, Berrien County, Niles City, p. 264D; Pitrone and Elwart, *The Dodges,* 5–6; Latham and Agresta, *Dodge Dynasty,* 12; "They Knew John Dodge," *Detroit News,* 17 January 1920, 7; "Mayor Bonine Summons City Officials"; and "City Suspends Business to Honor Negro Drayman," *Detroit News,* 26 January 1927, 25. Both of the family histories have misidentified Tom Davis as the employer. In his August 1913 interview with the *Niles Daily Star,* John Dodge mentioned driving a cow for fifty cents a week and later carrying sacks of bran out of freight cars "*with* Tom Davis."

12. Pitrone and Elwart, *The Dodges,* 5; U.S. Census of Population, 1880, Michigan, Berrien County, Niles City, 268D; and "Mayor Bonine Summons City Officials." In a newspaper article published at the time of John Dodge's death in January 1920, Cyrus Bowles's last name is spelled "Boles."

13. U.S. Census of Population, 1880, Michigan, Berrien County, Niles City, p. 260D; and Pitrone and Elwart, *The Dodges,* 5. The U.S. Census of 1880 includes Frederick Bonine, age sixteen, the son of the physician Evan J. Bonine.

14. Pitrone and Elwart, *The Dodges,* 4–5; and Latham and Agresta, *Dodge Dynasty,* 11.

15. Letter, John F. Dodge to Lloyd Brothers Company, Toledo, 21 June 1912, letter books, MBHA.

16. "Former Niles Men Made Good"; and "The 'Dodge Boys' Started Here," *Niles Daily Star,* 9 July 1979. Latham and Agresta, *Dodge Dynasty,* 15, claim that the proposed gift was only $50,000 and was offered in 1917.

17. William Taylor, Jr., *An American Colossus: A Small Town, a River and a Railroad Yard* (Niles, MI: Niles Railroad Historical Association, 1995), 125, 126; "Building Boom Shows Gains of 151 New Houses," *Niles Daily Star,* 31 July 1919; *Luedders' Historical and Pictorial City Directory of Niles, Michigan, July 1925* (Coldwater, MI: Otto E. Luedders, 1925), 21; and "Did You Know, . . ." *Niles Daily Star,* 9 July 1979.

18. Brenda Beadenkope, "Niles Honors Native Sons with Historic Marker," *Niles Daily Star,* 18 November 1996. The marker came as a result of efforts by the Dodge Brothers Club, particularly John Velliky, and several local historians and enthusiasts.

19. Joseph S. Tuttle obituary, *Niles Daily Star,* 24 June 1921, 2; "Good Old Days in Niles, Fifteen Years Ago," *Niles Daily Star,* 2 September 1925; Stirling Bowen, "Niles, Stunned by Grief, Mourns Its Favored Son," *Detroit News,* 17 January 1920, 7; and "Mayor Bonine Summons City Officials."

20. Latham and Agresta, *Dodge Dynasty,* 15–17; Pitrone and Elwart, *The Dodges,* 6–7.

21. Jack Norbeck, *Encyclopedia of American Steam Traction Engines,* 3rd rev. ed., ed. George H. Dammann (Sarasota, FL: Crestline, 1984), 209; and Eugene H. Moak, "Brief History of Port Huron Engine & Thresher Company," 15 December 1982, p. 55, typescript found in the Michigan Room, St. Clair County Library, Port Huron, Michigan.

22. *Battle Creek and Marshall City Directories, 1882* (Coldwater, MI: A. G. Needham, 1882); and *Battle Creek City Directory for 1884* (Battle Creek, MI: W. F. Curtis, 1884), 96, 189.

23. *Battle Creek Daily Moon,* 6 March 1884, 4; 13 August 1884, 5; 25 October 1884, 4; and 25 November 1884, 4.

24. *Port Huron and St. Clair County Directory, 1883* (Port Huron, MI: C. E. Meech, 1883); *Port Huron City and St. Clair County Directory for 1885* (Detroit: R. L. Polk, 1885), 171; and *Port Huron and St. Clair County Directory, 1888* (Detroit: R. L. Polk, 1888), 175. The directories and the manuscript "1884 Michigan Census for St. Clair County" are found in the Michigan Room of the St. Clair County Library.

25. Moak, "Brief History of Port Huron Engine & Thresher Company," 55, 65; William L. Jenks, *St. Clair County, Michigan: Its History and Its People* (Chicago: Lewis, 1912), 2:785; and "Death Claims Eugene Moak: Prominent Industrialist Dies in Home Wednesday," Port Huron *Times-Herald,* 1 September 1930, 1.

26. *Detroit City Directory for 1888* (Detroit: R. L. Polk, 1888), 482; and Latham and Agresta, *Dodge Dynasty,* 19.

27. *Detroit City Directory for 1880* (Detroit: R. L. Polk, 1880), 126; *Detroit City Directory for 1882* (Detroit: R. L. Polk, 1882), 128, 735; "John Dodge's Life Story: A Man of Terrific Energy," *Detroit News,* 20 October 1915, 12; Pitrone and Elwart, *The Dodges,* 8; and Latham and Agresta, *Dodge Dynasty,* 17–18.

28. "Quit Brother's Door for Death: John F. Dodge Stayed Near Horace's Sickroom until Stricken," *Detroit News,* 16 January 1920, 1, 2.

29. "A Canvass of the Agricultural Implement and Iron Working Industries of Detroit," in *Eighth Annual Report (1890) of the Bureau of Labor and Industrial Statistics of the State of Michigan* (Lansing: W. S. George, State Printers, 1891), 116–19.

30. Parke, Davis & Company, *Complete Catalogue of the Products of the Laboratories of Parke, Davis & Co.* (Detroit: Parke, Davis, 1954), 210, describes the contents of Elixir 130. Latham and Agresta, *Dodge Dynasty,* 25–26, and Pitrone and Elwart, *The Dodges,* 10, identify the medicine as Formula 131, probably repeating the mistaken memory of some Dodge family member. There is no record of Parke, Davis ever producing a Formula 131.

31. Mrs. Wilfred C. Leland and Minnie Dubbs Millbrook, *Master of Precision: Henry M. Leland* (Detroit: Wayne State University Press, 1966), 55.

32. *Detroit City Directory for 1891* (Detroit: R. L. Polk, 1891), 1758; *Detroit City Directory for 1894* (Detroit: R. L. Polk, 1894), 2040; *Windsor Directory, Including Sandwich and Walkerville* (Ingersoll, Ontario: Union, 1894), 31–32, 36; and Pitrone and Elwart, *The Dodges,* 9.

33. Walter G. Griffith Reminiscences, October 1951, 2–5, Ford Motor Company Oral History Project, HF.

34. Latham and Agresta, *Dodge Dynasty,* 24–25; and U.S. Patent Office, "Horace E. Dodge and John F. Dodge, of Detroit, Michigan, Bicycle-Bearing, Specification Forming Part of Letters Patent

No. 567,851, dated September 15, 1896. Application filed July 20, 1895. Serial No. 556,595. (No model)." This is the only example of Horace's name appearing before John's on any document where both are listed. The advertisement for the E. & D. Bicycle appeared in the Windsor *Evening Record*, 16 April 1896, 1.

35. *Windsor Directory* for 1896, 20, 31, 35; 1897–98, 18, 29, 34; and 1899, 17, 27, 32; *1899 Business and Professional Directory of Detroit and Surrounding Towns* (N.p., 1899), 439, 451; and Latham and Agresta, *Dodge Dynasty*, 27. John Dodge's personal E. & D. Bicycle, which he supposedly rode to work until 1905, is in the collections of the Detroit Historical Museum.

36. "The Evans and Dodge Bicycle: Scores High in New York; Its Distinct Features a Revelation to the American Manufacturers and Riders," Windsor *Evening Record*, 16 February 1897, 4; "Typograph Works: Great Activity in Our Bicycle Factory," *Evening Record*, 19 November 1897; "City Siftings," *Evening Record*, 11 January 1898, 8; Neil F. Morrison, *Garden Gateway to Canada: One Hundred Years of Windsor and Essex County, 1854–1954* (Toronto: Ryerson, 1954), 159–60; and "New Bicycle Riding School at the Windsor Curling Rink," Windsor *Evening Record*, 31 March 1898, 5.

37. Glen Norcliffe, *The Ride to Modernity: The Bicycle in Canada, 1869–1900* (Toronto: University of Toronto Press, 2001), 107, 113; William Humber, *Freewheeling: The Story of Bicycling in Canada* (Erin, Ontario: Boston Mills, 1986), 55; and "Mr. Evans Leaves Today: Mr. Dodge Is Removing Machinery at Indianapolis to Hamilton," (Windsor) *Evening Record*, 18 December 1899, 4.

38. C. B. Glasscock, *The Gasoline Age: The Story of the Men Who Made It* (New York: Bobbs-Merrill, 1937), 200–201, and Theodore F. MacManus and Norman Beasley, *Men, Money, and Motors: The Drama of the Automobile* (New York: Harper and Brothers, 1929), 22–24, offer chronologies that differ by a year. Glasscock has John Dodge assuming control of the National Cycle plant in Hamilton in December 1899. MacManus and Beasley claim that John Dodge became the manager in Hamilton in January 1899 and resigned from National Cycle a year later, which would have made John and Horace "at liberty" for all of 1900. This is an improbable scenario because the Dodges started their machine shop in Detroit no earlier than October 1900. The Glasscock chronology fits the remaining facts much better.

39. Norcliffe, *Ride to Modernity*, 113–14; Glasscock, *Gasoline Age*, 201.

40. Pitrone and Elwart, *The Dodges*, 9–10; Latham and Agresta, *Dodge Dynasty*, 20; and *Detroit City Directory for 1893* (Detroit: R. L. Polk, 1893), 428.

41. Pitrone and Elwart, *The Dodges*, 11–13; Latham and Agresta, *Dodge Dynasty*, 20–22; *Detroit City Directory for 1893*, 428; *Detroit City Directory for 1894*, 459; *Detroit City Directory for 1898* (Detroit: R. L. Polk, 1898), 507; and *Detroit City Directory for 1899* (Detroit: R. L. Polk, 1899), 520. Anna's name on her marriage certificate (29 July 1896) is "Thompson."

42. Latham and Agresta, *Dodge Dynasty*, 27–29; Glasscock, *Gasoline Age*, 201; Pitrone and Elwart, *The Dodges*, 12; and Norcliffe, *Ride to Modernity*, 115.

43. *Detroit City Directory for 1901* (Detroit: R. L. Polk, 1901), 164, 545.

44. "Dodge Bros.' New Establishment, One of the Most Complete Machine Shops in Michigan—Everything New and Up to Date. Builders of Special Machinery and High Speed Pleasure Yachts," *Detroit Free Press*, 1 September 1901, pt. 2, p. 6; "John Dodge's Life Story: A Man of Terrific Energy," *Detroit News*, 20 October 1915, 12; Leland and Millbrook, *Master of Precision*, 61. "Dodge Brothers' New Auto Parts Plant Occupies 24 Acres: Most Modern Manufacturing Facilities Known to the Industrial World," *Detroit News*, 15 January 1911, Automobile Section, 21. A Dodge Brothers invoice book with entries starting in October 1900 confirms the earlier start-up. Dodge Brothers letterhead used in 1925 included "Dodge Brothers Detroit, U.S.A.," in large typeface, followed by "Established 1900." John Parsons collection, Falls Church, Virginia.

45. George S. May, *R. E. Olds: Auto Industry Pioneer* (Grand Rapids, MI: Eerdmans, 1977), 157. An article, "Wonderful Plant of the Dodge Brothers in Detroit," *Michigan Manufacturer and Financial Record* 13 (26 April 1914): 1, states that the Dodge machine shop in the Boydell Building dated from 1900.

46. Ibid., 20–122, passim.

47. Ibid., 155–58, 177–83.

48. The invoice book is held in the archives of Oakland University's Meadow Brook Hall, Rochester, Michigan.

49. "Dodge Bros.' New Establishment."

50. "Dodge Brothers as Quality Producers of Cars," *Automobile Topics* 34 (13 June 1914): 379.

51. *Detroit City Directory for 1901,* 164; and "Dodge Bros.' New Establishment."

52. "Quit Brother's Door for Death," 2. According to the booklet published by Dillon, Read & Company, *The Dodge Dollar: Dodge Brothers Carry Goodwill on the Balance Sheet at One Dollar* (New York: Bowne, 1925), n.p., Vocelle, who was general superintendent of the forge and foundry, had worked for Dodge Brothers for twenty-five years. This volume is found in the John Parsons collection.

53. John F. Polacsek, "The Dodge Fleet of Lake St. Clair," in *Tonnancour: Life in Grosse Pointe and Along the Shores of Lake St. Clair,* ed. Arthur M. Woodford (Detroit: Omnigraphics, 1994), 91; "Flames Lick Up Eight Launches: Fire in Studer's Boat Works Did $25,000 Damage before Checked. Dodge Bros.'s Flyer, Olds's Racing Boat and Other New Power Craft Gone," *Detroit News,* 15 June 1904, 1; and Ineke Bruynooghe, *Chronicle of Horace Dodge's Steam Yacht SS Delphine* (Roeslare, Belgium: Crea Printing Industries, 2003), 30–32. The Bruynooghe book mislabels a photograph of the 1901 *Lotus,* identifying it as the 1904 *Lotus.*

54. "John Dodge's Life Story: A Man of Terrific Energy, Rose from Work Bench; Knows Men," *Detroit News,* 20 October 1915, 12.

Chapter Two

1. Leland and Millbrook, *Master of Precision,* 61–63.

2. Ibid., and May, *R. E. Olds,* 157–59.

3. Frederick L. Smith, *Motoring Down a Quarter of a Century* (Detroit: Detroit Saturday Night, 1928), 18; Latham and Agresta, *Dodge Dynasty,* 32–33; and Pitrone and Elwart, *The Dodges,* 15. Oldsmobile production figures are from Helen Jones Early and James R. Walkinshaw, *Setting the Pace: Oldsmobile's First 100 Years* (Lansing, MI: Oldsmobile Division of General Motors Corporation, 1996), 461.

4. City of Detroit, indexes to building permits issued by the Detroit Fire Marshall, 1880–1908, Microfilm No. 960, Permit No. 1084, issued 8 September 1902 for 238–240 Monroe Avenue, found in the Burton Historical Collection, Detroit Public Library; *Detroit City Directory for 1903* (Detroit: R. L. Polk, 1903), 861; and *Cycle and Automobile Trade Journal,* June 1903, 62, 63. The Dodge plant, with the new address (after 1920) of 682–714 Monroe Avenue, was demolished in the early 1960s for construction of the Walter P. Chrysler Expressway (Interstate 75).

5. Pitrone and Elwart, *The Dodges,* 17; Milo M. Quaife, *The Life of John Wendell Anderson* (Detroit: privately printed, 1950), 96–97; Reminiscence of John Wandersee, 6, Ford Motor Company Oral History Collection, HF; and "Horace Dodge Dies in Southern Home," *Automobile Topics* 60 (18 December 1920): 491, 498.

6. MacManus and Beasley, *Men, Money, and Motors,* 28; and Harry Barnard, *Independent Man: The Life of Senator James Couzens* (New York: Charles Scribner's Sons, 1958), 38.

7. "Memorandum of Agreement, John F. Dodge & Horace E. Dodge and Henry Ford & Alex. Y. Malcomson, Ford Motor Company, 28 February 1903," file 1, box 1, accession 95, "Agreements and Notes," HF; and Allan Nevins, with the collaboration of Frank Ernest Hill, *Ford: The Times, the Man, the Company* (New York: Charles Scribner's Sons, 1954), 228–32, 240.

8. MacManus and Beasley, *Men, Money, and Motors,* 29–31.

9. Ibid., 28–29. Unfortunately, MacManus and Beasley never specify where the advertisement appeared. A two-page ad for "The Fordmobile" appeared in the June 1903 issue of *Cycle and Automobile Trade Journal,* 44A–45, but with no such claim attached. However, an article on the Ford Motor Company in that same issue (p. 62), claims that 80 percent of the first 650 chassis built by Dodge Brothers for Ford were already completed.

10. "Ford Motor Company," *Cycle and Automobile Trade Journal,* June 1903, 61–63; and "Ford Motor Co.: It Has Been Organized to Build Autos under Ford's Patents," *Detroit Evening News,* 19 June 1903, 11.

11. Nevins and Hill, *Ford: The Times, the Man, the Company,* 235–38.

12. Donald Finlay Davis, *Conspicuous Production: Automobiles and Elites in Detroit, 1899–1933* (Philadelphia: Temple University Press, 1988), 94, 234n. 22.

13. Nevins and Hill, *Ford: The Times, the Man, the Company,* 231; John F. Dodge and Horace E. Dodge v. the Ford Motor Company, Appeal from the Circuit Court for the County of Wayne in Chancery, Michigan Supreme Court, *Record,* vol. 2, *Amended Bill of Complaint,* 26 April 1917, 507–9; and May, *R. E. Olds,* 201–3.

14. Dodge and Dodge v. the Ford Motor Company, 507–9.

15. John F. Dodge and Horace E. Dodge v. Henry Ford et al., State of Michigan, in the Circuit Court for the County of Wayne, Michigan Supreme Court, *Record,* vol. 1, pt. B, Transcript of Testimony Taken Before Samuel L. May, Circuit Court Commissioner, Testimony of 14 November 1916, pp. 109–11; and Glasscock, *The Gasoline Age,* 64.

16. Letter, John Wendell Anderson to Wendell Abram Anderson, 4 June 1903, J. W. Anderson MSS, accession 71, HF; Nevins and Hill, *Ford: The Times, the Man, the Company,* 230, 236, 238, 242, 615n. 23; and Quaife, *Life of John Wendell Anderson,* 102. The letter of 4 June 1903 is reprinted on pp. 94–102.

17. Nevins and Hill, *Ford: The Times, the Man, the Company,* 247.

18. August Degener Notebook, accession 187, HF; and Fred Rockelman Reminiscences, August 1952, 28, Ford Motor Company Oral History Project, HF.

19. Ford Motor Company, minutes of directors' meetings of 7 December 1903 and 22 August 1904, Minute Book, Secretary's Records, box 1, accession 85, HF; and Barnard, *Independent Man,* 60–61.

20. The time and pay records covering September 1903 to May 1906 are contained in a single large volume, which is found in the DCHC. For the Dodge brothers' boat-building activities, see Pitrone and Elwart, *The Dodges,* 29–30, 75, 110–11.

21. Nevins and Hill, *Ford: The Times, the Man, the Company,* 328.

22. Ibid., 231, 251.

23. Letter, James Couzens to the Dodge Brothers, 21 April 1906, box 1, Dodge Brothers Correspondence, 1904–1920, accession 893, HF.

24. John Wandersee Reminiscence, 13, 15–17.

25. Nevins and Hill, *Ford: The Times, the Man, the Company,* 279–83, 330, 340, 646; Ford Motor

Company, minutes of directors' meeting of 9 January 1906, Minute Book, Secretary's Records, box 1, accession 85, HF; and John Wandersee Reminiscence, 17. The Model K, manufactured from 1 October 1906 to 30 September 1908, was available in touring car and roadster versions, both retailing for $2,800.

26. Nevins and Hill, *Ford: The Times, the Man, the Company*, 272, 644; and letter, Ford Motor Company to Dodge Brothers, 3 January 1907, box 1, Dodge Brothers Correspondence, 1904–1920, accession 893, HF. For a detailed history of the Ford Piquette Avenue plant, see Trent E. Boggess, "The Piquette Avenue Plant: Birthplace of the Model T," *The Vintage Ford* 33 (November–December 1998): 15–27.

27. *Detroit City Directory for 1910* (Detroit: R. L. Polk, 1910), 2774; City of Detroit, indexes to building permits, 1908–1920, vol. 4, Permit No. 237, issued 2 February 1904 for 226–234 Monroe Avenue, found in the Burton Historical Collection, Detroit Public Library; letter, Dodge Brothers to Edison Illuminating Company, 24 February 1911, MBHA; and "Dodge Brothers' New Auto Parts Plant." The job records of Field, Hinchman & Smith are in the historical files of Smith, Hinchman & Smith (now the Smith Group) in Detroit. The Meadow Brook Hall Archives contain examples of early Dodge Brothers letterhead.

28. Nevins and Hill, *Ford: The Times, the Man, the Company*, 649.

29. Pitrone and Elwart, *The Dodges*, 13; and Agreement, Woodward Lawn Cemetery Association and John F. Dodge and Horace E. Dodge, 28 August 1901, folder "Cemetery Agreement," MBHA.

30. Pitrone and Elwart, *The Dodges*, 13, 25. John Dodge was so successful at keeping the marriage secret that Pitrone and Elwart were the first to publish evidence of it.

31. Ibid., 16–17, 25, 29, 33.

32. Ibid., 33–34, 66, 77, 92.

33. Ibid., 29, 38–39, 41; Thomas J. Holleman and James P. Gallagher, *Smith, Hinchman & Grylls: 125 Years of Architecture and Engineering, 1853–1978* (Detroit: Wayne State University Press, 1978), 63, 69–70; and W. Hawkins Ferry, *The Legacy of Albert Kahn* (Detroit: Wayne State University Press, 1987), 17, 77–79.

34. "Harsha Sells $100,000 Site: Deposed U.S. Clerk Gets Big Sum for Property Bought by Dodge Bros.," *Detroit News*, 18 September 1909, 1; "Dodge Bros. New Factory on Chene Street Will Be a Complete and Modern Structure," *Detroit News*, 31 July 1910, Financial Section, 1; and "Dodge Brothers' New Auto Parts Plant."

35. Grant Hildebrand, *Designing for Industry: The Architecture of Albert Kahn* (Cambridge, MA: MIT Press, 1974) barely mentions the Dodge factory. The archives of Albert Kahn Associates include the original drawings for the major buildings. For a detailed history of Dodge Main, see Charles K. Hyde, "'Dodge Main' and the Detroit Automobile Industry, 1910–1980," *Detroit in Perspective* 6 (spring 1982): 1–21.

36. The diary is found in MBHA.

37. "Dodge Brothers' New Auto Parts Plant."

38. "Dodge Bros. New Factory on Chene Street"; and "Dodge Brothers' New Auto Parts Plant."

39. Letters, Dodge Bros. to Detroit Illuminating Company, 6 March 1911; Dodge Bros. to Charles D. Fisk, 10 July 1911; and Dodge Bros. to Howard B. Bloomer, 24 July 1911, all found at MBHA; and *Detroit City Directory for 1911* (Detroit: R. L. Polk, 1911), 2858; *Detroit City Directory for 1912* (Detroit: R. L. Polk, 1912), 3072; *Detroit City Directory for 1913* (Detroit: R. L. Polk, 1913), 2578; and *Detroit City Directory for 1914* (Detroit: R. L. Polk, 1914), 2782.

40. "Dodge Brothers as Quality Producers of Cars," 383, 384; Hyde, "'Dodge Main,'" 4: and E. F. Lake, "A Modern Heat-Treatment Plant: New Features in Dodge Bros. Heat-Treatment Shop—

Cyanide Hardening," *Machinery* 21 (September 1914): 1–7. For a detailed, building-by-building history of the Dodge plant, see Charles K. Hyde, "Dodge Brothers Motor Car Company Plant," historical report completed for the National Architectural and Engineering Record, December 1980. The report can be found in the Library of Congress, the State of Michigan Archives, the Walter Reuther Library, and the NAHC.

41. Letters, Dodge Bros. to Albert Kahn, 7 March 1911, 14 and 30 September 1911, and 13 December 1911, MBHA.

42. Letters, Horace E. Dodge to Albert Kahn, 3 October 1911 and 3 February 1912, MBHA; Horace E. Dodge to Louis Kahn, 10 February 1912, MBHA.

43. "Dodge Brothers as Quality Producers of Cars," 377; "Wonderful Plant of the Dodge Brothers in Detroit," in *Made in Michigan,* a special expanded issue of *Michigan Manufacturer and Financial Record* 13 (25 April 1914): 73; and "The Tremendous Plant Created by the Dodge Brothers," *Michigan Manufacturer and Financial Record* 14 (8 August 1914): 4–7. The claim that the Dodges accounted for 60 percent of the value of Ford cars is on p. 4.

44. "Tremendous Plant," 383–84.

45. Ibid.

46. Lindy Biggs, *The Rational Factory: Architecture, Technology, and Work in America's Age of Mass Production* (Baltimore: Johns Hopkins University Press, 1996), 109–13; and Horace Lucien Arnold and Fay Leone Faurote, *Ford Methods and the Ford Shops* (New York: Engineering Magazine, 1915), 25–26.

47. John F. Dodge to James Couzens, 10 December 1915, box 2, James Couzens Papers, Manuscript Division, Library of Congress. I thank my colleague Philip P. Mason for bringing this letter to my attention.

48. Glasscock, *The Gasoline Age,* 210.

49. Letters, James Couzens, Secretary & Treasurer, to John Dodge, 6 and 15 June 1911, Dodge Brothers Correspondence, 1904–1920, box 1, accession 893, HF; Thomas Klug, e-mail correspondence with author regarding Dodge Brothers membership in EAD, 9 April 2002; "One Year in Detroit's Open Shops," an address by Frank P. Johnson to the members of the EAD on 17 February 1914, reprinted in *Detroit Saturday Night,* 7 March 1914, lists Dodge Brothers as members; and Steve Babson, *Working Detroit: The Making of a Union Town* (Detroit: Wayne State University Press, 1986), 20–21, 23, 31–33.

50. Letter, Dodge Bros. to Employers Association of Detroit, 13 May 1911; "#6 Reports," 13 May 1913; "R.M.W. Reports," 14 May 1913; and "#105 Reports," 14 May 1913, all in the MBHA.

51. John Dodge to A. Vocelle, Supt., Dodge Brothers, 6 November 1911, MBHA.

52. Dodge Bros. to Edward Russell, Hamtramck, 12 July 1912, MBHA.

53. William W. Lutz, "Beer on Job Proved Just a Bust, He Recalls," *Detroit News,* 22 January 1961, 13-A.

54. *Thirty-First Annual Report of the Department of Labor of the State of Michigan* (Lansing, MI: Wynkoop Hallenbeck Crawford, State Printers, 1914), 188, 221; "The Wonderful Plant of the Dodge Brothers in Detroit," *Michigan Manufacturer and Financial Record* 12 (27 January 1913): 1; "Wonderful Plant," *Michigan Manufacturer and Financial Record* 13 (25 April 1914): 1; "Tremendous Plant," 6; "Dodge Brothers as Quantity Producers of Cars," 377, 379; and H. Cole Estep, "How Dodge Brothers Plant Was Reorganized," *Iron Trade Review* 56 (6 May 1915): 909.

55. Letter, Dodge Bros. to Ford Motor Company, Attention Mr. C. H. Wills, 21 February 1911, MBHA.

56. Letter, Dodge Bros. to Ford Motor Company, Attention Mr. James Couzens, 22 April 1911, and Dodge Bros. to Ford Motor Company, Attention Mr. Diehn, 26 July 1911, MBHA.

57. Letter, John F. Dodge to Henry Ford, President of Ford Motor Company, 4 June 1912, MBHA. He began the letter, "Dear Henry."

58. *Ford Times,* 5, no. 2 (April–May 1912): 224.

59. "Agreement between the Ford Motor Company and the Dodge Brothers, July 1913," folder 7, box 1, Agreements and Notes, accession 95, HF. This contract does not mention a one-year's notice for cancellation and is not dated or signed, suggesting that it was the contract canceled when Dodge Brothers gave a one-year's notice of cancellation.

60. Letter, Dodge Brothers to James Couzens, Secretary and Treasurer of the Ford Motor Company, 17 July 1913, Dodge Brothers Correspondence, 1904–1920, box 1, accession 893, HF; and Ford Motor Company, Minutes of the Board of Directors, 18 and 21 August 1913, Secretary's Minute Book, box 1, accession 85, HF.

61. Richard Crabb, *Birth of a Giant: The Men and Incidents That Gave America the Motor Car* (New York: Chilton Book Company, 1969), 348–49.

62. MacManus and Beasley, *Men, Money, and Motors,* 172–74.

63. "Dodge Brothers to Manufacture Complete Cars," *The Horseless Age* 32 (20 August 1913): 288; and "News from Detroit: Dodge Company, Which Furnishes Ford Parts, to Build Own Car," *Motor Field* 27 (September 1913): 27. Early postcards of the Dodge factory before the 1914 expansion show two rows of houses immediately south of the plant.

Chapter Three

1. W.A.P. John, "His Job Came First: Why Frederick J. Haynes, President of Dodge Brothers, Sums Up His Business Philosophy by Saying That 'The Man Whose Job Comes First When Occasion Demands, Gives the Orders in the End,'" *Motor* 38 (September 1922): 51, and biography form, *Detroit News,* ca. 1922. In the biography form, Haynes indicated that he graduated from Cornell University, class of 1895, but all the other sources say that he never earned his degree.

2. John, "His Job Came First," 88.

3. Ibid., 88, 90; and B. C. Forbes and O. D. Foster, *Automotive Giants of America: Men Who Are Making Our Motor Industry* (New York: B. C. Forbes, 1926), 122–23.

4. John, "His Job Came First," 90; and Sinclair Powell, *The Franklin Automobile Company* (Warrentown, PA: Society of Automotive Engineers, 1999), 54–55.

5. Letters, John F. Dodge to Frederick J. Haynes, 18 and 22 April, 15 May, and 7 June 1912, MBHA; and John, "His Job Came First," 90.

6. "Dodges Will Manufacture Cars," *Motor World* 31 (23 May 1912): 28; and "Dodges to Manufacture a Six: Car to Appear Soon, Despite Rumors of Its Abandonment—Relations with Ford Company Remain Unchanged," *Motor World* 32 (22 August 1912): 5.

7. "Dodge Brothers to Manufacture Complete Cars," 287; "News from Detroit: Dodge Company, Which Furnishes Ford Parts, to Build Own Car," 27; "Two More Immense Plants for Detroit: Dodge Bros. to Withdraw from the Ford Co. and Start Manufacture of the Dodge Car, Similar to the Ford," *Detroit News,* 16 August 1913, 1; "Dodge Plans Further Disclosed," *Automobile Topics* 33 (28 February 1914): 168; and Powell, *The Franklin Automobile Company,* photographs on 134, 150.

8. "Granddaddy of Them All," *Chrysler Motors Magazine* 2 (January 1936): 10; and Don Butler, "Dodge Brothers: 'Good Enough Is Not Acceptable,'" *Car and Parts* 22 (April 1979): 48.

9. Dodge Brothers, *Directors' Minutes,* meeting of 1 July 1914; Special Meeting of the Stockholders of Dodge Brothers, 1 November 1917; and Special Meeting of the Board of Directors of Dodge Brothers, 26 December 1919, all in banker's box "Dodge Brothers 1," DCHC.

10. David Smith, "How John and Horace Made Good: The Untold Story of the Dodge Boys," *Detroit Free Press,* 17 April 1966, 13; Pitrone and Elwart, *The Dodges,* 62. Butler, "Dodge Brothers: 'Good Enough Is Not Acceptable,'" 50, cites Fred Lamborn, longtime Dodge Brothers machinist, as the source of information about John Dodge's methods for testing tires.

11. The notebooks are found in the Dodge Brothers company files in the NAHC. A printed note, "Property of Theodore T. Heidloff (Registered)," is taped to each of the three volumes. The notebooks include scores of vendors' calling cards, indicating an attempt to call on Haynes. Several lists of topics to be discussed with John F. Dodge, plus lists of factories visited in other cities, strongly suggest that Frederick Haynes was the author.

12. "Dodge Brothers as Quality Producers of Cars," 386, 389.

13. "Tremendous Plant," 5; Estep, "How Dodge Brothers Plant Was Reorganized," 909, 913, 946b; "Dodge Brothers to Erect Huge New Building," *Detroit News,* 16 October 1914, 18; Niran Bates Pope, *Dodge Brothers Works* (Detroit: Dodge Brothers, 1920), 18; and Holleman and Gallagher, *Smith, Hinchman & Grylls,* 75, 84, 94, 129. For a comprehensive history of the Dodge Brothers plant in Hamtramck, see Hyde, "'Dodge Main,'" 1–21.

14. Estep, "How Dodge Brothers Plant Was Reorganized," 909–16, 946b.

15. Ibid., 912–15.

16. *National Cyclopedia of American Biography* (New York: James T. White, 1926), 19:267; and Estep, "How Dodge Brothers Plant Was Reorganized," 913–16.

17. Niran Bates Pope, *Dodge Brothers Works* (N.p., n.d.), 7–8, Dodge Brothers corporate files, NAHC.

18. "Dodge Brothers as Quality Producers of Cars," 377; and Niran Bates Pope, *Dodge Brothers Works* (1920), pamphlet in the Dodge Brothers File, 4, NAHC.

19. "Dodge Brothers Choose Philp: Select Studebaker Sales Manager as General Manager of Sales—Deliveries to Commence in September—Sales Organization Plan," *Automobile Topics* 33 (18 April 1914): 713; "Assigning Men to Dodge Districts: Representatives of Dodge Brothers Start Out in Interest of the New Car—Philp Announces Additional Selections for Sales Department," *Automobile Topics* 33 (13 June 1914): 363; "Dodge Brothers Completes Organization of District Representatives," *Automobile Topics* 34 (4 July 1914): 626; "Dodge Brothers Reveal the Car They Will Make," *Automobile Topics* 35 (7 November 1914): 905; "Tremendous Plant," 6–7; and Sydney A. Cheney, *From Horse to Horsepower* (Melbourne: Rugby Limited, 1965), 115–16. Every issue of *Automobile Topics* between 23 May 1914 and 4 July 1914 included an announcement of the appointment of at least one Dodge Brothers district representative.

20. MacManus and Beasley, *Men, Money, and Motors,* 174–76.

21. Cheney, *From Horse to Horsepower,* 116–117, 121–29, passim.

22. Collection of Dodge advertisements, DCHC.

23. *Saturday Evening Post* 187 (10 October 1914): 38, and 187 (31 October 1914): 37.

24. *Automobile Topics,* 11 July 1914–26 December 1914, passim. Dodge Brothers ran a full-page advertisement every week during this period.

25. Thomas A. McPherson, *The Dodge Story* (Osceola, WI: Motorbooks International, 1992), 5, 7, identifies the driver as "Guy Arneel" in print but as "George Brown" in the famous photograph

in front of John Dodge's home. Butler, "Dodge Brothers: 'Good Enough Is Not Acceptable,'" 50, spells the driver's name "Ameel." The latter spelling is presumed to be correct, as it is also given in Dillon, Read & Company, *The Dodge Dollar*. The *Dodge Brothers Master Parts Book for February 15, 1927* and many other sources identify 14 November 1914 as the date for the first production car.

26. McPherson, *The Dodge Story*, 6; "Dodge Brothers' Test Cars Running," *Automobile Topics* 35 (3 October 1914): 537; "Dodge Brothers Reveal the Car They Will Make," 907, 910; and "Dodge Bros. Car Makes Its Debut: Official Announcement and Presentation to Public Is Made Today. New Machine Launched on Market at Big Plant with Luncheon as Feature," *Detroit News*, 10 November 1914, 1, 20.

27. "This Is 'Old Betsy,'" *Detroit News*, 8 April 1917, 13.

28. McPherson, *The Dodge Story*, 5. Technical specifications are from James T. Lenzke, ed., *Standard Catalogue of Chrysler, 1914–2000*, 2nd ed. (Iola, WI: Krause Publications, 2000), 183.

29. Cheney, *From Horse to Horsepower*, 132; "Dodge Brothers Put Their Car on View: New Offerings, at $785, Attracts Crowds of over Six Thousand People the First Day," *Automobile Topics* 36 (14 November 1914): 14; "Dodge Brothers Cars Draw Crowds," *Automobile Topics* 36 (21 November 1914): 91; "Dodge Receptions Stir Many Cities: Boston's Mayor Welcomes New Dodge Car at the Hub—Mounted Police Precede Triumphal March—Western Dealers, Too, Keep Pot 'A-Boiling,'" *Automobile Topics* 36 (5 December 1914): 247; and "Crowd Omaha Salesroom to View Dodge Brothers Car," *Automobile Topics* 36 (26 December 1914): 490. A Dodge Brothers booklet, *After Five Years* (1919), gives the date of the first delivery to a customer. The booklet is in the private collection of John Parsons, but excerpts are printed in *Dodge Brothers Club News*, May–June 1986, 7–10.

30. "Here Is Dodge Bros. Car of 'Mystery'" and "New Dodge Car Scores Great Hit in Atlanta," *Hearst's Sunday American*, 6 December 1914, 4-C; "Dodge Bros. Present Their New Car: A Five-Passenger, Four Cylinder Machine That Looks the Goods and Is Claimed to Live Up to Its Appearance," *Motor Magazine* 13 (January 1915): 58–60; and "The 17–24 H.P. Dodge Brothers Car," *Autocar* 35 (31 July 1915): 131–34.

31. Cheney, *From Horse to Horsepower*, 137–41; and Jim McLachlan, "The First DB in Australia," *Dodge Brothers Club News* 16 (August–September 1998): 20–21.

32. Ralph C. Epstein, *The Automobile Industry: Its Economic and Commercial Development* (New York: A. W. Shaw, 1928), 186, 337; Davis, *Conspicuous Production*, 33; Early and Walkinshaw, *Setting the Pace*, 462; and Terry B. Dunham and Lawrence Gustin, *The Buick: A Complete History*, 6th ed. (New Albany, IN: Automobile Quarterly, 2002), 570.

Chapter Four

1. Stan Grayson, "The All-Steel World of Edward Budd," *Automobile Quarterly* 16 (fourth quarter 1978): 353; and Vincent R. Courtenay, *Ideas That Moved America . . . The Budd Company at 75* (Troy, MI: Budd, 1987), 10–11.

2. Courtenay, *Ideas That Moved America*, 5; Michael Lamm and Dave Holls, *A Century of Automotive Style: 100 Years of American Car Design* (Stockton, CA: Lamm-Morada Publishing Company, 1996), 34; and Grayson, "The All-Steel World of Edward Budd," 355–56.

3. Lamm and Holls, *A Century of Automotive Style*, 31–33.

4. Courtenay, *Ideas That Moved America,* 12; Gilbert F. Richards, *Budd on the Move* (New York: Newcomen Society in North America, 1975), 7–10; and Grayson, "The All-Steel World of Edward Budd," 357.

5. "Body Schedule—First 40,000 Cars—Issued June 2nd, 1915," in Frederick Haynes Notebooks, vol. 2, NAHC. The document is marked "Mr. Haynes" and is stamped as received by Haynes on 3 June 1915.

6. Courtenay, *Ideas That Moved America,* 13; Haynes Notebooks, vol. 3, fols. 142–43, 176–81; and John R. Velliky and Jean Maddern Pitrone, eds., *Dodge Brothers/Budd Co. Historical Photo Album* (Detroit: Harlo, 1992), 43, 51, 57.

7. Allan Nevins and Frank Ernest Hill, *Ford: Expansion and Challenge, 1915–1933* (New York: Charles Scribner's Sons, 1957), 86–88, 90–91, 94; testimony of C. Harold Wills, 21 May 1917, State of Michigan Supreme Court, *Record, John F. Dodge and Horace E. Dodge v the Ford Motor Company,* vol. 2, *Appeal from the Circuit Court for the County of Wayne, in Chancery,* 588–90, HF; and letters, H. O. Richardson to Dodge Brothers, 12 July 1917, and Dodge Brothers to H. O. Richardson, 26 July 1917, Dodge Brothers Correspondence, 1904–1920, box 1, accession 893, HF.

8. Nevins and Hill, *Ford: Expansion and Challenge, 1915–1933,* 101–4, 110–11; and David L. Lewis, *The Public Image of Henry Ford: An American Folk Hero and His Company* (Detroit: Wayne State University Press, 1976), 99–101.

9. Nevins and Hill, *Ford: Expansion and Challenge, 1915–1933,* 105–11; Lewis, *The Public Image of Henry Ford,* 101–3; and John Wandersee Reminiscence, 53–54.

10. Lenzke, *Standard Catalogue of Chrysler,* 183; "Visit to Budd Plant, 5/21/15," in Frederick Haynes Notebooks, vol. 2; Butler, "Dodge Brothers: 'Good Enough Is Not Acceptable,'" 50; "Dodge Bros. Out with All Year Car: Is First Winter Model Company Has Built," *Detroit News,* 17 September 1915, 20; and Dodge Brothers winter car brochures for 1916, 1917, and 1918 models, DCHC. The special tops were made by the Rex Manufacturing Company of Connersville, Indiana, which remained in business into the late 1920s.

11. McPherson, *The Dodge Story,* 7–23; and Lenzke, *Standard Catalogue of Chrysler,* 183–85.

12. Don Bunn, *Dodge Trucks* (Osceola, WI: Motorbooks International, 1996), 11–15, 17; "Dodge Bros. Offer Commercial Model: Design Based on Passenger Car Chassis, but Several Parts Are Strengthened and Tires Are Bigger—Many Delivered to Government," *Automobile Topics* 48 (24 November 1917): 249; John C. Bittence, "Early Trucks," *Dodge Brothers Club News* 18 (August–September 2000): 21–22; brochure, "Dodge Brothers Business Car Chassis: Adaptable to a Wide Range of Special Body Equipments," ca. 1920, John Parsons collection; and Dillon Read & Company, *The Dodge Dollar,* 20.

13. McPherson, *The Dodge Story,* 16; and Lenzke, *Standard Catalogue of Chrysler,* 184–85. Most of the substantial changes made in 1914–19 are outlined in Butler, "Dodge Brothers: 'Good Enough Is Not Acceptable,'" 46–48, 50, 52–53, 56. Because of the constant improvements made to the Dodge Brothers vehicles, replacements parts were tied to vehicle serial numbers and not to the model year.

14. Nevins and Hill, *Ford: The Times, the Man, the Company,* 647; Early and Walkinshaw, *Setting the Pace,* 461–62; Dunham and Gustin, *The Buick,* 569–70; and Alfred P. Sloan, Jr., *My Years with General Motors,* ed. John McDonald with Catherine Stevens (Garden City, NY: Doubleday, 1964), 166–67.

15. "Index of Group Changes," Dodge Brothers, *Master Parts Price List, June 20, 1917;* and Dodge Brothers, Inc., *Now Drive the Car* (Detroit, 1926), 4. Both sources are in the John Parsons collection.

16. "Russell Huff, Keystone of Nation's Engineering Arch," *The Packard,* September 1926, found in the Russell Huff biography file, NAHC; and "Russell Huff Rites Today: Noted Automotive Engineer to be Buried Here in Evergreen Cemetery," *Detroit Free Press,* 21 March 1930.

17. "Dodge Brothers Makes Further Appointments: Directors of Advertising, Distribution, Service and Export Announced," *Automobile Topics* 58 (7 August 1920): 1462; and "George Harrison Phelps Goes in for Himself: Continues to Handle Dodge Brothers Advertising through Agency," *Automobile Topics* 64 (4 February 1922): 1110.

18. "The Creed of a Dodge Brothers Salesman," framed copy in MBHA and *From the Office of the Director of Advertising, Dodge Brothers Detroit,* monthly newsletter. The Meadow Brook Hall Archives has a near-complete run of these newsletters from October 1916 to April 1922.

19. Dodge Brothers, *Good Will* (1916), "Dodge Brothers 4," DCHC.

20. Dodge Brothers sales literature, DCHC.

21. Binghamton Motor Car Co., *Binghamton, Owego, Elmira Owners of Dodge Brothers Motor Car,* January 1916. Collection of Thomas J. Carpenter, Big Flats, New York.

22. A.H.E. Beckett, "'Charge of the Light Brigade,' Motorized Motor Cars Turn Tide for Pershing's Men in Chihuahua Skirmish," *Motor Age* 29 (1 June 1916): 21; Robert L. Rosekrans, "Bandits, Bullets, Battles—Dependability Is Born amid Violence as 'Old Betsy' Chugs on Stage," *Dodge News* 29 (January 1964): 4–5; "Taking the Finger Prints of Current Events," *Automobile Topics* 42 (15 July 1916): 982; Karla A. Rosenbusch, "Charge of the Brigadier's Dodge: 1916 Dodge Brothers Military Vehicle," *Automobile Quarterly* 39 (May 1999): 11–12; and Butler, "Dodge Brothers: 'Good Enough Is Not Acceptable,'" 53.

23. Konrad F. Schreier, Jr., "U.S. Army World War I Dodges," *Dodge Brothers Club News* (May–June 1988): 4, 6, 7; *After Five Years,* John Parsons collection, reprinted in *Dodge Brothers Club News* (May–June 1986): 7; "Dodge Brothers in the Army, Part I," *Dodge Brothers Club News* 19 (October–November 2001): 15, 17; "Small Trucks Ready for Q.M. Dept.," *Detroit Free Press,* 7 July 1918, pt. 4, p. 10; and "Boxed Motor Cars Leaving Detroit for France," Automobile Club of Southern California, *Touring Topics* 10 (November 1918): 19. The most detailed analysis of Dodge car and truck service in the First World War appeared in a five-part series, "Dodge Brothers in the Army," in *Dodge Brothers Club News,* 19 (October–November 2001): 14–18; 20 (December 2001–January 2002): 19–24; 20 (April–May 2002): 26–31; 20 (June–July 2002): 23–27; and 20 (August–September 2002): 19–23.

24. *From the Office of the Director of Advertising, Dodge Brothers Detroit* 2 no. 9 (6 December 1918): 4.

25. *The Good Will of an Army,* MBHA.

26. *From the Heart of a Soldier* (1921), box "Dodge Brothers 6," DCHC; and *From the Office of the Director of Advertising, Dodge Brothers Detroit* 6, no. 7 (25 November 1921).

27. Cheney, *From Horse to Horsepower,* 149–52, 155–58.

28. Ibid., 143–45.

29. Benedict Crowell, Assistant U.S. Secretary of War, Munitions Department, *America's Munitions, 1917–1918* (Washington, DC: U.S. GPO, 1919), 57–58; Pitrone and Elwart, *The Dodges,* 77; Clarence M. Burton, ed., *The City of Detroit, Michigan, 1701–1922* (Detroit: S. J. Clarke, 1922), 4:311–12; and Cleveland Moffett, "Why Germany Quit: Revealing for the First Time the Story behind the Fighters," *McClure's Magazine* 51 (May 1919): 34.

30. Pitrone and Elwart, *The Dodges,* 78–80; and Moffett, "Why Germany Quit," 34. Pitrone and others, including this author, have erroneously credited the Dodge brothers with manufacturing the

French 75-millimeter artillery piece, easily the most famous large gun of the First World War. Other American manufacturers in other cities made the recoil mechanisms for the 75-millimeter gun.

31. Articles of Agreement between Dodge Brothers and the United States of America, 1 November 1917 (execution completed 13 November 1917), banker's box "Dodge Legal," DCHC.

32. Smith, Hinchman & Grylls, Architects and Engineers, "Preliminary Specifications for Proposed Arsenal Building for Dodge Brothers, Detroit, Michigan, 25 October 1917," and "Arsenal Buildings, Dodge Brothers Plant #3 Preliminary Estimate, 14 November 1917," MBHA; "Dodges Build Huge Plant: Work Under Way on Munitions Factory; Contract Reported for $20,000,000," *Detroit News,* 31 October 1917, 1; "Acres of Concrete Laid for Floor of Munitions Factory," *Detroit News,* 2 December 1917, Real Estate Section, 2; "An Arabian Nights Stunt in Munition-Plant Building: How Dodge Bros. Made an Overnight Start on Their Big Job of Building the Recoil Mechanisms for the Cannon Pershing's Men Will Use in France," *Detroit Saturday Night,* 9 March 1918, 1; and Holleman and Gallagher, *Smith, Hinchman & Grylls,* 94, 211.

33. Sevellon Brown, *The Story of Ordnance in the World War* (Washington, DC: James William Bryan, 1920), 57–58, 64–67; and Benedict Crowell and Robert Forrest Wilson, *The Armies of Industry I: Our Nation's Manufacture of Munitions for a World in Arms, 1917–1918* (New Haven: Yale University Press, 1921), 65–66, 73–74, 89–90. This is volume 4 of a six-volume series, *How America Went to War: An Account from Official Sources of the Nation's War Activities, 1917–1920.* In Dillon, Read & Company, *The Dodge Dollar,* Lamborn's position at Dodge Brothers is listed as "superintendent, method and equipment division," which included responsibility for the placing of machinery within the plants. The description included the following: "During the war had responsible position at Dodge Brothers Ordnance Division."

34. Crowell and Wilson, *The Armies of Industry,* 1:66; Crowell, *America's Munitions, 1917–1918,* 58, 77; and Moffett, "Why Germany Quit," 34. One of Horace Dodge's notebooks, titled "Operations on 155 MM Howitzer Sleigh and 155 MM Rifle Cradle," lays out the 77 and 38 distinct consecutive operations, respectively, needed to produce these components. The notebook, dated 1918, is found in box "Dodge Brothers 4," DCHC.

35. Only a few scattered memoranda and letters have survived relating to these disagreements: Memorandum, Office of the Inspector of Ordnance, U.S.A., 20 May 1918, no author; Dodge Brothers Interoffice Memorandum, Harry H. Williams to A. L. McMeans, 7 June 1918; and letter, Willis B. Palliser, First Lieutenant, Office of the Inspector of Ordnance to John F. Dodge, 10 June 1918, all in MBHA.

36. "Dodge Brothers Honored at Patriotic Dinner," *DAC News* 2 (July 1918): 32; and "Will Show Big Guns in Parade: Cannon from Front to be Contribution of Dodge to Victory March," *Detroit Free Press,* pt. 1, p. 10.

37. Dodge Brothers, *Directors' Minutes,* Special Meeting of the Board of Directors, 28 June 1919 and 9 July 1920, banker's box "Dodge Brothers 1," DCHC; and Wesley W. Stout, *"Tanks Are Mighty Fine Things"* (Detroit: Chrysler Corporation, 1946), 17–18.

38. "Marshall Foch Devotes Part of Brief Visit in Detroit to Inspect Dodge Brothers Works," *From the Office of the Director of Advertising, Dodge Brothers Detroit* no. 6 (11 November 1921), NAHC. Dodge Brothers Company also published *A Mechanical Triumph* (Detroit: Dodge Brothers, 1921), a twenty-three-page illustrated booklet to mark Foch's visit to the Dodge Brothers plant (Dodge Main) on 7 November 1921. The booklet is found at the NAHC. A French version of the same booklet, *Un triomphe de la mechanique,* is in box "Dodge Brothers 4," DCHC. An earlier version of the identical pamphlet, dated 20 January 1919, but with no title, is also found in that box, suggesting that it was simply reprinted for the Foch visit.

39. Lloyd E. Griscom, *The Automotive Pioneers: Industrious Adventurers* (Palmyra, NJ: S. J. Publications, 1967), 95; Burton, *The City of Detroit,* 3:253; and *National Cyclopedia of American Biography,* 19 (New York: James T. White, 1926), 267.

40. The most complete schedule of all the activities is found in the booklet *Second Annual Convention, Dodge Brothers District Representatives, Detroit, May Sixteenth to May Twentieth 1916,* found in the MBHA. Summaries of the fourth (1918), fifth (1919), and sixth (1920) meetings indicate the same basic schedule. Menus from the first (1915), third (1917), and fifth (1919) banquets at the DAC are found in the John Parsons collection.

41. "Brilliant Dinners on the Card Once More," *DAC News* 3 (June 1919): 38; newsletter, *From the Office of the Director of Advertising, Dodge Brothers, Detroit* 4, no. 3 (6 June 1919); *After Five Years, Dedicated to the Sales Organization of Dodge Brothers, Commemorating the Fifth Annual Banquet Given at the Detroit Athletic Club, May Twenty Second, Nineteen Hundred Nineteen* (Privately printed, 1919); and "District Representatives in Annual Convention; French Wins Golf Trophy," *From the Office of the Director of Advertising, Dodge Brothers, Detroit* 5, no. 2 (4 June 1920). *After Five Years* was printed in a limited edition of thirty copies. The NAHC has the title page and table of contents for this book, but not the volume itself. The only known surviving copy is in the John Parsons collection.

42. Burton, *The City of Detroit,* 4:312.

43. Horace Lucien Arnold and Fay Leone Faurote, *Ford Methods and the Ford Shops* (New York: Engineering Magazine, 1915). The most thorough discussions of Ford's breakthroughs are Stephen Meyer III, *Labor Management and Social Control in the Ford Motor Company, 1908–1921* (Albany: State University of New York Press, 1981), 9–36; and David A. Hounshell, *From the American System to Mass Production, 1800–1932: The Development of Manufacturing Technology in the United States* (Baltimore: Johns Hopkins University Press, 1984), 217–61.

44. Quoted in "Dodge Brothers as Quantity Producers of Cars," 383.

45. Lindy Biggs, *The Rational Factory: Architecture, Technology, and Work in America's Age of Mass Production* (Baltimore: Johns Hopkins University Press, 1996), 96–105, 108–11, describes the factory layout and material handling systems at the Ford Highland Park plant.

46. Arnold and Faurote, *Ford Methods and the Ford Shops,* 5, 77–83, 114; Estep, "How Dodge Brothers Plant Was Reorganized," 909–16, 946b; and Nevins and Hill, *Ford: The Times, the Man, the Company,* 644.

47. Walter P. Chrysler and Boyden Sparkes, *Life of an American Workman* (New York: Curtis, 1937), 191.

48. Estep, "How Dodge Brothers Plant Was Reorganized," 946b; and postcards, ca. 1920, John Parsons collection.

49. Roy S. Drake, *Dodge Brothers Works* (Detroit: Franklin, n.d.), n.p.

50. Niran Bates Pope, *Dodge Brothers Works* (Detroit: Dodge Brothers, 1919), 10; Dodge Brothers, *Directors' Minutes,* meeting of 15 May 1919, banker's box "Dodge Brothers 1," DCHC; "Dodge Plant Is Building: Program Involving $8,000,000 Expresses Confidence in Future Business," *Detroit News,* 27 February 1921, Financial Section, 12; Hyde, "'Dodge Main,'" 10–11; and Nevins and Hill, *Ford: The Times, the Man, the Company,* 648.

51. Greg Kowalski, *Hamtramck: The Driven City* (Charleston, SC: Arcadia, 2002), 22, 31; and Olivier Zunz, *The Changing Face of Inequality: Urbanization, Industrial Development, and Immigrants in Detroit, 1880–1920* (Chicago: University of Chicago Press, 1982), 291, 354.

52. "Dodge Brothers as Quality Producers of Cars," 383.

53. J. Walton Schmidt, "Information for the Committee on Education," 10 January 1916, and compilation of employment statistics, large firms, 1 June 1916, Americanization Committee of Detroit Papers, BHL. For a detailed examination of the ACD, see Anne Brophy, "'The Committee . . . has stood out against coercion': The Reinvention of Detroit Americanization, 1915–1931," *Michigan Historical Review* 29 (fall 2003): 1–39.

54. Nevins and Hill, *Ford: The Times, the Man, the Company,* 647; Nevins and Hill, *Ford: Expansion and Challenge, 1915–1933,* 393; Davis, *Conspicuous Production,* 96; and Epstein, *The Automobile Industry,* 345.

55. Chris Sinsabaugh, *Who, Me? Forty Years of Automobile History* (Detroit: Arnold-Powers, 1940), 300; and Tad Burness, *Cars of the Early Twenties* (New York: Galahad, 1968), 89.

56. *The American Car since 1775* (Kunztown, PA: Automobile Quarterly, 1971), 138–39.

57. Dodge Brothers, *Directors' Minutes,* meeting of 15 May 1919, banker's box "Dodge Brothers 1," DCHC.

58. Letter, William G. Mather, President of the Cleveland-Cliffs Iron Company, to John F. Dodge, 23 December 1919, box 1, Dodge Brothers Correspondence, 1904–1920, accession 893, HF; and Nevins and Hill, *Ford: Expansion and Challenge, 1915–1933,* 208–10.

Chapter Five

1. Gregg D. Merksamer, *A History of the New York Auto Show, 1900–2000* (Atlanta: Lionheart, 2000), 56; Pitrone and Elwart, *The Dodges,* 94–97; and "Influenza Spreads through Chicago: 10,000 Nurses Needed; Cases Now Total 4,000," *Detroit News,* 20 January 1920, 19.

2. Pitrone and Elwart, *The Dodges,* 97–98; "Horace Dodge Past Pneumonia Crisis: Brother Also Reportedly Improving in New York Hotel," *Detroit Free Press,* 11 January 1920; "Dodge Brothers Both Recovering: No Setback Feared, Said Auto Manufacturers' Physician," *Detroit Free Press,* 12 January 1920; "Condition of John Dodge Is Critical, Wife Said to Be at Bedside: Brother Improves," *Detroit Free Press,* 13 January 1920; James Swinehart, "John F. Dodge Unconscious: Motor Manufacturer Critically Ill in New York Hotel to Pneumonia," *Detroit News,* 13 January 1920; "John Dodge Has Chance: Automaker May Survive Illness, Physician Says," *Detroit Times,* 13 January 1920; James Swinehart, "Dodge's Condition Slightly Better: Physician Reports Progress of Pneumonia Checked," *Detroit News,* 14 January 1920; and telegram, 8:12 a.m., New York, 13 January 1920, Matilda Dodge to Miss Amelia V. Rausch, Meadowbrook [*sic*] Farms, Rochester, MI, MBHA.

3. "Dodge's Men Pall Bearers: 16 Veteran Employees of Factory to Carry Casket of 'The Boss' to Grave," *Detroit News,* 16 January 1920, 1; "Toil-Stained Hands Carry Dodge's Body: Dead Auto Magnate Home in Coffin on Car He Had Chartered for Vacation. Remains Accompanied by Wife, Kin, Friends," *Detroit Journal,* 16 January 1920, 1; and "Toilers Bear Dodge Casket: Body of Auto Magnate Carried from Station through Lane of Workers," *Detroit Free Press,* 17 January 1920, 1.

4. "Toilers Bear Dodge Casket"; "Thousands See John F. Dodge Placed in Tomb: All Walks of City's Life Are Represented in Final Rites," *Detroit Times,* 17 January 1920, 1; "Tribute to Dodge Paid by Toilers: Long Queue of Workers Files before Bier of Former 'Boss' and Friend," *Detroit Journal,* 17 January 1920, 2; and "John Dodge's Body Is Laid in Vault: Fifteen Intimate Friends Witness Final Rites," *Detroit Free Press,* 11 February 1920, 11. "Toilers Bear Dodge Casket" indicates that the number of pallbearers had been reduced from sixteen to ten. An article, "'Old Guard' Receive Body of John Dodge," *Detroit Journal,* 17 January 1920, 2, shows sixteen men and provides their names. A

photograph in the *Detroit News,* 18 January 1920, 14, of the casket being moved at Woodlawn Cemetery, however, shows only ten pallbearers.

5. "Toil-Stained Hands Carry Dodge's Body," 2; and "Tribute to Dodge Paid by Toilers," 2.

6. "Thousands See John F. Dodge Placed in Tomb," 1.

7. "Tribute to Dodge Paid by Toilers," 1.

8. "John F. Dodge, Address by Rev. Joseph A. Vance, Pastor of the First Presbyterian Church, Detroit, at the funeral of John F. Dodge, at 33 E. Boston Boulevard, 2 p.m., Saturday, January 17, 1920," MBHA.

9. Burton, *The City of Detroit,* 3:254.

10. Newspaper clippings scrapbooks, MBHA; letter, Matilda Rausch Dodge to the S. J. Clarke Publishing Company, 16 December 1921, and invoice, S. J. Publishing Company for Mrs. John R. Dodge, 2 April 1922, found in folder "Letters Regarding John Dodge Biography after June 1920," MBHA. John Dodge's biographical sketch can be found in Burton, *The City of Detroit,* 3:250–54.

11. Dodge Brothers, *Directors' Minutes,* Special Meeting of 29 January 1920; Special Meeting of 28 May 1920; and Annual Stockholders' Meeting, 20 July 1920, all in banker's box "Dodge Brothers 1," DCHC.

12. Dodge Brothers, *Directors' Minutes,* Special Meeting of the Board of Directors, 27 November 1920, banker's box "Dodge Brothers 1," DCHC.

13. Ibid.

14. "Effort to Buy Dodge Plant Likely: New York Interests Long Have Sought It; Death of Both Brothers May Make Efforts Successful, Detroit Bankers Feel," *Automotive Industries* 43 (16 December 1920): 1237, 1239.

15. Letter, H. E. Dodge to Dodge Brothers Dealers, 27 January 1920, *From the Office of the Director of Advertising, Dodge Brothers Detroit* 4, no. 12 (20 February 1920): 1; and "Half Million Motor Cars: Dodge Brothers Employees Take Part in Impressive Ceremonies," *From the Office of the Director of Advertising, Dodge Brothers Detroit* 5, no. 4 (9 July 1920): 2, 3.

16. "Lingering Illness Kills Dodge, Grieving over Brother's Death: Horace Dies on Vacation in Florida," *Detroit Journal,* 11 December 1920, 1.

17. "Horace E. Dodge Dies in Florida: Detroit Automobile Manufacturer Succumbs Suddenly at Palm Beach Home," *New York Times,* 11 December 1920; "Horace Dodge Dies in Southern Home: Surviving Brother of Famous Firm Succumbs after Long Decline—Had Never Recovered Shattered Health—The Business an Imposing Monument," *Automobile Topics* 60 (18 December 1920): 489; "Doctor Nails Rumor over Dodge Deaths: Did Not Die from Drinking Bad Liquor, He Says," *New York News,* 15 December 1920; and Certificate of Death for Horace Elgin Dodge, 11 December 1920, State of Florida Bureau of Vital Statistics, issued by Palm Beach County, Florida.

18. "Dodge Funeral on Wednesday: Body to Arrive Tuesday Morning; Will Be Laid beside Brother," *Detroit News,* 11 December 1920, 1; and "Toilers to See Dodge Tonight: Body to Lie in State from 5 to 9 p.m., Coming on Special Train; Symphony Honors Friend," *Detroit News,* 13 December 1920, 1.

19. "Dodge Requiem in Music Room: Bronze Coffin Rests Midst Roses in Rose Terrace, Family Home," *Detroit News,* 15 December 1920, 1, 2; "Dodge at Rest with Brother: Body of Auto Magnate Laid beside That of Lifelong Partner in Vault," *Detroit Free Press,* 16 December 1920, 1; and "Dodges Together, Brothers in Tomb: Funeral Procession of Horace Passes by Factory," *Detroit News,* 16 December 1920, 1.

20. T. R. Fassett, "In Memoriam to Horace E. Dodge," *Detroit Journal,* 15 December 1920.

21. Latham and Agresta, *Dodge Dynasty,* 154–56.

22. Bernard M. Baruch, *Baruch: The Public Years* (New York: Holt, Rinehart and Winston, 1960), 61–62; and "Doctor Nails Rumor over Dodge Death."

23. "Hebraizing the Dodges," *Detroit Saturday Night,* 9 July 1921, sec. 1, p. 1.

24. C. T. Schaefer, "What's in a Name?" *Motor Life* 26 (October 1926): 35, 47; and U.S. Patent Office, "Trade-Mark for Certain Named Motor Vehicles and Parts Thereof," Number 131,027, registered 10 January 1922.

25. Burial Records for Ivy S. Dodge, Woodlawn Cemetery, 19975 Woodward Avenue, Detroit; "Dodge Brothers Erect Handsome Mausoleum of Egyptian Design," *Detroit Journal,* 30 January 1915, 12; and Cyril M. Harris, ed., *Illustrated Dictionary of Historic Architecture* (New York: Dover, 1977), 187–88. Currently, the Dodge mausoleum, which has twelve crypts, contains the remains of John F. Dodge, first wife Ivy S. Dodge, and son John Duval Dodge; Horace E. Dodge, wife Anna Thomson Dodge, and son Horace E. Dodge, Jr.; and Andrew Gehman Dodge, son of Horace E. Dodge III. The remains of two of the three children of John F. Dodge and Matilda Rausch Dodge (Anna M. Dodge and Daniel George Dodge) were originally in the Dodge mausoleum as well but were transferred in July 1962 to a newly built adjacent mausoleum for Matilda Rausch Wilson and husband Alfred Wilson.

26. Glasscock, *The Gasoline Age,* 197–98.

27. Ibid., 206–7.

28. "John F. Dodge Pays $10,000 for 'Monks at Play': Purchases Canvas for His Brother Horace E. Dodge, Grosse Pointe. Picture Has Attracted Admiration of Thousands; Was Purchased Abroad in 1892," *Detroit News,* 30 August 1912, 1, 2.

29. The loving cup is in the private collection of John Parsons.

30. Latham and Agresta, *Dodge Dynasty,* 89.

31. "Group Policy No. 40 Issued to Dodge Brothers by the Aetna Life Insurance Company of Hartford, Connecticut," policy for Ray L. List in the amount of $1,000, dated 6 December 1919, John Parsons collection.

32. Photographs in box "Dodge Brothers 1–1897–1919," DCHC; program, "Dodge Brothers Excursion, July 15, 1916," and booklet, "Count Your Calories," Dodge Brothers Girls Athletic Association, 1920, both in the MBHA; Latham and Agresta, *Dodge Dynasty,* 89.

33. "Lays down His Baton: Liberati Was One of Bandmasters' Aristocracy," *Detroit News,* 8 November 1927; Dodge Brothers Concert Band programs, 27 December 1918 and 25 February 1919, both in MBHA; program, "Luncheon, Dodge Brothers Eastern Dealers, Ritz Carlton Hotel, New York, Wednesday January Seventh Nineteen Hundred Twenty," MBHA; program, "Dodge Brothers Concert Band, Detroit Armory, March Twenty Ninth, Nineteen Hundred Twenty" and "Today's Entertainers: Dodge Brothers Industrial Band," folder "Dodge Brothers Concert Band," box "Dodge Brothers 2–1920/1923," DCHC; and "Dodge Band Plays for Prison Inmates," *Detroit Times,* 17 May 1920.

34. John C. Dancy, *Sand against the Wind: The Memoirs of John C. Dancy* (Detroit: Wayne State University Press, 1966), 128–31.

35. Niran Bates Pope, *Dodge Brothers Works* (July 1920), 9–10.

36. "Dodge Brothers' Lives Threatened: Employee Who Wanted $5-a-Day Scale Arrested," *Detroit News,* 19 April 1918, 1; "Dodge Black Hand Case Now in Court: John Olejnik Is Now Facing Serious Charges," *Detroit News,* 18 July 1918, 17; and "Man Who Threatened Dodges Goes to Prison," *Detroit News,* 19 July 1918, 10.

37. Miscellaneous memoranda, John Dodge to Mr. McMeans, 16 December 1919, folder for 1919, Dodge Brothers Correspondence, 1904–20, box 1, accession 893, HF.

38. Davis, *Conspicuous Production,* 40–47.

39. Charles H. Bennett Reminiscence, 35–36, Ford Motor Company Oral History Collection, HF. Bennett did not indicate precisely when this incident occurred.

40. George M. Holley Reminiscence, 111, Ford Motor Company Oral History Collection, HF.

41. Malcolm W. Bingay, *Detroit Is My Own Home Town* (New York: Bobbs-Merrill, 1946), 43–44.

42. "Dodge and Oakman Nabbed on Capias: Arrested in Conjunction with $25,000 Damage Suit Filed by T. J. Mahon Whom They Beat Up," *Detroit Times*, 21 January 1911, 2; "Oakman-Dodge Taken on Capias: Assailants of Thomas J. Mahon in Barroom Trouble Arrested on Lawyer's Complaint; Charges Wanton Injury, Asks Damages of $25,000; Defendants Released by Judge Murphy on Bail Bonds of $2,500 Each," *Detroit Free Press*, 21 January 1911, 5; and Pitrone and Elwart, *The Dodges*, 48.

43. Bingay, *Detroit Is My Own Home Town*, 44–45.

44. Ibid., 43.

45. Letters, John F. Dodge to Police Commissioner F. H. Croul, 10 July 1911, and John F. Dodge to Miss Angie Clara Chapin, Wellesley College, Wellesley, Massachusetts, 11 December 1911, MBHA.

46. Letters, Horace E. Dodge to H. C. Dunston, St. John's School, Manlius, New York, 11 October 1911, and Horace E. Dodge to L. A. Grigsby, St. John's School, Manlius, New York, 17 October 1911, MBHA.

47. Davis, *Conspicuous Production*, 95; Bingay, *Detroit Is My Own Home Town*, 43; and Pitrone and Elwart, *The Dodges*, 30.

48. Latham and Agresta, *Dodge Dynasty*, 95–98; Arthur Pound, *Detroit: Dynamic City* (New York: D. Appleton-Century, 1940), 301; letter, Horace E. Dodge to the Michigan Fire & Marine Insurance Company, 17 July 1911; letter, H. E. Dodge to Grinnell Brothers, Detroit, 13 November 1913; H. E. Dodge to the Michigan State Telephone Company, Detroit City Gas Company, and Edison Illuminating Company, 21 December 1911; and a series of letters, Horace E. Dodge to Tiffany & Company, New York, 22 June 1911–17 November 1911. All of the letters are found in the MBHA.

49. Polacsek, "The Dodge Fleet of Lake St. Clair," 91; and "Other New Power Craft Gone," *Detroit News*, 15 June 1904, 1; Pitrone and Elwart, *The Dodges*, 29; and Dodge Brothers, *Time and Pay Records*, 1906, DCHC.

50. Polacsek, "The Dodge Fleet of Lake St. Clair," 91–92; Earl Brannock, *Queen of the Chesapeake and Hudson* (Cambridge, MD: Frank Gumpert, 1986), 14–15; "Fastest Boat Is Christened: Dodge Bros. Launch Hornet II, Speediest of All Crafts," *Detroit News*, 19 April 1910, 6; National Museum of American History, Smithsonian Institution, Deed of Gift record (28 February 1958), courtesy of Paul F. Johnston, Ph.D., Curator of Maritime History; D. W. Fostle, *Speedboat* (Mystic, CT: Mystic Seaport Museum, 1988), 114–18; "Manufacturer Named New Commodore of Detroit Motor Boat Club," *Detroit Tribune*, 9 December 1913; "H. E. Dodge New Motor Boat Club Commodore: Tributes Paid W. E. Scripps on His Retiring," *Detroit News*, 9 December 1913, 8; and "H. E. Dodge Heads Motor Boat Club: William E. Scripps Retires as Commodore after Serving Four Terms," *Detroit Free Press*, 9 December 1913.

51. Brannock, *Queen of the Chesapeake and Hudson*, 13; "Horace Dodge's New Yacht Launched: 'Nokomis' Is Handsome Pleasure Craft," *Detroit News*, 20 December 1913, 16; "Marconi Wireless Telegraph Company of America Complimentary Frank," which expired on 31 December 1917, is in the private collection of Ron Fox of Detroit; and Bruynooghe, *Chronicle of Horace Dodge's Steam Yacht Delphine*, 37–38. The *Detroit News* (20 September 1931, Rotogravure Section) reprinted a photograph of John and Horace Dodge and friends bidding farewell to the *Nokomis*, but misidentified the boat as the *Delphine*.

52. Polacsek, "The Dodge Fleet of Lake St. Clair," 92–93.

53. Ibid., 93.

54. Ibid., 94.

55. "'Francis'—Largest Express Cruiser," *Motor Boat,* 25 December 1920, 36–37; and "Francis, the New Dodge Cruiser," *Power Boating,* January 1921, 25–27.

56. Polacsek, "The Dodge Fleet of Lake St. Clair," 94, 97–100; Jay Ottinger, *The Steam Yacht Delphine and Other Stories* (Sea Level, NC: Jay Ottinger, 1994), 9–18; Ross MacTaggart, *The Golden Century: Classic Motor Yachts, 1830–1930* (New York: W. W. Norton, 2001), 105–13; George E. Van, "Mrs. Dodge's Delphine Is Steaming Home," *Detroit Times,* 15 May 1959; David McKay, "Former Dodge Yacht Sails Again—Overseas," *Detroit Free Press,* 11 January 1992, 7A; and Douglas Ilka, "Ex-Dodge Yacht Delphine Gets Face-Lift: New Belgian Owners Want to Restore Vessel's Splendor," *Detroit News,* 13 March 1998.

57. Pitrone and Elwart, *The Dodges,* 103–11; and Latham and Agresta, *Dodge Dynasty,* 150–54. The private collection of Ron Fox of Detroit includes jeweler Cartier's invoice to Horace Dodge for the five-strand pearl necklace (24 May 1920) and an acknowledgment from Cartier (23 June 1920) of Horace Dodge's payment of $925,000 for the two pearl necklaces.

58. Pitrone and Elwart, *The Dodges,* 38–39; Latham and Agresta, *Dodge Dynasty,* 61–62. The quotation from the New Year's gathering is from "Stories of John Dodge," *Detroit News,* 16 January 1920, 27.

59. Pitrone and Elwart, *The Dodges,* 89–90; Latham and Agresta, *Dodge Dynasty,* 142–43, 177–79; and "Dodge Building Mansion on Lake St. Clair Shore," *Detroit News,* 24 July 1919, 1, 2.

60. *Detroit Saturday Night,* 20 December 1913, 16; Latham and Agresta, *Dodge Dynasty,* 104–5.

61. Albert Nelson Marquis, ed., *The Book of Detroiters: A Biographical Dictionary of Leading Living Men of the City of Detroit* (Chicago: A. N. Marquis, 1908), 105, 116, 126, 143, 173, 283.

62. Ibid., rev. ed. (Chicago: A. N. Marquis, 1914), 104–5, 127, 149, 182, 302.

63. *The Detroit Club: Articles of Association, Rules and Regulations, Officers and Members* (Detroit: Detroit Club, 1913); and *Detroit Club: Articles of Association, By-Laws and House Rules, Officers, and Members* (Detroit: Evans-Winter-Herb, 1940), 75; "John Dodge," *National Cyclopedia of American Biography* 19 (New York: James T. White, 1926), 267; and "Horace E. Dodge," in Burton, *The City of Detroit,* 4:312. Arthur Woodford graciously provided the information on the Detroit Club.

64. Grace L. Ainsworth, "Concerning Mr. Dodge's Gift," *The Club Woman, Official Organ of the Detroit Federation of Women's Clubs* 4, no. 8 (May–June 1913): 305; "Dodge Gives Home to Women's Clubs: Federation Elects Officers and Plans Year's Work," *Detroit News,* 25 April 1914; "Beautiful Homes of Women's Clubs to Open on Friday: Federation Club House, Gift of John F. Dodge, Ready for Occupancy," *Detroit News,* 23 January 1916, 14; Adele Page, "John Dodge—An Appreciation," *The Club Woman* 12, no. 6 (February 1920): 311–13; and "$10,000 Promised for Rescue Home: Teams Organized at Banquet Begin Work Wednesday to Raise Funds," *Detroit Journal,* 19 April 1916. The Detroit Federation of Women's Clubs building is still standing.

65. "Red Cross Seals Sell Fast Here: Big Record Is Made at Manufacturing Plants," *Detroit Free Press,* 22 December 1913; "Tubercular Aid Posters Placed: Sale of Seals in Drug Stores beyond Expectations, Says Mrs. John F. Dodge," *Detroit Free Press,* 6 December 1913; "Gift of $12,000 Swells Fund for Tuberculosis Sanitarium; Check Given to Save Children," *Detroit News,* 3 February 1914; and "Gift Assures New Home for Care of Tubercular Children," *Detroit Journal,* 3 February 1914.

66. Pitrone and Elwart, *The Dodges,* 82.

67. Davis, *Conspicuous Production,* 105; George B. Catlin, *The Story of Detroit* (Detroit: Detroit News, 1926), 682; and Minutes of the Directors' Meetings of Orchestra Hall, 23 April 1919–14

November 1930 and Minutes of the Directors' Meetings of the Detroit Symphony Society, vol. 1, 20 May 1919–24 September 1931, Detroit Symphony Society Papers, BHC. Davis claims that Horace Dodge, William H. Murphy, and Paul Gray each donated $150,000, while Catlin put Horace's Dodge's donation at $100,000.

68. Pitrone and Elwart, *The Dodges,* 210; "Resolution on Death of Mr. Horace E. Dodge," Meeting of January 3, 1921, Minutes of the Directors' Meetings of the Detroit Symphony Society, vol. 1, Detroit Symphony Society Papers, BHC; "2 Give $50,000 for Orchestra: Mrs. Horace E. Dodge and William H. Murphy Each Pledge $25,000," *Detroit News,* 13 February 1921, 1; and minutes from various meetings of the directors of Orchestra Hall and the Detroit Symphony Society, 1919–30, Detroit Symphony Society Papers, BHC.

69. Folders, "Dodge Brothers Income Tax Returns," and "Dodge Brothers-Data on Contributions Not Challenged," box 4, accession 96, Dodge Estate-Legal, HF; "Pastor Announces $250,000 Dodge Gift to Church," *Detroit News,* 19 January 1920, 1; "Dodge's Luncheons to Detroit School Pupils Continued in Last Days: Auto. Maker Wrote Check for Year Just before Starting for New York," *Detroit News,* 20 January 1920, 1; "Dodge Community House Ready: Welfare Home Built by Gift Fund to Be Dedicated Nov. 19," *Detroit News,* 14 November 1925; and "Memorial to John Dodge: Thousands Play in This Community House Given by Auto Maker," *Detroit News,* 22 January 1927, 10.

70. Pitrone and Elwart, *The Dodges,* 53, 93, 105; "Orphan Home Given $50,000 by Dodges: Donation Will Be Used for New Building," *Detroit News,* 20 November 1920, 7; "Horace Dodge as His Friends Knew Him: Was Skilled Organist," *Detroit Journal,* 11 December 1920, 2; "Dodge Funeral on Wednesday"; and Jefferson Avenue Presbyterian Church, *New Church Register, Record No. 2,* "Chronological Roll of Communicants," Miss Delphine Ione Dodge, Received by Examination, 14 April 1912; Mrs. Christina A. Dodge, Received by Certificate, 6 April 1913; and Horace E. Dodge, Received by Examination, 1 June 1913.

71. Latham and Agresta, *Dodge Dynasty,* 144; and "J. F. Dodge and H. E. Dodge Subscriptions," compiled in 1923, MBHA.

72. Melvin G. Holli, *Reform in Detroit: Hazen S. Pingree and Urban Politics* (New York: Oxford University Press, 1969), 150–56; and Arthur M. Woodford, *This Is Detroit, 1701–2001* (Detroit: Wayne State University Press, 2001), 105–7.

73. Latham and Agresta, *Dodge Dynasty,* 81–82; miscellaneous outgoing John Dodge correspondence as water board commissioner, 18 July 1905 to 31 June 1909, MBHA; Minutes, Board of Water Commissioners, City of Detroit, Detroit Archives, BHC; "John Dodge's Life Story: A Man of Terrific Energy," *Detroit News,* 20 October 1915, 12; Davis, *Conspicuous Production,* 250n. 12; and *The 100th Annual Report of the Department of Water Supply, City of Detroit, for the Fiscal Year Ended* [sic] *June 30, 1952* (Detroit: Board of Water Commissioners, 1953), a-18.

74. "Appoints Dodge on Water Board: Mayor Marx Names Him to Succeed Basil A. Lempke. He Is First Commissioner Announced; Served in Same Capacity during Codd Administration," *Detroit News,* 3 February 1913, 1; "John Dodge's Life Story: A Man of Terrific Energy," *Detroit News,* 20 October 1915, 12; and letter, J. G. Everson to John Dodge, 30 June 1911, MBHA.

75. Davis, *Conspicuous Production,* 76, 163.

76. Graeme O'Geran, *A History of the Detroit Street Railways* (Detroit: Conover, 1931), 274; "Mahon Third M. O. Commissioner: Leader of Street Railway Men Named with Stringham and Dodge," *Detroit News,* 28 May 1913, 8; "Operate Railway: Commission to Be Appointed by Detroit Mayor; They Will Have Charge of Street Car Lines under Municipal Ownership," *Traverse City Eagle,* 8 June 1913; "Has Trouble Securing Man for Car Board: Competent People Not Hankering for Non-Salaried Position, Mayor Declares," *Detroit Times,* 23 July 1913; "James Couzens Accepts

Appointment as Member of Railway Commission: Financier Will Act with John Dodge and Wm. D. Mahon in Fight for Municipal Ownership of Detroit's Traffic System. All Three Men Have Long Advocated City's Possession of Street Car Service," *Detroit News,* 29 July 1913, 1; and "John F. Dodge Named President of Railway Board at First Session," *Detroit News,* 1 August 1913.

77. "John Dodge Made No Study of M.O. While in Europe: Had Stomach Ache on Arrival Home and Avoids Talk," *Detroit Journal,* 2 July 1913; "Dodge Returns; Ill from Long Trip in Train," *Detroit Journal,* 4 July 1913; "John F. Dodge Found Municipal Ownership in Europe a Great Success: Street Railways in Great Britain Are Operated by Cities," *Detroit News,* 17 July 1913, 1, 2; "Fishes Listen to Marx Confab on Dodge's Yacht: Mayor and Advisors Take to Deep to Discuss Trolley Measure," *Detroit Free Press,* 18 July 1913; and "Journal Forces Marx Back into M.O. Fold; Dodge Used as Pivot: Dodge Quoted in 'Hot' Interview; He First Declared He Had Not Studied M.O. in Europe, But Is Now Provided with Glowing Eulogisms When Needed by Administration," *Detroit Journal,* 19 July 1913. According to Marion Marzolf and Marianne Ritchie, *Matilda R. Wilson: Mistress of Meadow Brook Hall* (n.p., ca. 1962), 5, this was the only time Matilda accompanied John on a European trip.

78. O'Geran, *History of the Detroit Street Railways,* 270–74, 278–79; and Davis, *Conspicuous Production,* 163.

79. "Mahon Quits Street Railway Board; Says It's Playing Politics," *Detroit Journal,* 21 April 1914; "Mahon Resigns from Street Railway Board," *Detroit Times,* 21 April 1914; "Quit for Good, Mahon Asserts: Street Railway Commissioner Declares It Will Do Mayor No Good to Ask Reconsideration," *Detroit News Tribune,* 22 April 1914; "Mahon Thinks Marx Crowd Is Knocking M.O.: Resigns Because He Believes Mayor Is Playing D.U.R.'s Game, Friends Say," *Detroit Times,* 22 April 1914; and "Wilkie Named for Traction Board: Water Commissioner Will Take Place Vacated By William D. Mahon," *Detroit Times,* 23 April 1914.

80. "Couzens' Activity Displeases Marx Machine Crowd: Say Commissioner Is Taking Glory from John Dodge," *Detroit Journal,* 12 May 1914; "Marx Starts 16-Mile Line for D.U.R., Extending Rights over Streets, Digging M.O.'s Grave: Mayor Marx Pours Out Champagne at Grave of M.O.— Couzens Urges: 'Don't Let Car Co. Build Another Foot,'" *Detroit Journal,* 14 May 1914, 1; and "Dodge Blocks Plan of D.U.R. on Cross-Town: Cars Run over Junction Line in Tour of Inspection. Company Had Hopes of Putting in Its Style of Curve," *Detroit News,* 16 October 1914, 1.

81. "John Dodge's Life Story: A Man of Terrific Energy," *Detroit News,* 20 October 1915, 12. O'Geran, *History of the Detroit Street Railways,* 311–15, offers a slightly different version of the Dodge-Mahon confrontation.

82. "Proof That John Dodge Pays Taxes in City of Detroit," *Detroit News,* 18 September 1915, 1; and "Wedding Will Not Prevent Dodge Speech: Commissioner to Deliver Address during Daughter's Reception. Will Speak at Big Armory Meeting Saturday Night," *Detroit News,* 29 October 1915, 2.

83. Barnard, *Independent Man,* 104, 105; William W. Lutz, *The News of Detroit* (Boston: Little, Brown, 1973), 46; and Davis, *Conspicuous Production,* 164.

84. "Dodge and Haass off Street Railway Board," *Detroit News,* 14 January 1919, 1; Minutes of the Meetings of the Board of Street Railway Commissioners, Detroit Street Railway Collection, Burton Historical Collection, Detroit Public Library; O'Geran, *History of the Detroit Street Railways,* 291; Davis, *Conspicuous Production,* 166, 167; and Barnard, *Independent Man,* 114–16, 126–28, 133.

85. Norman Beasley and George W. Stark, *Made in Detroit* (New York: G. P. Putnam's Sons, 1957), 225–26.

86. Burton, *The City of Detroit,* 3:253; Davis, *Conspicuous Production,* 105, 255n. 4; Barnard, *Independent Man,* 84, 106; *Official Roll of the Delegates and the Alternates to the Sixteenth Republican National Convention at Chicago, June 7, 1916,* comp. James B. Reynolds, Secretary, Republican National Committee, 10–11, MBHA; letters, John F. Dodge to Charles Evans Hughes, 13 November 1916, and Charles Evans Hughes to John Dodge, 21 November 1916, Dodge Brothers Correspondence, 1904–20, box 1, accession 893, HF; letters, John Wanamaker to John Dodge, 24 October 1916, and John Dodge to John Wanamaker, 27 October 1916, Dodge Brothers Correspondence, 1904–20, box 1, accession 893, HF; letter, Cameron Currie to Thomas H. Newberry, 13 February 1918, box 1, Truman Newberry Papers, Burton Historical Collection, Detroit Public Library; "Report Puts Dodge in U.S. Senate Race: Dispatch Says He Discussed Ambition with Friends," *Detroit News,* 16 March 1918, 1; "Dodge Denies He's Out for Senate: Motor Car Builder Says He Will Not Be Candidate," *Detroit News,* 19 March 1919, 1; "Wise Ones Say Marx Will Run," *Detroit News,* 3 July 1918, 1; and letters, Frank O. Lowden to John F. Dodge, 7 January 1920, and William E. Hull (Lowden for President Campaign Committee) to John F. Dodge, 10 January 1920, Dodge Brothers Correspondence, 1904–20, box 1, accession 893, HF.

87. "Gillespie Denies Dodge Home Has Extra Protection: Willing to Supply Special Officers Only If Residents Pay Bill," *Detroit Free Press,* 21 August 1913.

88. "Marx and Dodge Auto Hits Woman, Policeman Says: Then Speed [*sic*] Forward without Stop, He Charges," *Detroit Journal,* 3 October 1913; "Mayor Furious When Asked of Motor Incident: 'None of the Journal's Business!' Shouts Executive," *Detroit Journal,* 4 October 1913; and "Dodge, in Secret Session, Fined $50 as Auto Speeder: Trial Held on Quiet in Trombley's House; Result Contradicts Marx's Story Motor Was Not Going over 15 Miles," *Detroit Journal,* 9 October 1913.

89. "Horace Dodge Does Not Heed Warrant," *Detroit News,* 2 November 1916, 7; "Names H. E. Dodge as Under-Sheriff: Sheriff-Elect Announces Millionaire's Appointment," *Detroit News,* 3 December 1916, 1; and "Dodge Storm-Bound with Four Slayers: Millionaire Under-Sheriff Pays $1,000 for Private Car," *Detroit News,* 21 February 1918, 1.

Chapter Six

1. Dodge Brothers, *Directors' Minutes,* meetings of 27 November 1920, 7 and 13 January 1921, 19 July 1921, 13 October 1921, 6 January 1922, 28 February 1922, and 15 March 1922, banker's box "Dodge Brothers 1," DCHC.

2. Dodge Brothers, *Directors' Minutes,* meeting of 15 March 1922, banker's box "Dodge Brothers 1," DCHC; and "People Given Parks by Dodge Brothers," *Automobile Topics* 67 (9 September 1922): 323.

3. Dodge Brothers, *Directors' Minutes,* meeting of 16 December 1924, banker's box "Dodge Brothers 1," DCHC; Latham and Agresta, *Dodge Dynasty,* 79–80; and "Dodge Firm Gives State Park Site: Value of 2,400 Acres on Munuskong Bay Put at $80,000," *Detroit News,* 3 March 1925, 25.

4. "Michigan State Parks: Their Location, Convenience Equipment and Privileges, 1926"; "State Parks," *Michigan Gazetteer, 1931–32,* 63; and "Island Lake Dodge Brothers No. 1 State Park," Parks Division, Michigan Department of Conservation, ca. 1940, all found in the vertical file "Dodge Brothers," Niles Community Library, Niles, Michigan.

5. Dodge Brothers, *Directors' Minutes,* meeting of 31 December 1921, and Stockholders' Meeting of 18 July 1922, both in banker's box "Dodge Brothers 1," DCHC.

6. Dodge Brothers, *Directors' Minutes,* meetings of 18 July 1922, 2 November 1922, and 3 January 1924, banker's box "Dodge Brothers 1," DCHC. The letter, dated 13 December 1923, came from Sidney T. Miller, Anna Thomson Dodge's attorney.

7. Dodge Brothers, *Directors Minutes,* special meetings of 30 June 1922 and 15 December 1922, banker's box "Dodge Brothers 1," DCHC.

8. Forbes and Foster, *Automotive Giants of America,* 134; and Dillon, Read & Company, *The Dodge Dollar.* 20.

9. Dodge Brothers, *Directors Minutes,* Special Meeting of the Stockholders, 27 December 1922; Special Meeting of the Board of Directors, 12 and 26 February 1924, all in banker's box "Dodge Brothers 1," DCHC; "$39,600,000 Sewage Disposal Plan Accepted by Council: Committee's Recommendations Taken under Advisement," *The Detroiter* 17, pt. 1 (21 December 1925): 9; "Orders Dodge Site Acquired: Council Tells O'Neil to Begin Condemnation for Sewage Disposal Plant," *Detroit Times,* 12 October 1927, 18; and copy of a letter from the Special Committee on the (Wayne) County Sewage Disposal System to the Board of Supervisors, Wayne County, 22 January 1930, appended to *Sewage Disposal for the City of Detroit, December, 1925,* n.p.

10. Dodge biography file, David Beecroft Papers, King Collection, NAHC.

11. Dodge Brothers, *Directors' Minutes,* meetings of 15 and 30 March 1922, banker's box "Dodge Brothers 1," DCHC.

12. Robert C. Laurens, "A History of the Matheson Automobile," *Antique Automobile* 14 (September 1950): 99–105; "Matheson Is Dodge Brothers' Service Manager," *Automobile Trade Journal* 19 (May 1916): 89: "Dodge Brothers Makes Further Appointments," *Automobile Topics* 58 (7 August 1920): 1462; "Matheson-Houghton Resign Their Posts in Dodge Brothers," *Automobile Topics* 73 (1 March 1924): 212; "Injuries Fatal to Car Builder: Charles Matheson, 63, Killed in Wisconsin; Was Reared Here," *Grand Rapids Press,* 13 August 1940, 3; Dodge Brothers, *Directors' Minutes,* meeting of 26 February 1924, banker's box "Dodge Brothers 1," DCHC; and "Matheson Resigns as Dodge Sales Head: Two Other Officials Quit the Organization," *Detroit News,* 2 March 1924, sec. 1, p. 21.

13. Letters, Walter P. Chrysler to Leo M. Butzel, 17 March 1924, and Mrs. Alfred G. Wilson to Charles W. Matheson, 19 December 1928, both in the John Parsons collection; "Chrysler Officials Man DeSoto Corp.: Separate Organization Sponsors 'Mystery' Car," *Automobile Topics* 89 (28 April 1928): 989; Michael J. Kollins, *Pioneers of the U.S. Automobile Industry,* vol. 3, *The Financial Wizards* (Warrendale, PA: Society of Automotive Engineers, 2002), 100; and "Injuries Fatal to Car Builder." Matheson (22 March 1876–12 August 1940) was actually sixty-four at the time of death.

14. Dodge Brothers, *Directors' Minutes,* Special Meeting of the Board of Directors, 15 August 1922, banker's box "Dodge Brothers 1," DCHC; and McPherson, *The Dodge Story,* 34–35.

15. Dodge Brothers, *Directors' Minutes,* meeting of 15 December 1921, banker's box "Dodge Brothers 1," DCHC; "Dodge Brothers Have All-Metal Business Coupe," *Motor World* 71 (7 June 1922): 33; "New Dodge Brothers All-Steel Coupe," *Motor Age* 41 (8 June 1922): 12; "Dodge Brothers Out with Its New Coupe," *Automobile Topics* 66 (10 June 1922): 301; "All-Steel Business Sedan Being Produced by Dodge," *Automotive Industries* 47 (14 September 1922): 539; and Robert Palmer, "The 1923 'All-Steel' Business Sedan: A Quantum Leap in Technology," *Dodge Brothers Club News* 17 (June–July 1999): 18.

16. Lenzke, *Standard Catalogue of Chrysler,* 186; McPherson, *The Dodge Story,* 29; Bunn, *Dodge Trucks,* 25–34; and Dillon, Read & Company, *The Dodge Dollar,* 20.

17. "Dealers Given Opportunity to Popularize 'Dodge Brothers March'—Music Is Now Ready," undated materials distributed at the 1921 New York Automobile Show, found in folder "Dodge

Brothers Concert Band," box "Dodge Brothers 2, 1920/1923," DCHC; Pitrone and Elwart, *The Dodges,* 210; and "Dodge Brothers Jewelry," MBHA.

18. Dodge Brothers sales brochure, 1924 models, DCHC; and "More Than Ever: Character and Dependability," *Saturday Evening Post,* 1 May 1926.

19. Dodge Brothers, Inc., *Now Drive the Car.*

20. Roy Chapman Andrews, *The New Conquest of Central Asia: A Narrative of the Explorations of the Central Asiatic Expeditions in Mongolia and China, 1921–1930* (New York: American Museum of Natural History, 1932), 5, 12–13; *On the Trail of Ancient Man: A Narrative of the Field Work of the Central Asiatic Expedition* (New York: G. P. Putnam's Sons, 1926), 11; and "Fur Traders Turn to Dodge Cars: Mongolian Fur Hunters Take a Leaf from Andrews's Book," *Detroit Free Press,* 24 February 1924, pt. 4, p. 3.

21. Roy Chapman Andrews, *Under a Lucky Star: A Lifetime of Adventure* (Garden City, NY: Blue Ribbon, 1943), 229.

22. Andrews, *The New Conquest of Central Asia,* 13, 329; Charles Gallenkamp, *Dragon Hunter: Roy Chapman Andrews and the Central Asiatic Expeditions* (New York: Penguin Putnam, 2001), 184; and H. Taylor Patterson, "Roy Chapman Andrews: Across China by Dodge," *Car Classics,* April 1974, 41.

23. "Bears in Dodge Go Calling: Pair of Grizzlies Given to Coolidge; 'Idaho Bill' Brings Them from Mexico in Dodge Car," *Detroit Free Press,* 16 December 1923, pt. 3, p. 9; and "Dodge Brothers Cars Help Elect Coolidge," *Detroit Sunday Times,* 9 November 1924, pt. 3, p. 11.

24. "World Record for Dodge Car: Million Autos in First Nine Years Set New Mark, Executives Claim," *Detroit Free Press,* 23 December 1923, pt. 1, p. 6.

25. *Dodge Brothers Sales Bulletin, Convention Number,* "Commemorating the Ninth Annual Meeting of Dodge Brothers Dealers, New York, January 9, 1923, Hotel Pennsylvania," box "Dodge Brothers 2, 1920/1923," DCHC, and in the John Parsons collection. A scattering of menus and programs from various regional meetings held during this period in Detroit, Boston, Chicago, and Kansas City have survived in the MBHA, NAHC, DCHC, and the John Parsons collection.

26. Forbes and Foster, *Automotive Giants of America,* 137.

27. Dillon, Read & Company, *The Dodge Dollar,* 11–12; and "Address of John A. Nichols, Jr., Delivered before Dodge Brothers Dealers, Pennsylvania Hotel, New York City, January 9th, 1923," John Parsons collection; and box "Dodge Brothers 2, 1920/1923," DCHC.

28. Dodge Brothers, Inc., *Manual of Uniform Accounting System for Dodge Brothers Dealers Up to Fifty Cars,* rev. ed., March 1926; *The Assets of a Dodge Brothers Dealer in Banking Terms,* May 1923; Frederick J. Haynes, *The Sound Progress of Dodge Brothers Business,* August 1924, both in box "Dodge Brothers 6," DCHC; Dillon, Read & Company, *The Dodge Dollar,* 11–12; and Forbes and Foster, *Automotive Giants of America,* 136–37.

29. The quotation is from Norman G. Shidle, "Confidence in Future of Industry Shown by Dodge Purchase: Ultra-Conservative Banking Interests Now Regard Automobile Business as Preferred Investment. Compete for Chance to Get In," *Automotive Industries* 52 (9 April 1925): 649.

30. Sales Letter No. 465, "Second Hand Cars," from C. W. Matheson to All Dodge Brothers Direct and Associate Dealers, ca. 1920, and Sales Letter No. 974, "Curbstone Dealers," from G. H. Phelps to All Dodge Brothers Direct and Associate Dealers, ca. 1922, both in the John Parsons collection; *Stolen Car Bulletin* 1, no. 13 (1 June 1921), box "Dodge Brothers 4," DCHC; and Haynes, *The Sound Progress of Dodge Brothers Business.*

31. Dealer's Agreement between Dodge Brothers, Detroit, USA, and Stewart C. Maxcy, Thomasville, GA (expires 30 June 1921), dated 18 June 1920, signed by C. W. Matheson, Acting General Sales Manager, box "Dodge Brothers 4," DCHC.

32. "Order, Dodge Brothers Motor Vehicle, issued by Dashiell Motor Company, 2412 Michigan Avenue, Chicago, Illinois," from the private collection of Mel Bookout, Niles, Michigan.

33. Sales agreement, from the private collection of Thomas J. Carpenter.

34. Dillon, Read & Company, *The Dodge Dollar,* 7–9.

35. Dodge Brothers, *Book of Information, Dodge Brothers Motor Vehicles,* 16th ed. (April 1923), John Parsons collection.

36. Dillon, Read & Company, *The Dodge Dollar,* 14–17.

37. Shidle, "Confidence in Future of Industry Shown by Dodge Purchase," 649.

38. Michael E. Keller, *The Graham Legacy: Graham-Paige to 1932* (Paducah, KY: Turner, 1998), 19–23.

39. Ibid., 25–27.

40. Ibid., 31–35.

41. Graham Brothers *Minute Book,* 12 January 1917–6 May 1919, in banker's box "Dodge Brothers 1," DCHC.

42. Keller, *The Graham Legacy,* 35–39, 43–45; and Bittence, "Early Trucks," 23.

43. Ibid., 47; "Death Breaks Life-Long Triad of Triumphant Graham Brothers," *Automotive Industries* 67 (20 August 1932): 246; Haynes, "The Sound Progress of Dodge Brothers Business," speech delivered in August 1924, box "Dodge History 4," DCHC; and Bittence, "Early Trucks," 23.

44. Dodge Brothers and Graham Brothers reports to National Automotive Chamber of Commerce for 1925, corporate records for Dodge Brothers and Graham Brothers, NAHC.

45. Keller, *The Graham Legacy,* 47–52.

46. Lawrence H. Seltzer, *A Financial History of the American Automobile Industry* (Boston: Houghton Mifflin, 1928), 12; *The American Car since 1775,* 139–41; and "Dodge Sales Highest in '24: Increase of 35.6 Per Cent over Best Previous Year, 1923, Shown by Records," *Detroit News,* 18 January 1925, sec. 10, p. 30.

47. Epstein, *The Automobile Industry,* 345; Sloan, *My Years with General Motors,* 59; and C. C. Edmonds, "Tendencies in the Automobile Industry," *American Economic Review* 13 (September 1923): 429.

48. Dodge Brothers, *Directors' Minutes,* meetings of 18 July 1922, 19 April 1923, and 7 October 1924, banker's box "Dodge Brothers 1," DCHC; and "Dodge Brothers Plan New Huge Body Plant," *Detroit News,* 17 September 1922, pt. 1, p. 28.

49. "The Works of Dodge Brothers (Canada) Limited," four-page undated brochure, courtesy of Harry Reding, Irricana, Alberta, Canada.

50. John, "His Job Came First," 92, 94. The interview in *Forbes Magazine* was reprinted in Forbes and Foster, *Automotive Giants of America,* 121–40.

51. Manufacturers' Appraisal Company, *Appraisal, Dodge Bros. Detroit, Mich., March 23, 1925,* banker's box "Dodge Brothers 2," DCHC.

52. "Dillon, Read Group Buys Dodge Motors for over $175,000,000: Sale for All Cash, Biggest on Record, Ends a Keen Battle with General Motors," *New York Times,* 1 April 1925, 1, 2.

53. George M. Hassett, "Dodge to Stay Independent: Same Management Will Be Kept, Assert Bankers, Telling Plans; 146 Million Price Rumor," *Detroit News,* 2 April 1925, 1; and "Dillon's Career Crowned by Dodge Deal Strategy," *Detroit News,* 2 April 1925, 2.

54. Forbes and Foster, *Automotive Giants of America,* 131–33; Kennedy, *The Automobile Industry,* 170–72; Dodge Brothers, *Directors' Minutes,* Stockholders' Meeting, 7 April 1925; Special Meeting of the Stockholders, 30 April 1925; and Special Meeting of the Board of Directors, 30 April 1925, all in banker's box "Dodge Brothers 2," DCHC. The assets of Dodge Brothers, a Michigan corporation, were transferred to the new legal entity, Dodge Brothers, Inc., a Maryland corporation.

55. "Dodge Widows among Richest," *Detroit Times,* 2 May 1925, 1, 2; "Dodge Agents Receive Check: Last Step in Sale of Huge Auto Plant Taken When Stockholders Get $146,000,000," *Detroit Free Press,* 2 May 1925, 1; and original copy of the check, dated 1 May 1925, John Parsons collection.

56. Latham and Agresta, *Dodge Dynasty,* 159; "John D. Dodge Fighting Sale: Court Refuses Temporary Injunction to Tie Up Deal, But Summons Mrs. Dodge. Sister's Estate Involved," *Detroit News,* 4 April 1925, 1, 2; and "Dodge's Suit Is Dismissed: Widow Shows Sale of Plant Does Not Affect Capital Stock, Only Assets. Petitioner Is Criticized," *Detroit News,* 8 April 1925, 1, 2.

57. Chester Merrill Withington, "Dodge in Decade Jumps to Third among Auto Makers of World," *New York Evening Post,* 14 November 1925, F-7.

Chapter Seven

1. The changes in the four-cylinder offerings between 1926 and 1928 are confusing at best. Design changes were frequent, and some models overlapped. For example, Dodge Brothers produced the 126/127 series from 2 January 1927 to 22 March 1927, the 124 series between 22 March 1927 and June 1927, and the 128/129 series of four-cylinder cars from 21 June 1927 to 27 July 1928. John Bittence, e-mail communication with author, 29 January 2004.

2. William Z. Ripley, *Main Street and Wall Street* (Boston: Little, Brown, 1927), 86–87; and Kennedy, *The Automotive Industry,* 171. Ripley cites the Dillon, Read takeover of Dodge Brothers as an outrageous example of financiers removing control of corporations from the rightful owners, the stockholders. Apparently, this was a common technique in American business in the 1920s.

3. Letters, Robert M. Shedden, Dillon, Read & Company, to Mrs. Anna Thomson Dodge, 22 May 1925; T. R. Wheeler, Dillon, Read & Company, to Mrs. Anna Thomson Dodge, 7 July 1925; and "Summary Account, October 14, 1925," all in Horace E. Dodge papers, BHL.

4. Dodge Brothers, *Directors' Minutes,* meetings of 26 August 1924 and 16 December 1925; Dodge Brothers, Inc., *Annual Report to the Stockholders for the Year Ended* [sic] *December 31, 1925,* 7; American Appraisal Company, "Grand Summary, Graham Brothers Properties," 31 December 1925; all found in banker's box "Dodge Brothers 2," DCHC; "Dodge Brothers Big Program Is Launched, Buys Truck Unit as Graham Brothers Enter Management," *Automobile Topics* 80 (28 November 1925): 215; "Graham Truck Sold to Dodge: Sum Paid for Control in Manufacturing Company Kept Secret. New Officials Are Named," *Detroit News,* 23 November 1925; "A Trinity of Faith: 3 Graham Brothers Rise to Success, Join Dodge," *Detroit News,* 24 November 1925, 14; and Keller, *The Graham Legacy,* 54. Two legal agreements between the Grahams and Dodge Brothers, Inc., both dated 2 October 1925, covering the immediate sales of 51 percent of Graham stock and the Dodge Brothers, Inc., option on the remaining 49 percent, are found in folder "Graham Brothers–Dodge Brothers Agreements," box "Chrysler/Dodge, 1928," DCHC.

5. "Dodge Announces Graham Purchase: Official Statement Is Made by Wilmer," *Detroit News,* 15 May 1926, 2; Dodge Brothers, *Directors' Minutes,* meetings of 14 April 1926 and 25 January 1928;

and *Annual Report to the Stockholders for the Year Ended* [sic] *December 31, 1926,* 6, all in banker's box "Dodge Brothers 2," DCHC.

6. Keller, *The Graham Legacy,* 54, 100, 117.

7. Dodge Brothers, Inc., *Annual Report, 1925,* 3; and *Directors' Minutes,* May 1925 through June 1928, both in banker's box "Dodge Brothers 2," DCHC.

8. "Wilmer Picked to Head Dodge: Dillon, Read Member Elected President: Grahams Sell Their Stock. F. J. Haynes Is Chairman," *Detroit News,* 15 April 1926, 1; "Dodge Chiefs Resign Offices: Wilmer, Haynes and Waterfall Take Advantage of Merger to Retire," *Detroit News,* 4 August 1928, 3; "Haynes Heads Durant Board: Former Dodge Brothers Chairman Is President of Reorganized Company," *Detroit News,* 17 January 1929, 1; and Powell, *The Franklin Automobile Company,* 247–48, 254, 263.

9. Dodge Brothers, Inc., *Annual Report, 1926,* 3; *Directors' Minutes,* meetings of 14 April 1926 and 21 July 1926, both in banker's box "Dodge Brothers 2," DCHC.

10. Hugh Allen, *The House of Goodyear: A Story of Rubber and of Modern Business* (Cleveland: Corday & Gross, 1943), 49–51; and John C. Gourlie, "New President Discusses Future Policies of Dodge," *Automotive Industries* 54 (22 April 1926): 677–79.

11. Gourlie, "New President Discusses Future Policies of Dodge," 679; and Dodge Brothers, *Directors' Minutes,* meeting of 17 June 1925, both in banker's box "Dodge Brothers 2," DCHC.

12. "Dodge Brothers Expand Factory: Plans Will Increase Output to 1,500 Cars Daily," *Detroit News,* 19 July 1925, sec. 1, p. 2; "Greater Dodge Factory Begun: Boost in Output to 1,500 Cars a Day Aimed at for Jan. 1 by Officials," *Detroit News,* 2 August 1925, sec. 10, p. 2; "Dodge's $8,000,000 Additions Under Way: 1,000 Additional Employees Will Be Required in Eight New Units to Be Ready January 1," *Detroit News,* 20 September 1925, sec. 11, p. 8; and "How Dodge Plant Is Expanding," *Detroit News,* 20 September 1925, sec. 11, p. 5.

13. Bittence, "Early Trucks," 25–26; John C. Bittence, "Catch These Buses!" *Dodge Brothers Club News* 17 (February–March 1999): 22–24; Bunn, *Dodge Trucks,* 34–36; and Graham Brothers, *Trucks for Professional Hauling and Warehousing Industries* (Detroit, 1926), 44–51.

14. "Dodge Brothers [sic] Bring Dealers Here: 2,500 to Arrive in Special Trains Wednesday; Program Will Last Three Days," *Detroit News,* 3 January 1926, sec. 10, p. 2; "2,500 Witness Dodge Exhibit: 135 Vehicles Shown to Dealers after Firm Reveals Its Price Reductions," *Detroit News,* 7 January 1926, 27; "Dealers to Get Dodge Offices: Dillon Says 2 Directors for Firm Will Be Named from Sales Branch," *Detroit News,* 8 January 1926, 34; and "Dodge Brothers Add Two Dealers to Board: Brooklyn and Los Angeles Men to Be Elected," *Detroit News,* 10 March 1926, 37.

15. Dodge Brothers, Inc., *Annual Report, 1926,* 6; and McPherson, *The Dodge Story,* 48–52.

16. "Dodge Brothers Now Has 5-Bearing Shaft," *Automotive Industries* 55 (23 September 1926): 512; and Dodge Brothers, Inc., *Now Drive the Car,* 6–18.

17. Epstein, *The Automobile Industry,* 346.

18. Ibid., 339, 344; and Dodge Brothers, Inc., *Annual Report to the Stockholders for the Year Ended* [sic] *December 31, 1927,* 6–7.

19. Dodge Brothers, Inc., *Annual Report, 1927,* 5–6.

20. McPherson, *The Dodge Story,* 53–58.

21. "Dodge Designs Surprise Car: Six or Eight Cylinder to Be Ready Soon, Wilmer Tells Dealers," *Detroit News,* 6 January 1927, 24; "Convention Visitors Inspect Dodge Plant: Company Builds Factory for Surprise Car," *Detroit News,* 8 January 1927, 5; "New Dodge Unit Work Speeded: Huge Addition Must Be Ready by March 15, Will Help Meet Output Demand," *Detroit News,* 16 January 1927, pt. 10, p. 5; "Dodge Rushes Its 'Six' Plant: Building Is Up and Machines Are Now Being Put in to Start

Production," *Detroit News,* 3 April 1927, pt. 10, p. 1; and "Factory Has Its Own Final Test Track," *Detroit News,* 7 August 1927, pt. 10, p. 1.

22. "The Page Turns to Dodge Brothers Senior," *Automobile Topics* 86 (21 May 1927): 130–37, 143; Athel F. Denham, "Dodge's New Six Announced—Sedan Is $1,595," *Automotive Industries* 56 (28 May 1927): 790–93; and Athel F. Denham, "The New Dodge Senior Six at $1,595 Is Announced," *Automobile Trade Journal* 31 (June 1927): 49–51.

23. A. Robert Donn, "Senior Six Advertising, 1927–1928," *Dodge Brothers Club News* 13 (August–September 1995): 19–21; Early and Walkinshaw, *Setting the Pace,* 464–65; and Dunham and Gustin, *The Buick,* 572.

24. Bruce K. Brown and John C. Bittence, "Presenting the Dodge Brothers Senior Six, Part 1," *Dodge Brothers Club News* 19 (August–September 2001): 22, 25; and William Wagner, *Continental! Its Motors and Its People* (Fallbrook, CA: Aero, 1983), 43.

25. Athel E. Denham, "Dodge Lowers Prices as New 'Four' Is Introduced," *Automotive Industries* 57 (16 July 1927): 76–78; "'Fastest Four Cylinder Car in America,' Says Dodge Brothers," *Automobile Topics* 86 (16 July 1927): 880–83, 894; and Nevins and Hill, *Ford: Expansion and Challenge, 1915–1933,* 457.

26. Quoted in Dodge Brothers, Inc., *Annual Report, 1927,* 6–7.

27. "Dodge Smaller Six—The Victory," *Automobile Topics* 88 (7 January 1928): 788–89: 846; Athel F. Denham, "Body Construction Is Feature of Dodge 'Victory Six,'" *Automotive Industries* 58 (7 January 1928): 8–10; and "Over the Hills in the Victory Six," *Automobile Topics* 89 (14 April 1928): 828–32.

28. John C. Bittence, "The 'Monopiece Body,' A Budd/Dodge Brothers Victory Everyone Forgot," *Dodge Brothers Club News* 18 (August–September 2000): 16–20; and K. W. Stillman, "50 Per Cent Fewer Parts Used in New Budd Bodies," *Automotive Industries* 58 (10 March 1928): 406–8.

29. E. E. Thum, "Many Advantages Realized in Body of All-Steel Design: Aside from Carrying Stresses, Which Was Main Objective, It Has Reduced Weight, Lowered Center of Gravity, Made for Less Vibration and Simplified Production," *Automotive Industries* 59 (15 September 1928): 370–72; "New Body Years Ahead in Engineering Design: Unique Body—Chassis Construction Achieves Greater Strength and Stability. Insures Better Road Performance, More Comfort, Greater Safety," *The Dotted Line, Dodge Brothers, Inc.* 20 (January 1928): 8–9; "50 Per Cent Fewer Parts Used in New Budd Bodies," *Automotive Industries* 58 (10 March 1928): 406–8; and Charles K. Hyde, *Riding the Roller Coaster: A History of the Chrysler Corporation* (Detroit: Wayne State University Press, 2003), 89–90.

30. Athel F. Denham, "Dodge Announces New Light Six to Replace Four," *Automotive Industries* 58 (31 March 1928): 506–8; and "Dodge Discards Four for Six," *Automobile Topics* 89 (31 March 1928): 642–44.

31. Bunn, *Dodge Trucks,* 37–41; and Dodge Brothers, *Graham Brothers Trucks, Commercial Cars and Motor Coaches* (Detroit, 1928).

32. Dodge Brothers, Inc., *Annual Report, 1925,* 7; and "Percy Owen Joins Dodge Brothers: Government Chief Resigns to Be Director of Foreign Sales," *Australian Motorist,* 1 December 1925, 237–38, found in Scrapbook Number 7, Percy Owen Collection, NAHC.

33. "Percy Owen Quits Dodge Brothers after First Year: Resignation Comes Suddenly; Will 'Go Fishing,'" *Automotive Daily News* 3 (5 August 1926); and "Dodge Exports Gain 22.7%," *Automotive Daily News* 3 (22 October 1926).

34. R. Carl Hicks and George D. Babcock, *Report on the Automobile Situation in the World and Europe,* 28 May 1927, typescript, 3–5, NAHC.

35. "Financial Data Concerning Automotive Manufacturers," *Automotive Industries* 58 (18 February 1928): 226; and John C. Gourlie, "Automotive Securities Gain 50% in Value in Year," *Automotive Industries* 58 (7 April 1928): 539–41.

36. L. L. Stevenson, "Orders Briefs in Dodge Deal: Supreme Justice Studies Injunction Plea in Fight to Stop Merger," *Detroit News,* 27 June 1928, 11.

37. "Operating Statement, Chrysler Corporation & Subsidiaries versus Willys-Overland & Subsidiaries, as of December 31st, 1927," 22 May 1928, box "Chrysler/Dodge 1928," DCHC.

38. Dodge Folders, box "Chrysler/Dodge, 1928," DCHC.

39. "Economic Advantage of the Plan," box "Chrysler/Dodge, 1928," DCHC.

40. Chrysler and Sparkes, *Life of an American Workman,* 190–91, 197; "Chrysler," *Fortune* 12 (August 1935): 37; Jeffrey I. Godshall, "DeSoto: Walter Chrysler's Stepchild," *Automobile Quarterly* 20 (first quarter 1982): 72–73; and Beverly Rae Kimes, "Plymouth: Walter Chrysler's Trump Card," *Automobile Quarterly* 5 (summer 1966): 80. The revelation that Walter Chrysler made an abortive offer to buy Dodge Brothers, Inc., from Dillon, Read & Company in 1926 comes from a lengthy article in *Fortune* based on an in-depth interview with Chrysler, who must have revealed this information. See "Chrysler," *Fortune* 12 (August 1935): 37.

41. B. C. Forbes, "Chrysler Tells How He Did It," *Forbes* 23 (1 January 1929): 30; "Chrysler"; John C. Gourlie, "Chrysler-Dodge Merger Embraces 8,000 Dealers," *Motor Age* 54 (7 June 1928): 33; Walter Boynton, "Chrysler-Dodge Combine Will Have 9,000 Dealers, Covering All the World," *Automotive Daily News,* 5 June 1928, 1–2; and *Six Years' Progress of Chrysler Motors,* 20 November 1929, p. 7. The last source, found in the DCHC, gives an overall breakdown by location.

42. "The Big Three," *Automotive Daily News,* 4 June 1928, 4.

43. Root, Clark, Buckner, Howland & Ballantine, "The Clayton Act," 13 June 1928, box "Chrysler/Dodge, 1928," DCHC.

44. Dodge Brothers, Inc., *Directors' Minutes,* meeting of 29 May 1928 and special meeting of 29 June 1928, both in banker's box "Dodge Brothers 2," DCHC; Chrysler and Sparkes, *Life of an American Workman,* 192–96; George Hassett, "$450,000,000 Stock Involved in Merger: Consolidated Chrysler-Dodge Organization Will Be Third in Auto World, Trailing Only General Motors and Ford," *Detroit News,* 30 May 1928, 1–2; "Chrysler and Dodge Brothers Unite to Form Third Largest Producer," *Automotive Industries* 58 (2 June 1928): 853, 857; Gourlie, "Chrysler-Dodge Merger Embraces 8,000 Dealers," 32–33, 38; John C. Gourlie, "Dodge-Chrysler Merger Unites Two Great Properties," *Automotive Industries* 58 (9 June 1928): 863–64; and Arthur M. Leinbach, "What the Chrysler-Dodge Merger Means to Security Holders: Terms of Consolidation Analyzed—Now Third Largest Automobile Manufacturer," *The Magazine of Wall Street* 42 (16 June 1928): 304–5, 362–33. Dillon, Read's near failure to come up with 90 percent of all categories of stock is confirmed in Nicholas Kelley's Oral Reminiscences, interview of 20 February 1953 by Wendell Link, Columbia University Oral History Collection, leaves 249–50.

45. Stevenson, "Orders Briefs in Dodge Deal"; and Dodge Brothers, Inc.–Chrysler Corporation, *Report on the Sale or Exchange of the Property and Assets of Dodge Brothers, Inc., to or with the Chrysler Corporation* (Detroit, 1928), 7–9, 32–35, Exhibit 114, box "Dodge Legal," DCHC.

46. "Chrysler Confidential Bulletin Number 390," 2 June 1928, DCHC; and "Dodge Car Dealers Hold Meeting Here: Officials Hear Chrysler on Company's Plans," *Detroit News,* 20 December 1928, 54.

47. John Bittence, e-mail communication with the author, 29 January 2004; and "Dodge Senior Six Has New Body Lines, Increased Power," *Automotive Industries* 59 (8 September 1928): 331–33.

48. Walter P. Chrysler, "What Chrysler Engineers Have Found Out about Dodge Brothers," *Literary Digest* 97 (13 October 1928): 71.

49. "Price Reduced on New Truck: Dodge Offers One-Ton Machine in Eight Styles for $745," *Detroit News,* 25 August 1929, pt. 6, p. 3; "Chrysler Pays Dodge Tribute: He Talks on Restoration of Prestige before Executives on First Anniversary," *Detroit News,* 15 September 1929, pt. 6, p. 5; Richard M. Langworth and Jan P. Norbye, *The Complete History of Chrysler Corporation, 1924–1985* (Skokie, IL: Publications International, 1985), 93; McPherson, *The Dodge Story,* 115; and "The Dodge Ram," folder "Dodge Ram," box "Emblems 3, Dodge," DCHC.

50. "The Big Three."

Retrospective

1. For the Ford branch assembly system, see Gerald T. Bloomfield, "Coils of the Commercial Serpent: A Geography of the Ford Branch Distribution System, 1904–1933," in *Roadside America: The Automobile in Design and Culture,* ed. Jan Jennings (Ames: Iowa State University Press, 1990), 40–51.

2. Nevins and Hill, *Ford: The Times, the Man, the Company,* 574–87, discusses Ford's increased autocratic approach to his business and his growing rigidity and isolation as early as the mid-1910s. The fates of Henry Ford's main lieutenants are delineated in Ford R. Bryan, *Henry's Lieutenants* (Detroit: Wayne State University Press, 1993).

3. The three full-length biographies of Durant paint the same picture of his personality and style: Lawrence R. Gustin, *Billy Durant: Creator of General Motors* (Grand Rapids, MI: Eerdmans, 1973); Bernard A. Weisberger, *The Dream Maker: William C. Durant, Founder of General Motors* (Boston: Little, Brown, 1979); and Axel Madsen, *The Deal Maker: How William C. Durant Made General Motors* (New York: John Wiley, 1999). For Walter P. Chrysler's disputes with Durant, see Hyde, *Riding the Roller Coaster,* 7–12.

4. For "Sloan on Sloan," see Alfred P. Sloan, Jr., with Boyden Sparks, *Adventures of a White-Collar Man* (New York: Doubleday, Doran, 1941) and *My Years with General Motors.* A recent scholarly biography, David Farber, *Sloan Rules: Alfred P. Sloan and the Triumph of General Motors* (Chicago: University of Chicago Press, 2002), offers perceptive insights into Sloan and his company.

5. The most comprehensive discussion of the changing marketing strategies of the American automobile industry is found in James M. Rubenstein, *Making and Selling Cars: Innovation and Change in the U.S. Automotive Industry* (Baltimore: Johns Hopkins University Press, 2001).

6. "Gift Endows History Hall: $130,000 in Memory of Dodge Brothers," *Detroit News,* 12 January 1946, 19.

7. Don Tschirhart, "City Council Gets Look at Dodge Fountain Plans," *Detroit News,* 19 October 1971, A-3. The text for the Dodge Fountain plaque is found in the John Parsons collection.

Appendix

1. This lineage is based on "The Dodge Diary," 1, no. 3 (January 1987), a newsletter published by the Dodge & Allied Surname Organization (Las Vegas), found in "Family Genealogy" file, MBHA. Most of the details are confirmed by the published genealogies listed in note 2.

2. Robert Dodge, *Report, Full, Authentic, and Complete, of All the Proceedings of the Memorable First Reunion of the Dodge Family in America* (New York: E. S. Dodge, 1879), 7; Joseph Thomson

Dodge, *Genealogy of the Dodge Family of Essex County, Massachusetts, 1629–1894* (Madison, WI: Democrat, 1894), 25–26, 41, 71–72, 59, 96–97; and *Cemetery Records of Niles Township in Berrien County, Michigan* (St. Joseph, MI: Genealogical Society of Southwestern Michigan, 1996), 24.

3. U.S. Census of Population, 1850, New Hampshire, Merrimack County, Newbury, p. 154; and Michigan Daughters of the American Revolution, Algonquin Branch, *Berrien County, Michigan Cemetery Records of All Persons Born before 1867* (DAR, 1930), 169.

4. U.S. Census of Population, 1860, Michigan, Berrien County, Niles City, pp. 257, 276; U.S. Census of Population, 1870, Michigan, Berrien County, Niles City, p. 301R; U.S. Census of Population, 1880, Michigan, Berrien County, Niles City, p. 262; State of Michigan Death Records, Liber A, Berrien County, pp. 26, 51, 274; and Michigan Daughters of the American Revolution, Algonquin Chapter, *Berrien County, Michigan Marriage Records, 1839–1867* (St. Joseph, MI, 1938), 97.

INDEX

Index

Index

Index

Index

Index